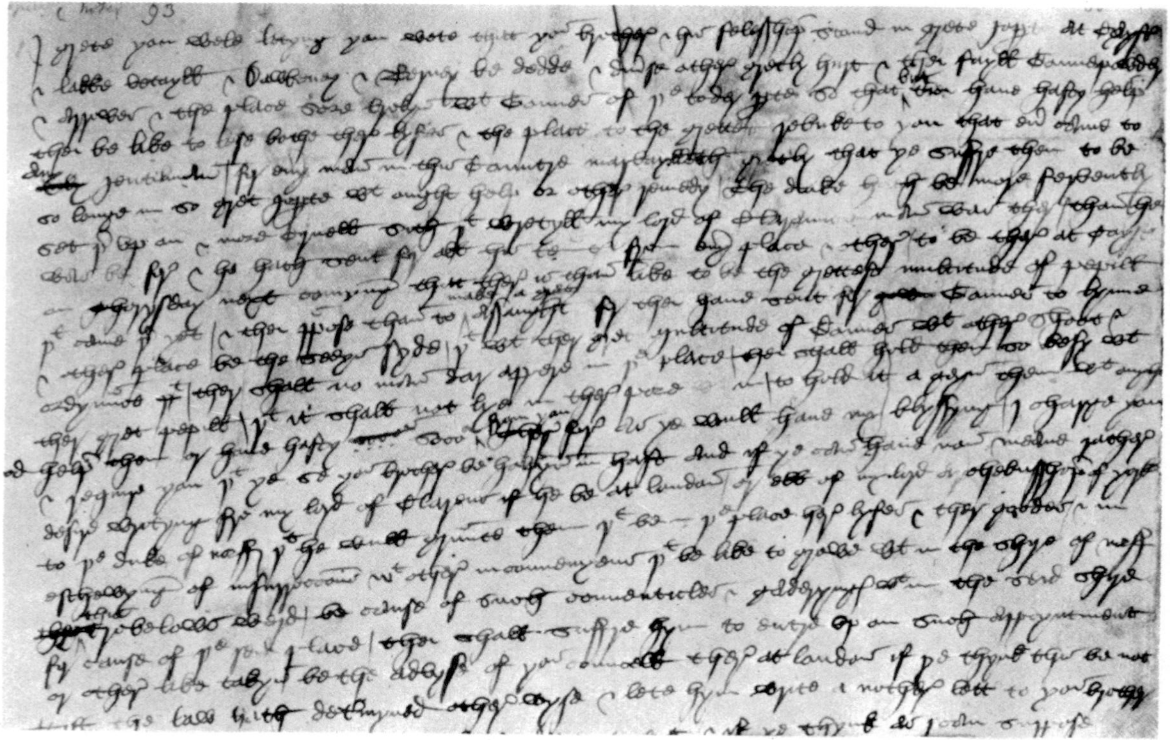

Facsimile of Paston Letter, No. 620 ll. 1—23, Br. Mus. Add. Mss. 34889 f. 88.

THE
ENGLISH PRONUNCIATION
AT SHAKESPEARE'S TIME

AS TAUGHT BY

WILLIAM BULLOKAR

WITH

WORD-LISTS
FROM ALL HIS WORKS

BY

R. E. ZACHRISSON

———•———

AMS PRESS
NEW YORK

PE
1141
Z3
1970

TO

MY WIFE

INTRODUCTION

The present investigation was begun as early as 1911, and was ready for printing in 1913, when I published my book on the Pronunciation of English Vowels 1400—1700. In the meantime it has been revised and much added to. It has now a two-fold object. In the first place it aims at giving a detailed analysis of Bullokar's pronunciation of English as reflected in his spelling. Moreover, I have once more gone through the entire evidence on the early New English pronunciation, availing myself of the fresh material that has come to light, and the investigations that have been published on the subject. The various sounds have been dealt with in the same order as in my book on the English Vowels, which consequently serves as a basis for the general discussion of the pronunciation of the early New English vowels and diphthongs. After having given a survey of the development of one particular sound, I have endeavoured to fix the approximate value assigned to it by Bullokar, and I have also given an account of words which contain this particular sound in Bullokar's pronunciation, but which are pronounced differently at the present time. The ground that is covered is consequently the early New English pronunciation from about 1400 to the time of Shakespeare, with the main stress laid on the Shakespearean period.

Of the many valuable books and papers on the early New English pronunciation which have appeared during the last few years, I do not hesitate to place in the foremost rank two works by Professor Wyld, History of Modern Colloquial English and Studies in English Rhymes from Surrey to Pope. Professor Wyld has enriched our knowledge of the early New English period with a wealth of material from sources which had not previously been examined for philological purposes. He lays great stress on the importance of occasional phonetic spellings, which often are a safer guide to the actual pronunciation than the rules of the grammarians. His interpretation of the evidence is characterised by a combination of ingenuity and commonsense and a wholesome sceptical attitude towards so called established truths. According to my views, he is inclined to overestimate the rôle played by class dialect in the early New English period, and in many cases he should have made a clearer distinction between phonetic variants and phonetic spellings. A closer scrutiny of the many fresh sources he has brought to light will lead to safer results concerning many details, but his general results are on the whole safe and supported by a sufficient number of conclusive forms. No impartial critic is likely to deny that Professor Wyld has broken new ground and has opened up many new paths for a succsessful exploration of the entire domain of early New English sound-history. Professor Wyld's book on English Rhymes does not settle the difficult questions to what extent the early rhymes reflect the actual contemporary pronunciation or to what extent they are traditional, influenced by the spelling or due to poetical licence, but his main thesis that the vast majority of early New English rhymes are, or were originally, based on identity or at least similarity of sound is undoubtedly correct.

Of great interest for our knowledge of 15th century English are the latest instalments of Professor Luick's Historische Grammatik der englischen Sprache, Professor Jordan's Handbuch der Mittelenglischen Grammatik, and Dr. Flasdieck's Forschungen zur Frühzeit der neuenglischen Schriftsprache.

The orthography in numerous original letters of the 15th century has been closely examined by Dr. Asta Kihlbom in A Contribution to the Study of Fifteenth Century English. Dr. Kihlbom's investigation is based on a detailed comparison between the language of autograph letters by well indentified persons from the middle and the latter half of the 15th century and that of the contemporary and official London and State documents investigated by Lekebusch.

Several details of the early New English pronunciation have been discussed in recent papers by Professor Luick and Professor Horn. The evidence of early Welsh sources, especially the Hymn to the Virgin, has been examined by Professor Förster and Professor Holthausen.

In this brief survey mentioning should also be made of Dr. Barnouw's Echoes of the Pilgrim Fathers' Speech, dealing with numerous Dutch renderings of English personal names in the early years of the 17th century, and Dr. Krapp's valuable and industrious work, The English Language in America, which incidentally throws much light on the English pronunciation also, especially in the 17th century.

Naturally the publication, during the few recent years, of so many valuable books and papers on the early New English pronunciation has highly advanced our knowledge of the subject. Several of the conclusions arrived at in my book The Pronunciation of the English Vowels will have to be modified in the light of the new material that has been adduced, and the new interpretations that have been proposed.

Concerning details, the reader is referred to the full discussion of the various sounds in the section headed Pronunciation. In this place only a few general remarks will be offered. Both Professor Luick and Professor Wyld have remarked that I have been too unwilling to assume the existence of more than one early New English pronunciation of a definite Middle English sound. In Englische Studien (52, 301) I pointed out that for several sounds, e. g. ME. *ę̄* in *sea* and ME. *ai* in *day,* I had assumed the existence of two pronunciations, one familiar or colloquial, the other more refined and perhaps somewhat archaic. At the same time, I willingly admit that in my earlier works I have dwelt too much upon the uniformity of early Standard speech. I am now convinced that not only the isolated words but also *one distinct sound* was often pronounced differently by different speakers. But I still maintain that this divergency is not, in the first place, due to dialectal importations[1] but principally to the existence in early Standard speech of advanced or colloquial forms of pronunciation, by the side of learned or more old-fashioned ones. This duplicity accounts for the pronunciations recorded for ME. *ā* and *ai* in *name* and *day*, for ME. *u* in *come*, ME. *ī* in *like* etc. Indeed, the struggle between old and new types of pronunciation constitutes one of the most remarkable features in the development of early Standard speech. Moreover, as I have already hinted at in a paper on the Essex dialect and the origin of Vulgar English (Engl. Studien 60, pp. 359 ff.), we have to reckon not only with vernacular importations into early Standard English, but also with phonetic changes indigenous in the speech-community which constitutes the dialectal area of London and its neighbourhood. The old-fashioned types of pronunciation were, as a rule, taught by English orthoepists, who endeavoured to set up an artificial Standard of speech, favoured principally by men of learning and used perhaps also in reading[2], whereas the advanced forms were in common colloquial use all over the country. In this respect class dialect may be said to have played an important rôle for differences in early Standard speech.

I do not think, however, that there was in in early New English the same gulf between Vulgar and Standard speech as there is now. In my previous writings I have endeavoured to show that the present duplicity does not go much farther back than the middle of the eighteenth century, and that it was the outcome of the great social revolutions that took place at this date.[3]

My distrust in the sound-analysis of the early English orthoepists and my confidence in the importance of the testimony of occasional spellings has been strengthened rather than weakened by my recent studies. With regard to phonetic spellings in

---

[1] Compare my criticism of the supposed wholesale importation of vernacular forms into early Standard speech (Anglia 38, pp. 430 ff.).

[2] Cf. Zachrisson, pp. 159 ff.

[3] Cf. Nordisk Tidskrift 1925, pp. 403 ff., Englische Stud., 60 pp. 355 ff.

early documents, I have to a great extent re-examined the
entire evidence with a view to eliminating all forms which are
not conclusive. In doing so, I have availed myself of all the
fresh material which has been brought to light, and have also
gone through some of the most important new sources, e. g.
the Stonor Letters and the Verney Memoirs.

In many doubtful cases I have scrutinised the MSS. of
individual letters and documents in order to ascertain the correct readings, some of which have been reproduced in facsimile.
The photographic copies of several letters did not come to hand
until the printing of my book had already begun. The results
of this palæographic examination tends, on the whole, to con-
firm the conclusions arrived at in my earlier writings. The only
group of spellings which proved to be inconclusive, were those
with *a* for *u* in *gun* in the fifteenth century. Moreover, only
one or two of the forms with *au* for *ou* in *house* can be implicitly relied upon.

The main object of the present work is to make the reader
acquainted with William Bullokar's amended system of orthography and the principles according to which it should be
interpreted. I have also tried to define the phonetic value of
the chief symbols used by Bullokar and account for all forms
of special interest for our knowledge of the early New English
pronunciation.

In giving examples illustrative of the various sound-changes
discussed, I have, as a rule, not aimed at completeness. Additional instances will generally be found in the word-lists, which
should always be consulted for investigations into the details of
early English sound-history.

I have, however, endeavoured to give full lists of words
containing oi, ooi, æ and e'. Moreover, all cases where Bullokar
deviates from the present usage, e. g. as to the distribution of
(s), (z), (þ), (ð) have been taken notice of.

Other orthoepists of an earlier or later date have frequently
been consulted, in the first place Smith and Hart, who were
contemporary with Bullokar, and Gill, our chief authority for

the pronunciation of the next generation. The fact that Bullokar's system (like that of all the other early English orthoepists) was very much influenced by the traditional spelling, makes it often impossible to arrive at any definite results as to the pronunciation of many isolated words.

None of the early English orthoepists have had so many books printed in the orthography devised by them as Bullokar. No less than four works comprising circa 400 pages have been handed down to our time. There is hardly one question of English sound-history which is not more or less fully illustrated in Bullokar's works. They will prove very valuable for the study of such difficult problems as quantity, vowels in front of r-combinations, and the distribution of the various oi- and e-sounds, to mention only a few instances. Is is not without pride Bullokar points out that 'vpon a doubt of true sounding of any worde, any man may resort to the doubtfull letter tenne generations hence, and there finde the vse, both of the olde, and cause of the change for Inglish spéech' (Book at Large, p. 279). Bullokar's amended orthography has previously been known to the philological world through Ellis' word-lists, which are faulty and unreliable in several respects, and from a dissertation by E. Hauck entitled Systematische Lautlehre Bullokar's (Marburger Studien, Heft 12, 1906) supplemented by an essay on Bullokar's life and the principles of his orthography in Jahresbericht über das Schuljahr 904/1905. Oberrealschule zu Marburg a. d. Lahn.

Both Ellis and Hauck have confined themselves to an examination of 'Booke at Large' of which only a small part (= fifteen pages) is printed in the orthography devised by the author. Consequently it is only a twentieth part of the whole material that has previously been investigated.[1] Hauck's account of Bullokar's pronunciation of vowels and diphthongs (the con-

---

[1] Ellis' and Hauck's chief mistake is to look upon Bullokar's forms as accurate phonetic notations, whereas they only represent an attempt to amend the historical spelling.

sonants are not dealt with) is chiefly of a descriptive character.[1]

Like nearly all his predecessors Hauck assumes that $\bar{\imath}$ was
not diphthongized (p. 68), that Bulllokar's [e'w] was (y˙) (p. 89),
although both his notation and definition of the sound clearly
point to a diphthongic pronunciation, that *ai* and *ei* were differently sounded (p. 99 ff.) etc. All through, Hauck makes too
little allowance for misprints, which are likely to abound in
Booke at Large, which was one of the first texts printed in the
orthography used by Bullokar.[2] Indeed Hauck (see p. 89) even
hesitates whether [eu] in leuk-warm is due to the omission of
the diacritic mark, or if it is to be interpreted as indicating a
pronunciation (ey)! Hauck seems often to have overlooked the
important part the 'derivative strokes' play for a correct interpretation of Bullokar's forms, and also makes various other
mistakes some of which will be pointed out below. Thus he
often mistakes the strokes, the so-called half-vowels ṁ, ń, ŕ
(rendered here as M, N, R) are provided with for lengthmarks,
and reads chańg' harṁ as cháng' hárm etc.

Some of the forms Hauck adduces from Book at Large,
I have not been able to find in the places indicated, e. g. tak
34, 7 (or. ed.), naked *ib.* 52, 19, whóʒ *ib.* 42, 11 [Here Hauck
has evidently read thóʒ as *whóʒ] etc. Sometimes one word is
mistaken for another, as when Hauck identifies rót 320 (or. ed.
49, 6) with Present English 'root' instead of 'rote' (of uncertain
etymology).

Uppsala, February, 1927.   **R. E. Zachrisson.**

---

[1] Cf. also Ekwall's criticism, Englische St., 1907, p. 430 ff.

[2] Cf. the following remarks in Bullokar's Fables of Æsop (1854), p. 4:
— I saięd be'fór that I be'gan pu̜blish*i*ng in Au̜gust 1580. So, that accord*i*ng
too the shew afór-sayed, I imprinted a Pamphlet for spel*i*ng, and the ordinary Primar too my græt chárg'eʒ: of the which im-pres*i*onʒ (too my
know*l*edg') thér ar not (of aſ sortʒ) thirty a-bród, aſ which I wish too be'
committed, whither I hau' committed their lýk, that iʒ, intoo the fier: for
som wil shew the ro̜wh-hewed wo̜rk, rather than the finished, pu̜lished, or
pu̜rg'ed, too slak or hinder the credit of the wo̜rk-man.

81 .   Of Jupiter and the Aap.

Iupiter grætly-dezyring too know whoo of mortal [creáturʒ] brotht-forth the trim-eſt yong-onʒ, commandeth what-soeuer liu-ing thing iʒ any-whær too be caled-togecher. They run-togecher too Iupiter from-euery-whær, the kynd of fowlʒ and bæſtʒ wær pre-ſent or comm :] among whoom when the aap cám-thither too, bæring hir il-fauored kit-lingʒ on hir arm, no-man could temperat or mæzur] him-ſelf]from lauhing, but Iupiter him-ſelf lauhed very-exceedingly too. The aap her-ſelf sayeth chær by-and-by, ye mary, Iu-piter too our iudg knoweth that my kitlingʒ grætly excel al how many soeuer be hér.

The moral.

Onʒ-owni iʒ faier too euery-ón: aʒ the pro-uerb iʒ. And elc-whær in Theocritus. Thoʒ thing that be læſt fair or fowleſt]ſem fair too ón louing them.

82 .   Of the ók and the red.

The ók being very-ful of diſdain and pryd goeth too the red, saying,if thu hau a coragios breſt or ſtomak,]com-on too the fiht

Ь   or

Facsimile of Page 89 in Bullokar's Æsop's Fables.

BULLOKAR'S ORTHOGRAPHY

I -- 26252.   K. Hum. Vet. Samf., Uppsala.   XXII: 6.

Bullokar's Works.

The following works printed in Bullokar's amended system of orthography have been preserved to the present day: Æṣop̃ Fáblź 1584 (= FA.) in the British Museum (C. 58 c. 23) and the Bodleian Library (Malone 366, Douce A. 51).

Booke at Large 1580 (= BL.) in Br. Mus. (C. 40 e. 4, C. 12 e. 23), Bodl. Libr. (Douce G. 516), and the Edinburgh Univ. Libr. (De. 3. 113).

Bref Grammar for English (= BG.) 1586, Bodl. Libr. (Tanner 67).

Pamphlet for Grammar (= PG.) 1586 (Tanner 67).

For a description of the various original editions, see Plessow, Palæstra (LII, pp. CXLIV—CXLIX), where all of them have been reprinted. I have collected my word-lists from these reprints. In order to ascertain the reliability of Plessow's reprints I have collated his text with that of the original editions. BL. has been compared with the original, page by page. In FA., BG., PG., numerous forms which were particularly interesting from a phonetic point of view, have been verified. I have also ascertained that the various copies of BL. and FA. in the Br. Mus. and the Bodl. Libr. are identical.

Plessow's reprints of Bullokar's texts do not contain many errors, considering how difficult it is to reproduce works of this kind faultlessly. I have noted the following instances:

Plessow's reprints	*Original editions*

Æṣop͡7 Fábĺż

p. 10 half	read haĺf¹.
p. 19 tabĺż	» tábĺż.
p. 26 prou'ok*i*ng	» prou'ók*i*ng
p. 32 beheld	» be'held.
p. 35 lýd*d*	» hýd*d*.
p. 45 ẹooneṭḥ	» ẹooineṭḥ, p. 75.
p. 46 shep	» she'p, p. 76.
p. 47 hau	» hau', p. 78.
p. 54 exc'ed*i*ng*l*y	» exc'e'd*i*ng*l*y, p. 89.
p. 56 sna*i*l	» snail, p. 93.
p. 64 táĺk	» taĺk, p. 106.
p. 67 moụth	» moụtḥ, p. 110.
p. 74 thihter	» thither, p. 122.
p. 101 renọwm²	» renọwm, p. 167.
p. 104 hárd*n*es	» hard*n*es, p. 171.
p. 104 clọth*i*ng	» clóth*i*ng, p. 172.
p. 108 lau'-of	» læu'-of, p. 179.
p. 118 oN*l*y	» ón*l*y, p. 194.
p. 161 saýʒ	» sayʒ, p. 266.
p. 163 diu'er	» diu'erṣ, p. 268.
p. 193 exc'ed	» exc'e'd, p. 293.

Sentenc'e͡7 of the

wýʒ Cato

p. 220 aný	read any, p. 9.
p. 222 frend	» fre'nd, p. 13.
p. 227 rithly	» rih*t*ly, p. 26.

---

¹ The first numbered page in FA. is p. 65.
² Incorrectly altered to renọwn, see Errata p. 392.

Book at Large

---

[1] ș for s in the orig. is an error.
[2] v for y in the orig. is an error.
[3] v for y in the orig. is an error.
[4] w for ew in the orig. is an error.
[5] lf for lf in the orig. is an error.
[6] th for ph in the orig. is an error.

p. 326 scaller*d*	read scatter*d*, p. 54.
p. 326 ýĺ	» yĺ, p. 54.
p. 321 (in the margin:) Why	» Wy', p. 50.

I the tables (after p. 330), where Bullokar's letters are re-produced, the following corrections in ink have been made:

Table I.

Section 1.   c' for c.

»   2.   C' and c' for C, c; G', g' for G, g.

»   3.   ad*i*c'ionż for adic'ionż; strýk7 for stryk7; witḥ for with.

»   4.   c' for·c; g' for g.

»   5.   C', c' for C, c; G', g' for G, g.

Table II.

Section 1.   R for r.

»   3.   bṭt for but.

»   4.   C' c' for C, c; G' g' for G, g.

»   6.   ón, ónly, tæchẹtḥ, ŋoṇ ṭoo for on, ońly, tæcheth, ŋou, too.

Bref Grammar.

p. 335 renọwn	read renọwm.[2]
p. 338 offendtḥ	» offendʒ.
p. 348 vʒ*e*d	» vʒed[3], p. 14.
p. 350 claṇʒe7	» claṇse7[4], p. 18.
p. 351 bóth	» both, p. 19.
p. 361 too lọu'ẹd	» loou'ẹd, p. 34.
p. 367 repe'*t*ed	» repét*e*d, p. 43.
p. 368 ịooinẹtḥ	» ịoinẹtḥ, p. 44.
p. 369 separát*e*d	» seperát*e*d, p. 45.

---

[1] Wy for Why in the orig. is an error.

[2] The first pages in BG. are not numbend.

[3] vʒed for vʒ*e*d in the orig. is an error.

[4] clause7 for claṇʒe7 in the orig. is an error.

p. 370 vȝed   read vȝed[1], p. 47.

p. 372 vȝed   » vȝed[1], p. 51.

p. 374 significaţion   » significaţon, p. 53.

p. 381 After 'ǫther graNte' is omitted: 'bųt too the ĕirż execùtǫrż, administrátorż and assignż of sųch feoffe warrante or graNte'.

p. 382 set-forth   read set-foorth, p. 64.

p. 384 gǫu'erNżng   » góu'erNżng, p. 67.

Bullokar's Life.

On Bullokar's life the following information ·is given in the Dictionary of National Biography. —

William Bullokar (1528?—1588?)[2] lived chiefly in London from about 1520 to 1590. In Queen Mary's time he served in the army under Sir Richard Wingfield, going into foreign service with him twice. He served afterwards under Toinings at Newhaven, and with Captain Turner in garrison. After having studied for some timȩ agriculture and law he resumed c. 1573 teaching, which he had been engaged in as early as 1550. He must have been a fairly good Latin scholar, as he translated Æsop's Fables and some other Latin works into English.

Bullokar as a Phonetician.

Considering the humble social position Bullokar occupied, it is not probable that he had time or opportunity to acquire great learning.[3] It cannot be proved that he was well acquainted with any other modern language than his mother-tongue. He

---

[1] vȝed for vȝed in the orig. is an error.

[2] Cf. Zachrisson, p. 168. Bullokar tells us several facts about his life in his preface to BG. pp. 333—338.

[3] Bullokar speaks of his literary predecessors, Smith and Hart, in terms of very great respect: 'I reioyced that men of such calling, learning, and experience, had trauelled in the like purpose', BL., p. 238.

may have had some knowledge of French and Italian, as in some instances he draws comparisons between the pronunciation of French and English sounds, and also translates some of the examples in BL. into French and Italian. Although Bullokar had studied the works of his predecessors Smith and Hart, his knowledge of phonetics was very superficial. He had no notion of the proper nature of a diphthong (cf. below p. 9), and could not always distinguish between voiced and voiceless consonants.[1] He uses his symbols of half-vowels without any discrimination, and his amended system of orthography is much influenced by the existing spelling. Considering the weaknesses alluded to, we cannot put implicit faith in his sound-descriptions, nor are all the forms given in amended spelling conclusive for the pronunciation of the time.

Bullokar's Amended Orthography. His classi= fication of sounds. Survey of symbols.

Like Smith and Hart, Bullokar also wanted to reform the old orthography. The reason why his predecessors failed is that 'they left out of their amendments diuers of the letters now in vse, and also brought in diuers of new figure and fashion' (p. 239), but 'for the sake of easy conference' the new orthography must not differ too much from the old (p. 272).

Hoping to meet with greater success, Bullokar forms the ingenious idea of *amending* ·(not reforming) the orthography by adding various diacritic marks to the old letters.· He prides himself upon not having left out any old letters or brought in any new: 'but where any letter was double or treble sounded I giue a little strike thereunto, for true and perfect difference' (p. 272).

---

[1] Thus he uses ȝ = (z) in the plural only after *l*, *m*, *n*, *r*, vowels and diphthongs (p. 270). He fails to see the relation between (f), (v) (p. 298), although he looks upon (s), (z), (Þ), (ð) as pairs.

He points out how important it is that a letter should be named as it is pronounced, so that the young pupils may not be misled in learning to spell and pronounce by divergency between the *alphabetic* sound of a letter and its pronunciation in a given word (p. 240). Consequently the system of ortho-graphy Bullokar uses is not purely phonetic.

The difference between the old and the new spelling is characterized by Bullokar in the following way: Of the 24 let-ters of the alphabet 10 are 'perfect, i. e. their names and sounds do always agree', viz. *a, b, d, f, k, l, m, n, r, x.* But of these only *a, b, d, f, k, x* are 'perfectly perfect', for *l, m, n, r* can and must also 'be used for halfe vowels'. All other letters are 'vnperfect', because 'every of them haue but one name and some of them haue two soundes, and some haue three soundes' (p. 253 f.). They must consequently be amended, so that nobody can have any doubt as to their proper sound.

According to Bullokar, there were 'eight English vowels of differing sounds', viz. [a] in *lack,* [æ] in *leak,* [e'] in *leek,* [i] in *lick,* [o] *lock,* [oo] in *look,* [ụ or y] in *luck,* [u or v] in *Luke* (p. 285). Of these [e', oo, v, u, æ] are always long, [a, o, i] can be both short and long (p. 283), [ụ, y] are always short.

Vowel length is indicated in various ways (p. 283): 'Some-times an accent point be set over: a, e, i, y, or o, thus á, ä, â, or that a, e, or y be doubled thus aa, ee, iy, yi'. To these symbols Bullokar adds a number of others 'which however agree to one or other of the letters before written, in name and sounde'. Thus [y] can be used indifferently for [i], and when [o], [oo] are pronounced like [ụ] they must be provided with diacritic marks (p. 282).

After having discussed the vowels, Bullokar proceeds to the diphthongs. His definition hardly enables us to settle what he understood by a diphthong. He says, 'when two vowels of diuers sounds com together in one sillable, they make a diph-thong, that is to say, they are both touched short in sound together'. This ought to imply that both vowels are heard short. But if so, Bullokar contradicts himself by also including

among the diphthongs [e'w], [ooy], as in ne'w, booil, with a long
vowel for their first elements. Moreover, we know from contemporary testimonies that other diphthongs, such as *ęu* etc., also
had a long vowel for their first element. This is also indirectly
admitted by Bullokar, when he writes cóld etc. with marks indicating vowel-length. Possibly the expression alluded to only
means that a diphthong is a sound composed of the two simple
vowels represented in the digraph. This is very probable, considering that Bullokar (p. 313) has simplified his definition in
the following manner: 'When twoo vowels or half vowels come
toogether in one sillable they are called a diphthong'. From
what he says on p. 286, it appears that he admitted the existence of diphthongs with the second element very faintly
sounded: 'note that when :w: is in a diphthong with any vowel
before it, then is the vowel perfectly sounded, and :w: is lightly
touched upon' etc. Bullokar may also have had an idea that
there were diphthongs with the first or last element long. Cf.
his statement (p. 314) as to the quality of a diphthong: 'every
diphthong is of as long time *or longer* than any long vowel'.
This may, however, only indicate that a diphthong composed
of two short vowels was, in Bullokar's opinion, of longer sound
than a single long vowel.

In his terminology Bullokar does not distinguish between a
diphthong and a digraph. See p. 283, where he places among
diphthongs the digraph *oa* < *ǭ*. He distinguishes, however, between diphthongs pronounced as one of the eight vowels, and
diphthongs distinct in sound from any of the vowels. To the
latter class belong [ay], [ey], [oy], [ooy], [au̯], [eu̯] < *ęu*, [ow] <
ǭu, [uy], to the former [oa] < *ǭ*, [ou̯], [o̜w] < *ū*, [e'w] < *ęu, u*,
BL. p. 285.

In spite of this attempt at a classification, Bullokar's general information is of such a confused character that we can
hardly suppose he was able to distinguish between a simple
and a diphthongic sound. This doubt grows almost to a certainty when we see that in his amended orthography he some-

times uses characters denoting diphthongs for simple vowels; cf. below p. 18.

Bullokar's orthographic system also includes a number of half vowels, i. e. consonants to which 'one or other superfluous vowel is joined sometimes before them and sometimes after them'. They are four: ɩ, м, ɴ, ʀ¹ (p. 267).

The consonants do not give occasion for any remarks. They are not classified according to phonetic principles but discussed, as they occur in the alphabet.

Table of Symbols.

I do not include some variants of *r, s, f, sh* which are no guides to the pronunciation and which are therefore disregarded in the lists also; neither do I consider it necessary to give here the symbols with derivation- or inflection-marks. In my lists I have rendered such marks in accordance with Plessow (see p. CXLIX), i.e. by italicizing the letters under which Bullokar has a 'derivative dot', and marking with hooks those that are provided with 'derivative or declynative strikes'.

I.

Vowels, and Diphthongs of the same sound as the Vowels.

a < ME.² ă.

á, aa, â, ä < ME. ā.

e < ME. ĕ.

e', e'a, e'æ, æ' < ME. ę̄.

æ, é, ee < ME. ę̄.

i, y < ME. ĭ.

---

¹ Bullokar also considers *s* (the plural ending) as a half vowel, because 'in time past it included the sound of the vowell :e: and the sounde of :s:'. For this 'half vowel' he uses the symbols ʓ and ż (269).

¹ It would *sometimes* have been more exact to have written < e. NE. instead of < ME.

i, y, ý, iy, yi < ME. *ī*.

o < ME. *ŏ*.

ó < ME. *ǭ*.

oo < ME. *ǭ*.

ǫ, ṳ, ɏ, ǫǫ, ǫ*o* < ME. *ŭ*.

oɏ, oṳ, ǫw, ǫǫw < ME. *ū*.

ù = u (sounded short in unstressed syllables, see PG. p. 388).

u, v, e'ɏ, e'ṳ, e'w < ME. *ēu, u*.

Diphthongs.

ai, ay, ei, ey	< ME. *ai, ei*.
aɏ, aṳ, aw	< ME. *au*.
eɏ, eṳ, ew	< ME. *ēu*.
oi, oy, ooi, ooy, uy[1]	< ME. *oi*.
ow, ów	< ME. *ǭu*.

Half Vowels.

ʟ	= ɏl.
M	= ɏm.
N	= ɏn.
R	= er.
ź, ʒ	= (e)s.

Consonants.

b	= (b).
c'	= (s).
c	= (k).
ch	= (tʃ), (k) only in Greek words.
d	= (d).
f	= (f).
g	= (g).
g'	= (dʒ).

---

[1] At least in some instances this symbol seems to correspond to ME. *oi*. Cf. below.

h¹ = (h) and the spirant in liht, browht etc.
į   = (dʒ).
k   = (k).
l   = (l).
m   = (m).
n   = (n).
p   = (p).
ph = (f).
q   = (kw).
r   = (r).
s   = (s).
ş   = (z).
sh = (ʃ).
t   = (t).
ţ   = (s).
th = (đ).
tḩ = (Þ).
u' = (v).
v' = (v).
w   = (w).
wh² = (wh).
x   = (ks).
ŋ   = (j).
ʒ   = (z).

_____

¹ In words where *h* is written but not pronounced, Bullokar often omits *h*, but writes an accent (ˇ) above the vowel that comes after *h*, e. g. ĕirz̧ (= 'heirs'), ĕrbʒ (= 'herbs') etc.

² For *wh* Bullokar uses a digraph in which the two letters are written together. In instances such as bǫwh, thrǫwh, w forms a diphthong with the vowel that precedes, so that ǫwh is here equivalent to the diphthong ǫw followed by the spirant h'. In a similar manner owh in tḩowht sowht etc. is equal to the diphthong ow + h. This seems to have escaped Hauch (pp. 12, 23), who thinks Ellis has erroneously rendered Bullokar's bǫwh, thrǫwh with buuʜ, thruuʜ in his palæotype. Ellis' transcriptions are, however, perfectly correct, for he looks upon Bullokar's ǫw as identical with (u:).

Bullokar's Orthography as a Criterion of the Contemporary Pronunciation.

To be able to form a correct opinion on Bullokar's writing we must keep in mind it is *not a phonetic system* but is only *an amended orthography*. According to Bullokar, one symbol could have two or three pronunciations, which he duly noted by adding 'prikes and strikes'. Bullokar *did* not or *would* not recognize, however, *that one symbol could have other sounds than those indicated by his diacritic marks*. Thus, if *u* was not pronounced [u] or [ɥ], or if *ou* was neither pronounced [ǫu] nor [ow], Bullokar, who prided himself upon *not altering*[1] the existing orthography,[1] was unable to register these pronunciations. In view of this, a great many of Bullokar's forms must be considered as due to the spelling. I will adduce a few instances to illustrate my thesis.

In some words (the majority of them borrowed from French) *ou* was a symbol for (u:) or (u). This sound is only occasionally indicated by Bullokar (ex. coop, coorc', moorn etc.). In most instances our author follows tradition and writes [oụ] for the sound of (u:), (u) (ex. boụrn, coụrc', coụrt, coụrtịǫs, moụrn, noụrshed, noụrc', poụp etc.).

In e. NE. *e* in some words was a symbol for *ĭ*. Thus Hart 1569 has *ĭ* in *England*, Butler 1633 *ĭ* in *even, evil*, Hodges 1644 *ĭ* in *England, English, evil* etc.[2] If any of these words were known to Bullokar *only* in the traditional spelling *e*, he

---

[1] If Bullokar occasionally has phonetic forms, by the side of those in the traditional spelling (crooch*t* ∼ crǫwch*e*d, coorc' ∼ coụrc'), the reason is that such doublets were also found in the existing orthography (see NED). The actual alterations of the old spelling Bullokar ventures to carry out are mainly confined to the introduction of æ for *ea*, the simplifying of double consonants, the omission of silent letters, such as the final *e* in *ee* and *ie*, *o* in *eo*, *g* in *gh* (ex. miht = 'might'), *l* in souldier, *b* in doubt, *g* in *gn* (ex. rein = 'reign'). See BL. p. 274 f.

[2] Deibel, p. 7*, is probably right in assigning the value *ĭ* to some of the words Smith 1568 spells with his modified *e*.

could denote the pronunciation *ĭ* only by turning *e* into [e']
(his usual symbol for (i:) < ME. *ę̄*); to alter *e* to [i] would have
been an unwarranted derivation from the existing orthography.
Hence Bullokar's [e'] may sometimes stand for *ĭ*. Here, with
certainty, belong E'ngland, and E'nglish', and also possibly
some other instances, such as che'rýż, e'u'ɴ, whe'ry etc. Cf.
below pp. 48, 51.

Bullokar's obvious inability to render the actual pronunciation in the above instances makes it highly probable that also
other forms, in which the pronunciation may have deviated considerably from the spelling, are influenced by the traditional
orthography. Thus ME. *ŏht > ouht* is always rendered with
ouht by Bullokar (ex. ouht, bouht, souht etc.), except in dauhter,
where the scribal tradition had authorized the form with *au*. In a
similar way ME. *ei* by the side of *ę̄* in such words as rec'eiu',
dec'eiu', conc'eiu', conc'eit etc. is invariably rendered with [ei].
For all we know Bullokar may have pronounced these groups
of words with [aɥ] and [æ] respectively, although his dependency
on the existing orthography did not permit him to 'amend'
bought to *bauht or rec'eiu' to *rec'æu'.

Such forms as be'e' (= 'bee') and he'ar (= 'hear') are good
illustrations of Bullokar's almost superstitious veneration for the
traditional spelling. He was not willing to amend 'bee' to *be'
or 'hear' to *he'r, because he did not know, or did not approve
of such spellings as *be, here* for *bee, hear*. He does not ven-
ture to write [ɥ] always for ME. *ŭ*, or [oɥ] for ME. *ū*, but pre-
fers to amend the various traditional symbols for these sounds,
i. e. *o* in *come* to [o̧], and *ow* in *now* to o̧w (as well as *u* to
[ɥ] and *ou* to [oɥ]).

---

[1] Lengthening could not have taken place here, as *ng* is followed by
l. When other authorities testify (i:) in these words, they have probably
been led astray by the orthography, and analysed (i) as (i:). In the part
of BL. which is printed in the ordinary orthography, Bullokar has the
spelling Inglish, where *I* necessarily indicates a short sound. This form
he did not consider good enough to be adopted into the amended orthography.

From what has been said above, it is obvious that in many instances the actual pronunciation *has not been rendered* or *could not* be rendered by the orthographical expedients Bullokar had at his disposal. In this respect it is very instructive to com- pare Bullokar's system with that of Hodges (1644), who was also a Londoner. Like Bullokar, Hodges was very anxious not to alter the existing orthography, and like his predecessor he hit upon the expedient of providing the various symbols with diacritic marks to show their different pronunciations. Hodges brought his system to great perfection. Thus he distinguishes between seven pronunciations of *u,* seven of *ou,* four of *ey* etc.[1], whereas in Bullokar's system the corresponding symbols are pronounced only in two ways or one.

We are hardly justified in assuming that the London pro- nunciation had changed so much during the sixty years that had elapsed between the publication of Bullokar's Book at Large and Hodges' Primrose. It is not to be doubted that Bullokar *also* pronounced his symbols in *more than two or three* different ways, although the deficiencies of his orthographic system did not permit him to denote *all the sounds of a certain symbol.*

We have now shown that Bullokar in several instances was unable to indicate the actual pronunciation of words with the orthographical devices he had at his disposal. It remains to be seen if he makes a consistent use of the possibilities of distin- guishing between the various sounds that his symbols afforded him. Unfortunately this has not always been the case. The traditional spelling crops up every now and then, frustrating the author's attempt at reproducing a perfectly amended spelling.

---

[1] Hodges' symbols of

u : 1) u=(*Λ*), ex. *bustle;* 2) û = (*ju:*), ex. *bugle;* 3) ṳ = (*u*), ex. *bushes, push, punish;* 4) ṳ = (*e*), ex. *bury;* 5) u̩ = (*i*), ex. *busy;* 6) ŭ = (*w*), ex. *guerdon;* 7) ṳ = mute *u*, ex *soul.*

ou : 1) o̱u = (*au*), ex. *bough;* 2) ou = (*Λ*), ex. *rough;* 3) ȯu = (*ɔ:*), ex. *bought;* 4) ôu = (*o:*), ex. *dough;* 5) o̅u = (*u:*), ex. *court;* 6) oͧu = (*u*), ex. *could;* 7) ou = (*ɔ*), ex. *cough.*

ey : 1) e̅y = (*ai*), ex. *eying;* 2) e̩y = (*ei*), ex. *they, prey;* 2) e͡y = ? (*i*), ex. *alley;* 4) ëy = (*e:*), ex. *key.*

In the sequel a series of errors will be discussed which are due to a faulty use of the symbols.

1. Digraphs have been kept in the following instances: great, hoar, feoffee, feofment etc.
2. Final mute *e* is kept in týme.
3. A diacritic mark has been omitted:
   a. Under o, u, v: anguish?, autŏr, consanguinatiu'7, languish?, lou' (twice), succǫr (< ME. *socouren*), vtterly, vnder, wort7 (< OE. *wyrt*), wǫǫd-dou' (< OE. *dūfe*) etc.
   b. after u, v: dryuℜ etc.
   c. after c: on*c*.
   d. under s: hǫwse7 etc.; cf. below on *s*; a diacritic mark has been erroneously added to s, in firṣt and probably to th in láth̩.
   e. under th; soṵth, fowR*t*h.

Theoretically, Bullokar opposes to the unnecessary doubling of consonants, but nevertheless often admits forms with double consonants into his amended orthography. Ex. matter, mattok7, poppet etc. etc.

Although Bullokar expressly tells us (p. 275) that mute letters were to be discarded from his amended orthography, he occasionally retains them, and writes comb, climb*i*ng, lamb, womb (but: dum = 'dumb'), conqer, two, and invariably soldꝑor, in accordance with the traditional spelling. The last example is the more remarkable as we are told in BL. (p. 275) that *l* in *souldier* is 'unsounded'. The keeping of *l* before *m, k,* in such instances as caɫm, baɫm, fólk7, waɫkęd, as well as of *(g)h* in general, is, in all probability, also due to the spelling. Occasionally Bullokar omits *(g)h* (ex. bǫwż, plǫw*i*ng) or inserts it where it has no etymological justification (ex. deliht, kiht).

Like most 16th cent. orthoëpists, Bullokar does not distinguish very carefully between long and short vowels. Thus he very seldom indicates the length of a vowel in a final position. Cf. the following instances of [o], [y], [e], for [ó], [ý], [e'] or [é]: pe-cok, gre-hoynd, graN*t*e, dy, denyęth̩, cry, by*i*ng, by,

no, mo, go, fro, ago, hær- ynto.[1] Bullokar writes [i], [y] promiscuously for ME. ī. He never denotes the length of [i]. This
habit of omitting the length-mark over [i], seems to have made
Bullokar also negligent with regard to [y], which often appears
without a length-mark when standing for ME. ī. Examples of
y for ī are lyc', yl, whyt*e*r, gy૩, entyc'*e*d, deu'y૩ etc.

The diphthong in *owe, old, folk* etc. (< ME. ǭu) is only
occasionally marked as long. For examples, see lists. Bullokar
may have omitted the length-mark also in other instances. This
question can hardly be settled without a special investigation.
I must caution the reader against putting *implicit* faith in Bullokar's evidence on this point.

Bullokar often writes [e] for [*e*'] or [æ] when final: gre-
hoynd, graɴte, pe·cok etc. He objects to denoting *n* merely
by a stroke above the vowel, but breaks this rule in several
instances and writes compo૩ic'iō etc.

Bullokar's dependency on the existing orthography is still
more apparent when he admits into his amended system irregular or phonetic spellings without any historical justification,
as for instance rooм, rouf૪[2], owerź[3] and perhaps chu૩[4], or etymological spellings, such as accǫmpt*e*d etc.

In rendering the vowels of unstressed syllables Bullokar is
very much influenced by the traditional spelling.

In many instances 'declynative strikes' and 'derivative pricks'
are omitted. Ex. hug'nes, nótábl̷, Secretary (cf. secret*a*ryż),
v૩ed (often) etc.

The preterites and participles of irregular verbs are not
always kept 'perfect in figure'. Cf. cræptt and crept etc.

The four signs denoting half-vowels are used by Bullokar
in a very arbitrary way. No doubt ĕ, ŭ were never pronounced

---

[1] ynto may be an error for *yntoo. Lediard has however (o:) < ME. ǭ
both in *to* and *unto* (see Zachrisson Anglia: Beibl. 1917, 80), and Chaucer
rhymes *to:* ME. ǭ.

[2] Here *ou* is due to analogical transference, see Zachrisson, p. 78.

[3] owerź is an inverted phonetic spelling of 'oar'.

[4] For an interpretation of this form, see Zachrisson, p. 85.

in many of the words where Bullokar writes м, n, ʀ, ʟ. Cf. the following instances: hólᴍ (= hóulum!), elᴍ and elm, condemɴ and condemn, conc'ernɪng and conc'ern, fawɴɪng(!), flowɴ(!), gʀau'(!), al-aʀᴍ (obviously due to folk-etymology, see NED)[1]. Formatives are often written with half-vowels on the analogy of their ground-words. Ex. angʀi < angʀ, entʀi < entʀ, disc'iplɪn < discipl, constʀuᴄtion < *constʀ (for *construe*).

By the examples given, we have seen what a disturbing influence the spelling exercises on Bullokar's amended system of orthography. With regard to the different forms we are bound to ask ourselves continually not only if they could be amended according to the principles Bullokar has laid down, but also if they have been amended. The influence of the spelling, though obvious in the case of Bullokar, made itself more or less felt in the works of all early orthoepists down to Cooper. There is very much truth in Cooper's observation that his predecessors were principally anxious to improve the orthography[2]. To render the actual pronunciation faithfully was a matter of secondary importance. This highly important fact has been far too much disregarded.

Bullokar was not satisfied with having amended the English orthography. He also invented some diacritic marks (= 'declynative strikes', 'derivative pricks') (see p. 315) to show derivation and inflection. This not only renders the use of his system more complicated, but also impairs the value of his marks of pronunciation.

Derived or inflected words are called 'formatives' by Bullokar, and 'too ke'p, formatiu'ʒ perfect in figùr' (see p. 387), he never alters the ground-forms, even if the pronunciation has changed by inflection or derivation. Thus, because

---

[1] Considering such anomalous forms as flowɴ and fawɴɪng it is hardly probable that these spellings indicate the development of a svarabhactic vowel, as in ME. *storem, harum*, e. NE. *morun, therell* ('earl') etc. Cf. Jordan § 146, 3, Luick § 446 n. 1, Wyld p. 299.

[2] '*praecipue cacographiam nostram emendare irritò studuerunt*' Jones, Cooper 12*.

scholar is derived from *school*, he does not write this word *sco-lor but scool*l*or, the preterite *read* is not written *red but ræd*d*. For other instances, see BL., p. 294. This practice often prevents us from drawing safe conclusions on the pronunciation of such forms. It is true Bullokar tries to amend matters by doubling the consonants after certain longvowels, when they are to be pronounced short in formatives. In his BL. (p. 294) he tells us that [ý], [e'a], [e'], [æ], [oo] are pronounced ĭ, ĕ, ŭ when followed by double consonants. To illustrate this rule the following instances will suffice:

ý = (i): abýd*d*; býtţ (pt.); chýlddĕrɴ,
æ = (e): ætţ (pt.); hæl*l*tḥ; cræpţt, lædḍ,
e' = (e): bre'dḍ (pt.); fe'd*d* (pt.),
oo = ŭ: doo*n*n,
ó = ŏ: cól*l*ɥor.

On the other hand, it is difficult to believe that [oo] in fool*l*y, scool*l*or was pronounced ŭ. No doubt the sound was the same then, as it is now. Consequently the doubling of consonants does not *always* show the sound. In some instances Bullokar does not remember to double the consonant. Thus hólo*w*, in all probability, is an error for hóllo*w*. He never seems to double *r*, ʒ, *s,* and more seldom *n*, which makes it doubtful how he pronounced the vowel in such words as diu'ýn*i*ty, aboųn-d*a*nt, compár*a*tiu', aspýr*a*c'ion, flọwʀ*i*shɪng, rýʒɴ. Also the pronunciation of the consonants is sometimes uncertain because of the derivation mark. Thus *s* may have been written for ʒ in lọws*i* and glasɴ on the analogy of the simple words lọws, glas.

These many inconsistencies ought to render us very cautious when attempting to draw conclusions on the pronunciation from Bullokar's forms. We have seen that disturbances and inaccuracies arise from three causes: (1) The limited scope of Bullokar's amended system of orthography often made it impossible to give the actual pronunciation of the words. (2) Bullokar allows the orthography to influence his system, even when it would have been possible to render the sounds with comparative accuracy. (3) Some forms are not conclusive owing to Bullokar's desire to keep 'formatives perfèct in figure'.

When due allowance has been made for the deficiencies pointed out in the previous discussion, we need not hesitate in crediting Bullokar's evidence. The old spelling-enthusiast has taken infinite pains over his system, in point of fact he seems to have spent no less than seven years in thinking it out.[1] It must be admitted that he tries to distinguish most carefully between the sounds proper to the symbols he has devised. The errors due not to the inefficiency of his system but to carelessness are very few in number. Let us also not forget that the texts from which the word-lists have been compiled comprise no less than 400 pages.

Jespersen (Hart, p. 19) has very little confidence in Bullokar's capacity as a reformer of the orthography. He thinks Bullokar uses his dots and accents in the most inconsistent way, and his system is characterized as 'confusion worse confounded'. This is a much too severe criticism. A comparison between Hart's phonetic transcriptions and Bullokar's amended orthography will show that Bullokar has worked out his system — faulty and confused though it may be — with more accuracy and consistency than Hart.

Standard of Pronunciation.

Nearly all previous writers have assumed with Ellis that Bullokar used a very refined, somewhat archaic pronunciation.

---

[1] 'In the end, about seuen yeares past, perceyuing more and more the great want of amendmend, I determined with my selfe to lay my priuat doings aside, which my abilitie was il able to beare, to prouide some remedie in a thing so needfull in my Countrie: since which time, I haue endeuored to finish mine enterprise, thinking at the first, to haue restreyned mine owne businesse for half a yeare, or such like time. But when I had entred into the secretes thereof, I found that I had taken a weightier thing in hand, and being entred therinto, could not giue ouer, vntill I had finished the worke herein shewed.' BL. p. 241.

This conclusion is solely based on a too literal interpretation of his evidence on the pronunciation of certain English sounds. As Bullokar did not hold a very high social position, it is probable that his pronunciation was identical with the one current among the middle classes. This conjecture gains in probability by the circumstance that his books contain several forms which are not mentioned — or even marked as vulgar — by other orthoepists.

Such dialectal, or at least colloquial, forms are:

[oo] in *stroke, go*; this latter form is noted by Price 1665, who also has some other dialectal forms.

[e'] in *dive* < OE. dialectal *dēfan* for *dȳfan*.

[aw] (for ow) in *craw* (if not an error).

[ý] (for e') in flýc' < OE. dial. *flȳs*.

[ǫ] (for oụ) in thǫʒand, where the shortening of *ū* to *ŭ* is due to the combination (zn), i. e. $(pu:zend) > (pu:zn)^{1} > (puzn)$. For ME. dial. forms with *o*, see Morsbach, p. 163.

[kn] for [gn] in knawẹth knawʌ; this pronunciation is considered as vulgar by Cootes 1569 (p. 27).

Lengthening of *a, o* in front of certain *r*-combinations is not evidenced by any other contemporary orthoepists.

Addition and loss of *d, t* after certain consonants, as in garnerd, talant?, wan, wanż, móld. For similar instances in the Mod. Engl. dialects, see Wright, EDG §§ 295, 306.

The occurrence of such dialectal or colloquial forms in Bullokar's texts does not support the theory that our author used an archaic pronunciation of the English sounds.

Although not conclusive in this respect, there are some forms in Bullokar's orthography which might indicate that he was a Northerner or least of Northern extraction.

According to NED. *craw* for *crow* is found only in Northern dialects. Nevertheless *aw* for *ow* is frequently found in early London documents (see Morsbach, Schriftsprache, 73, 83, Lekebusch, 70 f.). I do not think Lekebusch is correct in

---

[1] Hodges 1644 marks *a* and *d* as mute in *thousand*.

looking upon these as Northern forms, as they occur in Southern texts also, e. g. in Shillingford's letters (see Zachrisson, p. 50). Cf. also the material adduced by Dibelius 186 ff., Luick § 408, Jordan § 105 n. The Forms of this kind also occur in the Stonor and Cely Letters, and were consequently current in the speech of London (Kihlbom 177).

NED. is not correct in putting down *are* < OE. *erian* (cf. Bullokar's ár*i*ng) as án exclusively Northern form; cf. below, p. 37.

According to the same authoritative work such spellings as *rousch* for *rush* (cf. Bullokar's rǫwsh, sb.) and *bouthe* for *booth* (cf. Bullokar's boụth) are confined to Northern texts[1]. In English Vowels (pp. 54, 77, 208) I have shown, however, that *ou* occurs as a symbol both for (u) and (u:) < ME. ŭ, ǭ, in London documents, so Bullokar's forms may very well reflect Southern habits of spelling.

Bullokar has ŏ in dolt and dolt*i*sh. These forms may be influenced by Northern English *doll* (= 'dull') < OE. *dol* (see NED.). Cf. however, below.

Bullokar has [ó] in *spoon*. At the present time forms with (o:) for ME. ǭ are found only in Northern dialects (ō in *moon, soon, noon*, see Wright, EDG. § 162). It is more likely that Bullokar's spón is an error for spoon or due to analogy; cf. below, p. 48.

The form bǫstiǫs (= 'boisterous') is certainly not a Northern peculiarity. Cf. below.

The form brak sb. (=†brack) (cf. 6—8 *brak*, NED.) is evidently derived from the analogical infinitive *brake* (cf. Zachrisson, p. 58) with ā shortened to ă before *k* final. According to NED., *brack*, sb. (= 'ruptura') is still used in Scotland, but it will be shown in the sequel that such shortened forms were usual in early Standard English.

---

[1] It deserves to be pointed out that Smith's dou for *dūfe* proves him to be a native of the East of England. Smith was born in Essex, and in the adjacent dialects of Norfolk and Suffolk the corresponding form (*dʌu*) (*dɔu*) is found (Deibel 56*). NED. erroneously gives *dow* as an exclusively Northern form.

Moreover, we find forms which exhibit typically Southern features, e. g. flýc (= 'fleece') (cf. 4—6 *flies, flyes* NED.)[1], de'v' (= 'dive'), v'ád (= 'fade').

In Bullokar's vocabulary I have found few words which are characteristic of Northern English (cf. below).

Bullokar mentions several place-names, which, as far as they can be identified, are, as a rule, situated in or near London. Such names are Clapham, Waltham, Old Bailey etc. Bullokar also mentions two small places situated in W. Sussex, Bosham and Billingshurst. As he also comments upon the dialectal pronunciation of initial *th* in E. Sussex and Kent, it is probable that he had lived in or visited these parts of England.

All the dialectal forms Bullokar uses may have occurred in the speech of the capital.

From this survey we may conclude that Bullokar spoke the language which was current in London at the time when Shakespeare left his native town in order to try his fortune in the great City.

---

[1] OE. *flēos, flīes*. If Bullokar's flýc' is not a phonetic spelling with *i* for *e* (cf. owerz for 'oars', rouf for *roof*) it may go back to West Saxon *flȳs*.

PRONUNCIATION

Quantity.

In this place we will point out and exemplify some marked differences between Bullokar's pronunciation and the present pronunciation. To what extent such differences are due merely to carelessness, i. e. omission of length-marks, cannot be definitely settled without a special investigation into quantity in early New English. When forms with a long vowel occur by the side of those with short quantity, there is greater likelihood of an error having been made. The same may be said about the forms which occur only in BL., Bullokar's first work in the amended spelling. On the whole, the same peculiarities with regard to quantity are found however in the works of other early English orthoëpists contemporary with Bullokar, e. g. Smith, Hart, and Gill.

Many words derived from French or Latin, which have length in the present pronunciation, are given with a short vowel by Bullokar. Sometimes we find both length and shortness in the same words. This vacillation may, to a certain extent, be due to the fact that quantity is less decided in French than in English. Hence a French vowel was sometimes rendered with a short, sometimes with a long English vowel. Cf. hereon Morsbach in Festschrift für W. Fœrster, p. 327 ff. Morsbach's explanation can with particular advantage be applied to French words containing a vowel followed by r and a consonant. Here the modern forms generally presuppose a short vowel. In Bullokar we find a continual vacillation between forms with long and short quantity. The peculiarity we have discussed may conveniently be illustrated with the following examples.

Bullokar has a short vowel where Modern English
has length:

1. In originally stressed syllables: ac'[1], broche̹, grac' (~á),
    Jamż (~á), mac'~(á), neger, post (~ó) etc.
2. In originally unstressed syllables[2]: -ac'ion (always), agu,
    approch*i*ng, aswag', brac', dec'es*e*d, deu'o̹r (error?) (~ou̹r),
    embrac'*i*ng̹, eqal (~æ), fau'o̹r, femál, fu̹ndo̹r, fu̹nd*e*d,
    glory, glorio̹os, gratio̹s, Joȝeph, labo̹r, mau'is, moment,
    matron, misplac' (but always á in 'place'), natiu', natùr,
    nac'ion, not*e*d (~ó), paper, parent̹, patienti, prec'ept̹,
    Roman, reproch (~ó), reȝn (~æ), sau' (~á), sau'or,
    sau'ery, saf-gard, sacred, tast*e*d, trety, v'ary, v'arianc'
    etc.

Forms of a similar kind are given by Hart, e. g. *nature,
persuade, commodious, compose, folio* etc., and by Gill, as in *aged,
expectation, favour, Egypt, ingenious, material, cider, divide, silence, glorious, commodious* etc.

We may also compare the following early spellings: *esse*
('ease'), *ratte* ('rate'), Cely Papers 3, 42, *casse* ('case'), *begyll*
('beguile'), *endytted* ('indicted'), Paston Letters 685, 612, 641.
In the case of French words it is possible that the forms with
a short vowel were sometimes favoured, because they came nearer
in sound to their French equivalents. Words of the type *nation*
have nearly always a long vowel, but the sad word *ration,* which
the war made actual, was generally pronounced (ræʃən) in accordance with French habits of speech. Note also the distinction between (ei) in *patent,* and (æ) in the more foreign combination *letters patent.* Cf. also Luick § 425 b.

Bullokar has length, where Modern English has
shortness: hærɴ, plástar, tou̹ch (~ u̹) (error?), træȝùr, góu'erɴ-
*i*ng (for ŏ in this word, cf. below) etc.

Vacillation in French words where the vowel is followed

---

[1] Words containing *i* are omitted, as Bullokar here omits the length-
mark. Cf. p. 18.

[2] Here are also given verbs, such as *place, note* etc.

by r + a consonant: árt (~ a), archorż, chárg' (~a), córd, córs ('corpse'), charᴍ, fórc' (~ o), fork, fórg', gárd (~ a), gárdɴ (~ a), lárg' (~a), márɫ, párt (~a), pártᴚor, párc'*i*ng, pærlż, perc'~ pérc', rehærc' (~ e), scárc'*l*y (~ a), spórt (~ o), sórt (~ o), særch (~ e), særc'*e*d, vérs (~e) etc. Words of this kind are generally given with a short vowel by Smith, Hart, and Gill. Cf. however Hart's *a* long in *tart* (Jesp. 92), and *o* long in *force, waard* in early London documents, and *gaard* in Machyn (Wyld 142).

In some of them (e. g. *sport, forge* etc.) length is testified by later authorities e. g. Walker (as in PE. *scarce*). Alphabet Anglois seems to have length for *a* in *part, harp* (see Zachrisson 11). Spenser rhymes *regard : reared* (Gabrielsson 161).

Short ME. vowels which were lengthened in open syllables often appear with shortness. Here we may distinguish between three groups of words:

1. Words which in ME. were only dissyllabic: ou'er, cho3ɴ (~ ó), borɴ (~ o), eu'en. In ou'er lengthening has not taken place owing to weak stress. If cho3ɴ, eu'en and borɴ are not errors, the vowel may have been shortened before the following consonants. Hart has a short vowel in *graven*, and later orthoëpists testify shortness for *swollen* and *stolen*. Cf. Zachrisson, Anglia: Beiblatt 1918, p. 173. In the verbs the short vowel in the past participle may also be due to the analogy of infinitives with a short vowel. Cf. below p. 31.

2. Words which in ME. exhibited both dissyllabic and trisyllabic forms: bra3ɴ, beu'er, father, hau'ɴ, opɴ, rather, water (~á), wau'er etc. The short vowel is due to inflected forms.

3. Words which in ME. chiefly occurred in dissyllabic forms: brak(sb), crau' (~ á), fret (~ æ), gra3, lo3*i*ng (~ ó), wau' (~ á), stau'ʒ, ᴚok*e*d (~ ó). In some of these words the length-mark may have been omitted by carelessness. If the forms are correct the short vowel goes either back to certain ME. trisyllabic forms (*grasede,*

crauinde etc.) in which no lengthening took place, or is due to subsequent shortening in syncopated form such as *crav'd, crav's* < *craved, craves,* where it came to be placed before two consonants. Hart has a few similar forms (*o* short and long in *hope, a* short and long in *make, shape*), which Jespersen looks upon as errors. The form stau' may be a blending of *stăf* and *stāve*.[1] Gill has *ā̆* in *make*, *ē̆* in *speak*, Smith *ē̆* in *break*. Here and in other similar cases shortening may also have taken place before a single final consonant.

The uninflected forms have been generalised in næther, næther-móst.

Some words of this type, with originally a long vowel, have been shortened[1] in Bullokar, but remained with a long vowel in Present English: holy, leu'er[2] (~ e'), eu'ning (~ e'), wery (~ e' ~ æ).

Sometimes length in Bullokar corresponds to shortness in Present English: wépɴ (~e), se'ly.

In thoȝand, thoȝandth, shortening has taken place before the following consonants.

The usual Elizabethan form hoṵs-band (see NED.) is found by the side of huṣband.

Before *st* there is vacillation between short and long forms: Ester ('Easter'), est-wýnd, north-est, næst etc. Cf. Wyld, Rhymes, 98.

In one instance Bullokar gives nót (= nought) with length.

A long vowel is generally kept before a single final consonant: bæm, bród, brood, dæf, doou', gooc', græt, hoou'ȝ, look, took, thræd etc.

Before a dental shortening has taken place in bred, bredth, breth, blud, ded, deth, flṵd, gọọd, loth, red etc. before *k*

---

[1] Similarly Daines' *stāfe* (Brotanek XXII) may be a blending of *stāve* and *stăf*. I do not think *ā* is the forerunner of PE. (a:) in *staff*. In other instances Daines has a short vowel before spirants (see Brotanek XVIII).

[2] Cf. such late ME. and e. NE. comparatives as *gretter, depper, nĕrer* etc. See ten Brink, Chaucer 131, Jespersen, Hart 29.

in sik, before *n* in ten, doo*n*n etc., before *f*, *v* in lof, strau' (~ á).
In e. NE. a short vowel was not unusual in numerous words
of this type.

The shortening of a long vowel before a final consonant in
all probability goes back to late Old English and early Middle
English. It is indicated by the doubling of consonants both in
a final position and in inflected forms. Such spellings are found
in OE. texts, especially from the transition period, and in Ormulum.[1] There can be little doubt that similar spellings in
Layamon etc., such as *tock, tocken, hock, sock, stodde* for *took,
tooken, hook, sook, stoode* are not due to orthographical confusion, as is assumed by Morsbach (§ 54, n 3), but to the shortening of a long vowel in connected speech, when the following
word began with a consonant. The short vowel could be analogically extended to inflected forms.[2]

In early New English the doubling of consonants is usual
not only in such words as *fōt*, but also in *take* etc., where the
consonant had become final after the loss of *-e*. Here again
they are not confined to final position but also occur in inflected
forms.[3]

In the Shillingford Papers I have noted *heddes* and *sonner*,
in letters written by Henry VIII (ed. Ellis) *hoppe* ('hope', sb.)
and *wrytt* ('write'), and in the Verney Memoirs *bredd* I 85, *dell*
('deal') I 160, *brocke* ('broken') I 272, *macke, tackes* I 435, *tacke,
shacke* I 261, *tacken* I 237, *macke, hopp* ('hope'), *lick* ('like'),
spack (= 'spake', pres.) I 244, *a grit dele* I 241 etc. Similar
forms from the Paston Letters are *takke, spakke* 695, *stell* ('steal')

---

[1] Illustrative instances are adduced by Bülbring, § 548 ff., Morsbach,
§ 54, Jordan, § 27, Hackmann, Kürzung langer Tonvokale, pp. 4 ff., Schlemilch, Beiträge zur Sprache und Orthographie etc., p. 65, Zachrisson, English Place-Names and River-Names, p. 41 and the literature quoted there.

[2] Cf. *bock* ('book'), *seocke* ('sick'), *strætte* ('street'), *iuatte* (= *iwat*),
leoppe (= *hléopon*), *wisse* (= *wīse* sb.) etc. in Layamon (Luhmann, 59 f.,
Lucht, 12 ff.).

[3] Illustrative instances are adduced by the authorities already quoted,
especially Hackmann, by Zachrisson, p. 55, and Wyld, pp. 255 ff., and
Rhymes, p. 92.

464, from the Cely Papers *salle* ('sale') 10. The grammarian
Daines (pp. 25, 50) directs *o* in *stole*, vb., and *spoke,* vb., to be
pronounced short. Butler has short and long *i* in *drive* (Eichler 32) and short *i* in *leap* (Eichler 36).

Such shortened forms are particularly usual in letters written
by persons who were not well versed in orthographical matters.
For this reason they are rare in official documents. They are
more frequent in the Cely Papers than in the Paston Letters,
but they are few and far between in the Stonor Letters, where
the correspondents generally belonged to the higher and well
educated classes. Nevertheless we also find here such forms as
to wytt, whette ('to wit') no. 127, 151, *deppe,* no. 161, *gonne,*
no. 153, *lossyn* ('losing'), no. 151 etc. But in certain household
accounts (no. 233), which were probably written by a servant of
the Stonors and are distinguished by their cacography, there is an
abundance of forms with double consonants. In this document,
which only consists of two pages, we meet with the following
forms: *yenne* ('even', sb.), *renne* ('reign'), *wenne* ('wine'), *pessen*
('peas'), *elleys* ('eels'), *yerre* ('year'), *wette wenne* ('white wine').
The lowering of *ĭ* to *ĕ* in *wette wenne* conclusively proves that
the doubling of the consonant really indicates vowel-shortening.

The occurrence of hybrid spellings, such as *seelle* ('seal'),
gootten, maytters, sayff, cheyffe etc. in the Cely Papers (3, 124,
61, 120, 130), and *weell, fooll, feell, dyell* etc. in the Paston
Letters (703, 732, 745, 693) shows that there must have been
a considerable vacillation between a short and a long vowel in
words such as *foot, take, taken, open, nature* etc. in the colloquial language of the early NE. period. In modern dialects the
shortening of a long vowel before a final consonant is very
usual. Cf. Hackmann, pp. 44 ff. Consequently the orthographical evidence which has been adduced supports the forms of
pronunciation given by Bullokar.

As the vowel-shortening in *foot, sick* etc. took place in
early ME. (Ormulum, Layamon), and could be analogically transferred to inflected forms (cf. p. 31), it follows that the shortened
vowel could be subsequently lengthened in open syllables. This

may account for such dialectal forms as *hame*[1] ('home') in the Paston Letters (but cf. below) and Stane, Staines for Stone(s) in Southern English place-names and perhaps also for Bullokar's e' in *like* etc.

Bullokar har length in lót (~o) (from the inflected forms). In several words discussed in the sequel *ĭ* appears to have been lengthened to *ẹ̆*.

Lengthening of *ŭ* has taken place in loou'ẹd (once). This spelling is also found in the famous More MS., though not in the portion supposed to have been written by Shakespeare.

Before *r* + consonant Bullokar often has long forms or long and short forms promiscuously: bárɴ (~a), cárĺ, chórĺ (< *ceŏrl* < *céorl*), córɴ (~o), hórɴż (~o), thórɴ (~o), haụ-thórɴtre', qárɴ, wárɴ (~a), ɴárɴ etc.

It appears as if the OE. lengthening before certain consonantal combinations (*rd*, *rl*, *rn*) should have repeated itself in ME. times.[2]

The lengthening has taken place also in words where the vowel in early ME. must have been short, as in *barn* < OE. *bĕrn* < *berærn, quarn* < *cwĕrn* < *cweorn*[3].

Before combinations which did not cause lengthening in OE. times, the vowel has remained short: ars-hól, bark, cart, forty, harᴍ, hart, hors, short, warᴍ etc.[4]

The only apparent exceptions to this are fórmer, fórmer, fór (once)[5]. As appears from the spelling fórmer, with the deri-

---

[1] Cf. Staines, Mds., spelt with *a* in all early forms (960—1200) (Gover 79) and the following Essex place-names: Steeple cum Stanesgate, *Stanesgate* 1254—55 PF.; *La Stane* 1235—36, *Stane* 1250—51 PF; *Stains Upper, Lower, Middle, Stanes Field* in Tollerhunt D'Arcy (Waller, Essex Field Names 149, 275).

[2] This explanation is also given by Horn, p. 46. Such instances as *horn, corn, thorn* must, however, be kept apart from *hord, torn, lord, sport* etc. where Walker has ó̍. See Gabrielson p. 164 f.

[3] Note that 'harm' is wrongly given with á by Hauck, p. 32.

[4] The only word of this type in which OE. *ō* may have been kept is boord ('board') which regularly appears with (u:) < *ǭ*.

[5] In French words Bullokar has á, ó before all kinds of *r*-combinations. Cf. p. 29.

vative dot under *m*, the length-mark is due to a supposed etymological connection with *fore-* in *before, forepart* etc.

Fórmer is a parallel to cræptt, ætt, doown etc., where the vowel was pronounced short, although it is provided with a length-mark. Cf. above p. 20. Similarly fór has been influenced by *fore-* in fórmóst etc.

As far as I am aware, a vowel corresponding to ME. *ā̆*, *ǭ* is not evidenced for any of these words from other sources, with the exception of Butler's thorn' ~ thorn, which may be an error (Eichler 41).

Spencer rhymes *marred* (spelled: *mard*) : *stared, unbard*: *far'd*, but the vowel may have been short in all these. Anyhow, Bullokar has not length in forms of this kind. Pope has *hard: dared*, but also *star : air, star : bear*. Cf. Gabrielson, pp. 72 f., 160 ff. The long vowel in these words may be the forerunner of PE. (a:)[1].

In Writing Scholar's Companion and Right Spelling (see Kern, 36) *corn, horn* etc. are given with the same vowel as *go, old*. Ekwall (p. IX) has pointed out, however, that the long *o* in 'corn, horn' etc. probably was (ɔ:), for the author of W. S. Companion does not keep the sounds (o:) and (ɔ:) apart. In a similar manner (ɔ:) and (o:) are confused under *ō* long in Right Spelling and in Brightland's Grammar, which are based to a great extent on Writing Scholar's Companion. See Zachrisson, Anglia: Beiblatt 1914, p. 249 f., 1917, p. 80.

Miège (1685) directs *o* to be pronounced long before *rn*, but this long vowel may also be (ɔ:). See Spira, p. 144.

In certain Northern dialects (see Wright, EDG. § 87) we find *ō, ōr* in front of *rn, rd* (*ford, corn, horn* etc.), but this *ō* has probably developed from earlier (uə), which is found by the side of *ō* in the same words. Cf., hereon, my article in Anglia 1914, p. 422. Moreover *ō, uə* are not confined to position before *rd, rn*, but occur also before other combinations, such as *rt, rm* (*short, storm* etc.).

---

[1] This is probably also the case with the long vowel evidenced by Daines in *warne, barne* (see Brotanek XVIII).

In Northern dialects (see Wright EDG, § 37) we also find *ēr* at least in one of Bullokar's words with á, i. e. in *warn,* but the same sound also occurs in *arm, harm, harvest* etc. where Bullokar only has ă. Such a form **can** therefore hardly be considered equivalent to Bullokar's or be quoted in support of the theory that he was a Northener.

Under these circumstances it would be very tempting to look upon Bullokar's forms with á, ó as forerunners of Present English (a:), (ɔ:), on the hypothesis that the lengthening at first took place only before *rl, rn, rd.* Such a hypothesis cannot, of course, be proved, but it would at least give *raison d'être* to the forms, which otherwise are without a parallel. If so, Bullokar's á, ó in *carl, horn* etc. must have been qualitatively different from á, ó of other provenience. This is in itself not impossible, for we have already seen how in late spelling-books (o:) and (ɔ:) were confused under *o* long.

Before *ld* and *nd* Bullokar sometimes has length, whereas shortening has taken place in the modern forms: býld, se'ld, se'ldǫm, fre'nd, wýnd꞊ sb., etc.

The forms comb and womb (also in Smith, see Deibel 39*) exhibit . shortness against length in Present English. The retention of *b* makes it doubtful whether they are not re-produced in a wholly traditional garb.

Quality.

ME. *a, ā* in man, name.

Bullokar's statement that *a* is 'a perfect letter' ought to indicate that ă in *man* and ā in *name* were pronounced with exactly the same sound. Similar statements are made by Smith, Hart, and Gill. It is very doubtful if Smith and other grammarians, who looked upon ă in *man* and ā in *name* as qualitatively identical, actually pronounced them with exactly the same sound. From the classical authors, they had learned that there are five vowels, long and short *a*, *e*, *i*, *o*, *u*, and they may have applied this rule broadly to the English sounds, simply to make them fit in as closely as possible with the time-honoured classical vowel system. It is to be noted that the qualitative identity of *ă* short and *ā* long is chiefly taught by grammarians who were at the same time great classical scholars. I consider it quite possible that these grammarians may have looked upon (æ) and (ɛ:) or even a slightly palatalised (a) and (æ:) or (ɛ:) as identical from a qualitative point of view. In spite of his great classical learning, Smith confuses not only diphthongs and digraphs, but also diphthongs and simple vowels.[1] Other authorities, who are less biassed in their judgement, such as many French grammarians, and Englishmen, such as Mulcaster, Butler, and Hume, distinctly tell us that there was a qualitative difference between *a* in 'man', and *a* in 'name'.[2] Numerous phonetic spellings, such as *beck* for *back*, *gelon* for *gallon*, *teke* for *take* etc., enable us to conclude that *a* in *man* and *name* had a palatal pronunciation as early as the 15th century.[3]

It is uncertain whether *ă* in *man* was also pronounced as (a) in the 16th and early 17th centuries. The Frenchman Erondelle and the Englishman Wodroephe identify · English and French *ă*, but such statements occur much later, when in all probability *ă* was generally pronounced as (æ). When describing *ă*, Cooper (1685) says that it was pronounced with the middle of the tongue somewhat elevated *(a medio linguae ad concavum palati panlulum elevato)*, i. e. as (æ). Nevertheless he identifies this sound with the French and the German (a).

Arguments against the supposed pronunciation of *ā* in *name* as (a:) and *ai* in *day* as (a:i) in the 16th century are adduced

---

[1] Cf. Zachrisson, pp. 164, 207, 217 f.

[2] Cf. Zachrisson, pp. 120 ff., 187 ff.

[3] Cf. Zachrisson, pp. 56—62, and the more definite conclusions arrived at in Engl. Stud, 52, 316. Some of Wyld's (p. 198) instances of *e* for *ă* are not quite conclusive. Thus *sedness*, Palladius 10. 255, means 'sowing' from OE. *sǣd*. Attempts at sifting the material are made in English Vowels, *l. c.* Cf. also below.

in my essay Shakespeare's Uttal pp. 34 ff. Whether *ā* in *name* could be pronounced as (a:) in the 15th century is difficult to decide. To judge by the following spellings in the Paston Letters it looks as if the Continental *a* in French loan-words was sometimes replaced with (ɔ:), as in *vause* for *vase* and *spaw* for *spa* at a considerably later date: *reparaucion* 136, *lawberyd* 410, *laubore* 827. Similar early spellings, such as *laurde* (15th c.), *chaurge* (16th c.) are discussed in my book English Vowels, p. 62.

Bullokar's [a, á].

In the light of the previous discussion it is most probable that Bullokar pronounced *ă* in *man* as (æ). For reasons that will be given in the sequel he may have pronounced *ā* in *name* as (æ:), or more probably (ɛ:).

A palatal pronunciation of *ā,* at least before *r,* must also be inferred from the forms bár, bárż, she'-bár (= *ursus*) and áring (< OE. *erian*) as well as særc'*ed* (< ME. *saarce, sarsse,* see NED). Here *ār* has evidently coalesced in sound with *ĕr* in *bear,* vb. For other early instances of this sound-levelling, see Zachrisson, p. 52 n. and p. 57. Add.: *spares* (= 'spears'), Machyn, 203.

In imparatiu' and imparatiu'*ly ĕr* appears as *ăr.* In e. NE. there is a great vacillation between *ĕr* and *ăr* in loan-words of this type. Bullokar as a rule writes 'er'.

OE. *ǣ* appears shortened to *ă* in wrastl*i*ng. Vacillation between *e* and *a* is usual in such words in e. NE. See Grünzinger, More, p. 24.

ME. *ai* appears as á in explán and mál. Cf. 6—8 *explane,* NED., 5 *malys* NED. Forms of this kind do not necessarily indicate that *ai* and *ā* had been levelled under the same sound. See Zachrisson, 66.

In halter and alter *ă* has not passed into *au* before *l* + cons. These may be errors of the same kind as bald~baĺd etc. It is conceivable, however, that *ă* in alter is a learned Latin pronunciation. Hart has *ă* in *alter* (but also in native words), Gill *ă* in *exalt*. Cf. the present vacillation between (*æl*) and (*ɔ:l*) in *altercate, altercation, alternate, alternative* etc. See Jespersen 10. 36.

ME. *ai*, *ei* in day, obey.

The pronunciation of ME. *ai*, *ei*, in *day*, *obey* etc. is the greatest *crux* in early NE. sound-history. To begin with, there can be little doubt that *ai* and *ei* had coalesced in sound at this period. Bullokar distinguishes theoretically between *ai* and *ei*, but confuses them in his amended orthography by writing stey and stay for French *estaye*, pertain by the side of pertein, ageinst and against, weih and wayeth etc.

Phonetic spellings, such as *pailling*, *haist* for *paling*, *haste*, and *daly*, *ading* for *daily*, *aiding*[1] etc. and occasional rhymes with old *ā* and *ai* in the works of Spenser[2] and Shakespeare[3] indicate that *a* in 'made' and *ai* in 'maid' were pronounced with the same sound by many speakers in the 15th and 16th centuries. The earliest French grammarians direct *a* in *made* and *ai* in *maid* to be pronounced with the same vowel as the French word *être*, 'to be'. This points to a common pronunciation (ɛ:) for the long *a* in *made* and the diphthong *ai* in *maid*. According to the French grammarians, the ME. open *ę̄* in *meat* was also to be pronounced in the same way as the French open *ę̄*. A literal interpretation of these rules would lead to the assumption that at Shakespeare's time such words as 'made', 'maid' and 'meat' were all pronounced with the same sound. In English Vowels[4] I assumed that this identification was due to the inability of the French grammarians to distinguish between the long open *e* in *made*, *maid* and the long close *e* in *meat*. A different view is taken by Wyld, who maintains that ME.

---

[1] Cf. Zachrisson, pp. 64 ff., Engl. Stud, p. 315, Wyld, p. 248, Rhymes, p. 54.

[2] Gabrielson, p. 31.

[3] Vietor, p. 55 f.

[4] Cf. Zachrisson, pp. 125, 128.

ai, *ā* and *ę̄* had an identical pronunciation in the 16th century
and later.[1] Some of the arguments Wyld marshals in support
of this view are not conclusive. Cooper does not include *meat*
and *mate* among words with the same pronunciation. The two
words he couples are *meat* and *mete*, which both contain ME.
long open *ę̄*.[2] Spellings such as *spake* and *brake* (inf., past pp.)
do not necessarily indicate a levelling of *ā* and *ę̄* under the
same sound. It is at least very probable that *a* has been transferred analogically from the past tense to the infinitive[3] and the
past participle. Rhymes, such as *retrate : take* (*ā : ā*), *disdain :
mean* (*ę̄ : ę̄*), *clean : Seine* (*ę̄ : ę̄*) *streams : Thames* (*ĕ : ĕ*) and several
others, are not quite conclusive. Nevertheless some of the
rhymes adduced by Wyld unambiguously show that such words
as 'made', 'maid' or 'meat' were actually pronounced with the
same vowel. Such instances are *ease : days* (Surrey), *sea : obey*
(Grimald), *Nature : defeature* (Shakespeare), *mead : braid, sea : lay*
(Drayton), *sea : play* (Habington) etc. Cf. also *way : sea, par-
take : weak, flame : beam, pace : increase, laesie* ('lazy') *: creasie*
('crazy'), *state : seat, nature : feature, save : reave* (Spenser) noted
by Gabrielson, p. 65. Cf. also Krapp, 126 f.

Moreover, in a number of grammars and spelling-books
from the end of the 17th and the beginning of the 18th centuries several words containing ME. *ai*, *ā* and *ę̄* are directed
to be pronounced alike. In some of these words *ai*, *ei* may be
orthographical symbols for ME. *ę̄*, or indicate a pronunciation
with (e), which was mistaken for (e:) by the respective writers,
but others remain which indisputably point to a levelling of
ā, *ai* and *ę̄* under the same sound. This is particularly the case
with Brown's (1700) list of words, in which he directs *feign* to
be pronounced as *feane or fane*, *pray* and *prey* as *pra or pre*,

---

[1] Cf. Wyld, p. 210, Rhymes, p. 55.

[2] Cf. Cooper, p. 78 (ed. Jones).

[3] Cf. Zachrisson, p. 58. Spellings such as *brake(n)*, *spak(en)* are too
frequent to be occasional phonetic spellings. Cf. the following additional
instances from the Verney Memoirs: *spake*, inf. I 111, *spake*, pp. I 385, 430,
brake, pp. I 169.

and *weigh* as *way or wea*, and with certain rules concerning the pronunciation of *ea, ei* given by Strong (1676) and Dyche (1710).[1]

Consequently the combined evidence of rhymes and orthoëpists tends to prove that Wyld is correct in assuming that from about the middle of the 16th till the beginning of the 18th centuries ME. *ai, ā*, and *ę̄* were pronounced with the same sound by numerous speakers.[2]

I account for this in the following way. During the whole of this period ME. words containing *ę̄*, such as *sea, meat, ease* etc., had two pronunciations, an advanced one with (i:) (cf. below) and a more conservative one with half-close (e:), which became identical with the advanced pronunciation of *ā* and *ai* as (e:) in such words as 'made' and 'maid'. On the other hand, I cannot subscribe to Wyld's view that this conservative pronunciation of ME. *ę̄* has been kept in *great, break, steak*, and *yea*, where Present English (ei) may go back to early variants with *ā, ai*, or be due to the influence of related words with *ai, ĕ*.[3] This explanation also holds good for the present pronunciation of Hayes in Middlesex, which goes back to OE. *hǣse* (OHG. *heisi*) 'brushwood'. All the early forms are regularly spelt with *e*.[4] Spellings with *ey, ay* do not appear until the end of the 15th century, when, as we have assumed, *ā, ai* and *ę̄* had coalesced in sound. The name was now confused with such names as

---

[1] Zachrisson, pp. 197—201. There I have arrived at somewhat different conclusions, because I did not know of the numerous rhymes with *ai : ā : ę̄* which give more weight to the statements of Brown, Strong, and Dyche.

[2] Some occasional spellings with *e* for *ā*, or *ai* (cf. Zachrisson, pp. 56, 67) may possibly indicate that this levelling had taken place as early as the 15th century. Conclusive in this respect are such spellings as *neayle* ('nail') Ludlow Acconts late 15 c., and *steay, dealy, chearge, neame, teabull, pleace* in the Verney Memoirs, middle of 17 c. (Lady Penelope) I 420—422. More spellings of this kind, not all of them quite conclusive, are adduced by van der Gaaf, p. 348.

[3] Cf. Jespersen, II, 75, Zachrisson, pp. 58, and below, p. 48.

[4] Cf. *linganhese, lingahæse* 793, *Hesa* 1086, *Hese* 1232, 1291, 1316 (Gover, 42).

contain 'hay' from OE. *hege, gehæg,* and for this reason (ei) has been kept in the present pronunciation.

If the 16th century pronunciation of ME. *ę̄* as (e:) were due to the introduction of SW. dialectal forms into Standard English, some of these vernacular forms might certainly have survived, but such a dialectal origin of (e:) is unlikely.[1]

The early NE. pronunciation of *ę̄* in 'meat' as (e:) merely represents a stage in its development to (i:). At Shakespeare's time (mi:t) for *meat* was the advanced pronunciation objected to by Gill and all contemporary grammarians, (me:t) was the more conservative one, which, however, in the course of the 18th century was generally replaced by the present one with (i:).

The early English grammarians, Smith, Gill etc., did not approve of a common pronunciation for *ai, a, ea* in such words as *maid, made, meat.* They keep *ā* in *made* distinct from *ę̄* in *meat,* and direct *ai* in *maid* to be pronounced as a diphthong. A careful analysis of their rules renders it most probable that they distinguished between *ā, ai, ę̄* as (ɛ:) or (æ:), (ɛ:i)[2], (e:) as opposed to the colloquial pronunciation of *ā, ai, ę̄* as (e:). It is difficult to tell to what extent this distinction is based upon an actual pronunciation of a more conservative character or on a more or less artificial one. The diphthongic pronunciation of *ai* taught by later grammarians is to a great extent either dialectal (Daines) or theoretical (Wallis, Cooper).

A monophthongic pronunciation of *ai* is also mentioned by the early English grammarians, although they do not approve of it. It cannot always be ascertained if this monophthongic pronunciation is identical with the common pronunciation of *ā, ai* and *ę̄* as (e:), or if it is only a finicking and somewhat affected pronunciation of *ai* with a very close (e:).

---

[1] On the question of dialectal forms in early Standard English, see Zachrisson Anglia 1914, p. 432, Engl. Stud. 60, p. 354 f., Det engelska Riksspråket, pp. 399, 402 ff.

[2] Arguments against a current pronunciation of *ai* as (æi) with the first element short are adduced in English Vowels, p. 190, Shakespeare's Uttal, p. 35 f.

Alone among the English grammarians Hart directs *ai* and *ę̄* in *maid* and *meat* to be pronounced with an identical sound, distinct from that of *ā* in *name*. A literal interpretation of his rules would lead to the assumption that he favoured the common pronunciation of *maid* and *meat* with (e:), whereas he pronounced *a* in *name* with a more open sound (ɛ:) or (æ:)? It is conceivable, however, that he also pronounced *name* with (e:), but was reluctant to use the same notation for *ā* as for *ę̄*, because he wanted to bring the English vowel system as much as possible into accordance with the Latin one.[1]

The results arrived at in the present survey, which differ in several respects from the interpretation of the evidence attempted in English Vowels, may be briefly summed up as follows: —

At Shakespeare's time *ai, ā, ę̄* in *maid, made, meat* in colloquial speech were generally pronounced with the same sound, a half-close long *e* (e:). To judge by the rhyming usage and by the available orthographical and orthoëpistical evidence, this pronunciation dates as far back as the 15th century, and was in current use till the beginning of the 18th century, when the pronunciation of *ę̄* in 'meat' as (e:) became obsolete. Possibly but not necessarily for theoretical reasons, the majority of early English grammarians keep *ā, ai,* and *ę̄* distinct, probably as (ɛ:) or (æ:), (ɛ:i), and (e:). They also refer to a monophthongic pronunciation of *ai,* which in some cases (Mulcaster, Butler) is most likely to have been the colloquial (e:) — used both for *ā, ai* and *ę̄* — in others a finicking pronunciation of *ai* as (e:). From about 1650 the distinction between *ai* and *ā* is, as a rule, not kept up even by the English grammarians, who, however, like their French colleagues, on the whole,

---

[1] I prefer these alternative interpretations of Hart's [aˑ] and [eˑ] to the one suggested in English Vowels, p. 192. Note that Butler, although distinguishing between *ai, ā̄* and *ē̄*, nevertheless admits into his amended spellings such forms as *dazy* for *daisy* and *plas'* for *plaice* (Eichler 12, 13).

addhere to the pronunciation (e:) for ę̄ during both the 16th and 17th centuries.

Jespersen thinks that the common sound for *ai* and *ā* (and ę̄?) was (ei), as in modern English, which is possible, but cannot be actually proved.[1]

Bullokar's [ai, ei, ay, ey].

For general considerations it is most probable that Bullokar, who never confuses *ā* with *ai* in his amended spelling, at least theoretically, followed Smith and Gill in distinguishing between *ā*, *ai* and ę̄ as (æ:) or (ε:), (ε:i) and (e:).

In leiʒurż (cf. above, p. 15) *ei* is probably only a spelling for ę̄. Cf. *raison, plaise* etc. in London documents of the 15th century (Lekebusch 40 f.).

In lei-boụnd (= 'lea-bound', see NED: bound, sb.[1]) *ei* goes back to the ME. form *lēage* (an analogical formation to the nom. *lēah*). Smith has the same form, but Deibel, p. 27, has not hit upon the correct explanation.

As for *receive, deceive* etc., cf. above p. 15.

ME. ę̄, ẹ̄ in meat and meet.

We have already seen that ME. ę̄ in *meat* was pronounced as (e:) by some speakers in the 16th century. That *meat* and similar words could also be pronounced with (i:) appears from such phonetic 16th century spellings as *spyke, bryke, pryche*, rhymes with ę̄ and ẹ̄ in works by Spenser, Shakespeare etc., and the evidence of Gill.[1] I am now able to augment the evidence with a few more phonetic spellings, viz. *displisyd*, Stonor

---

[1] On the use of *ei* as a transcription for English *ai* (1751) and for *ā* and *ai* (1828), see Cardim, p. 10. But the distinction between *ai* and *ā* in Castro's grammar (1751) may perhaps be due to the spelling. Even a trained phonetician like Ellis was unable to distinguish between (ei) and (e:).

[1] Cf. Zachrisson, pp. 69, 203, Engl. Stud. 52, p. 325, Jones, Cooper, p. 33, Gabrielson p. 28, Wyld p. 209, Rhymes p. 60.

Letters no. 120, *chine* (1531), by the side of *cheane* ('chain'), St.
Mary at Hill, London (Zopf, p. 45), *iseylie* 1655 Verney Memoirs II, 27. The following spellings with *ea* for *ẹ̄* may also
indicate that such words as *meat* and *meet* were pronounced
with a common sound (i:): *peace* ('piece'), Ludlow Accounts, late
15 c., *creaple* ('cripple') Lyly (Wyld 133), *nead, indead, beleafe*
Verney Memoirs I, 296, 128, 73[1]. It is worthy of note that
Queen Elizabeth sometimes writes *ea* for *ee,* as in *deapest, seake,
beleaved* (Wyld, 137), and *i* for *ea,* as in *spike, bequived* (Wyld,
ibid.), and *plisd* (cf. MLR. XVI, p. 88). Hence it looks as if
the Virgin Queen herself was to be numbered among the of-
fenders (*mopsæ, bubulci et portiores!*) who excited the rage of the
conservative Gill, because they pronounced *leave* with (i:).[2]

Phonetic 15th century spellings such as *myte* ('meet'), *hire*
('hear') etc. and the unanimous evidence of the early grammarians prove that ME. *ẹ̄* in *meet, be* etc. was generally pronounced
as (i:) in early NE. times.[3] As far as I can judge, Luick's suggestion (Brandl Cel. Vol., p. 91) that spellings, such as *myte*
etc., indicate that ME. *ẹ̄* ad *ī* had coalesced in sound, is a mere
conjecture. In native words such a change may possibly have
taken place before *r*, hardly in other cases. When *ẹ̄* in *meet*
became qualitatively identical with *i* in *sit,* the symbol for the
short *i* was unconsciously chosen to represent the new long (i:)
which had developed from the ME. close *ẹ̄*. This is the simple
explanation of such spellings as *myte* for *meet* etc. For similar
reasons *o* was sometimes chosen to render graphically the new
(ɔ-)-sound that had developed from ME. *au* in *all, saw* (cf.
Zachrisson 82, Engl. Stud. 52, 312, Anglia: Beibl. 1917, p. 81).
Likewise *ou*, which was first used as a symbol for *ŭ* short

---

[1] Sometimes *ea* for *ẹ̄* may denote *ĕ* short, as in *head* ('heed'), Paston
Letters 732 (cf. *hedde = heed*, ibid. 733).

[2] Other instances are noted by van der Gaaf, p. 345. When these
forms are used by writers who do not render *ē̦* with *i*, it is of course possible to interpret them as due to orthographic confusion on the analogy of
street, streat etc. Bullokar (BL. 255) says that the best writers used *ea*
for *ē̦* and both *ea, ee, ie, eo* for *ẹ̄*. Cf. B.'s *ṭhæ'u'ʒ* for *thieves*.

[3] Cf. Zachrisson, pp. 70, 90, 129 etc., Wyld, p. 206, Jordan, § 277.

(*poule* = 'pull', *mouche* etc. Paston Ls.) was in e. NE. commonly adopted to denote the long (u:) that had developed from ME. *ō* (*houf, alouf, broum, touth* etc.). Cf. Zachrisson 54, 77, 84, 208. The fact that French (i) in loan-words is graphically represented with *e* (*frese* 1418 = 'friese', Luick, *ib.*) may, or may not, indicate that (i:) < *ę̄* dates as far back as the beginning of the 15th century. If the development of *ē* in *meet* has been parallel to that of *ō* in *do,* the change may even have begun in the 14th century (cf. below, p. 59, n. 2), although up to the present there is no conclusive evidence for such an assumption.

Bullokar's [æ, é, e', æ', e].

Bullokar keeps ME. *ę̄* in *speak* and *ę̇* in *be* well apart; *ĕ* and *ę̄* were identical in sound but differed in length. From the previous discussion we may conclude that Bullokar pronounced *ĕ, ę̄* as (è) and (e:).

Nearly all previous writers have assumed that Bullokar pronounced ME. *ę̇* in *be* as (e:). The sole reason for this assumption is that our author does not couple *ĭ* and *ę̇* as long and short. His definition of *ę̇* as 'a more sharpe sound between the old sound of the old name of :e: and the name of :i:' does not permit us to draw any safe conclusions. Deceived by the orthography Bullokar overlooked the fact that *ī* was pronounced as a diphthong, and coupled it with *ĭ*. Hence he could not very well recognize *ę̇* as the long of *ĭ*, but described it as a long vowel without any short correspondent. Nevertheless, in some instances he unintentionally couples *ę̇* with *ī*, i. e. when he uses *e'* as a notation for *ĕ* pronounced as (i). See above p. 14 f.

In the sequel full lists of words with [e'] and [æ] will be given.

Bullokar's æ, é etc. in words of native or Scandinavian origin[1] corresponds to:

---

[1] Words the quantity of which is uncertain because of the derivative mark, have been excluded. Some very early Latin loan-words are given here.

1. ME. *ę̄* < OE. *ēa:* bæm, be'ræu'*e*d, dæf, æk, flæʒ́, græt, hæp, læp*i*ng, stræmʒ́.
2. ME. *ę̄* < OE. *ǣ* < G. *ai + i:* at-læst, clæn, dæl sb., æch, hæl vb., hæt, lædęth̨, læst, læu', læn, læn*n*es, mæn, mæn*i*ng, sb., ræch, sæ, sprædęth̨, tæch, tæʒ̈ęth̨, ynlæst, whæt, whæt*n*.
3. ME. *ę̄* < OE. *ǣ* < WG. *ā:* bræth*i*ng, bræth̨, blæt, ræd, Ræd*o*r, sæt, wépnʒ́.
4. ME. *ę̄* < OE. *e, eo* etc. in open syllables: be'næth, bræk, clæu'd̨ ('cleaved'), æt, ætℜ, fræt, in-stæd, læk, mét (vb. = 'measure'), mæl ('flower'), næther, næther-móst, qæn (< OE. *cwene*), ræp, ræpoŗʒ́, sæl, spæk, spæk*o*r, stæd, stælęst, swæl, thæʒ̈, træd, wæl, wæʒ̈ĺ, wæu'*i*ng.
5. ME. *ę̄* < Scand. *ei:* wæk, wækn*e*d.
6. ME. *ę̄* < *ě* before *st*: næst.
7. OE. *ēo:* cræp, cræp*i*ng.
8. ME. *ę̄* of uncertain origin: cræk*i*ng (probably of imitative origin), mæsh*e*d (? < M. Du. *mæsche,* NED.).

On cræp and næst, cf. pp. 30, 48.

Bullokar's æ in words of French or Latin origin corresponds to:

1. ME. *ę̄* < OFr. *e:* bæk, bæst, c'æs, extrém*i*ty, fæst, læg, métʀ næt*n*es, repétęd, træʒ̈ùr, ʒ̈æl, ʒ̈ælǫos.
2. ME. *ę̄* < OFr. *ę* < earlier *ai, ei:* appæʒ̈, decræc', dis-æʒ̈e⁊, entræt, ægĺ, æʒ̈i, entrét*i*ʒ́, fæt, incræc'ed, pæc', pæc'*a*bĺ, plæz, ræʒ̈ɴ, trætic'.
3. ME. *ę̄* < OFr. *eie, ee:* mæn, adj., mæn, sb.
4. OFr. *e* followed by *a* in the next syllable: cræturʒ́.
5. Latin *e* in words of late introduction: æqal, prætor, præ-i̯ooin*i*ng*l*y.
6. Latin *oe, ae* in proper names: Tiphæas.

With regard to words under 5., see the detailed and instructive account given by Ekwall, Jones §§ 194 ff. There can be little doubt that Latin *ē, ae, oe* was pronounced with a vowel corresponding to ME. *ę̄* in e. NE. Whether this was the case in ME. also is not equally certain. According to Baret (1573), *meus, Deus* were 'in old time' pronounced 'more thinly like ee' (see Zachrisson, p. 37). The interchange between *ẹ̄* and *ę̄* seen in many words belonging here, may be accounted for on the assumption of a ME. pronunciation with *ę̄* and an early New English one with *ẹ̄*.

Bullokar's e', æ' in words of native or Scandinavian origin corresponds to:[1]

1. ME. *ę̄* < OE. *ēo (īe)*: be', be'e', be'twe'n, cre'p*i*ng, fle'c', fre', fre'nd, kne'ż, le'u'er, me'k*e*r, pre'st, re'd, se', se'*n*, the', vb., the'f, thæ'u'ʔ, thre', tre', we'dʔ, whe'l.

2. ME. *ę̄* < Anglian *ē* or (after palatals) late WS. *ē* < WG. *ā:* che'ʒ, de'd, e'l̦, e'u'ning, ew-she'p, gre'dy, she'p, se'ly, sle'p, stre'tʔ, spe'ch, ᵹn-me't, we'd, ᵹe' ('ẏea').

3. ME. *ẹ̄* < Anglian *ē* < *ēa* before palatals: le'k ('leek').

4. ME. *ẹ̄* < OE. *ē* < *ō + i:* be'se'chẹd, bre'd, vb., bre'dọr, fe'd, fe'l, fe't, ge'c', gre'n, he'd, he'lż, me't*e*st, vb., qe'n, se'k, se'mẹth, spe'd*i*, spe'd*i*ly, te'th, we'p.

5. ME. *ẹ̄* < OE. *ē* < *ēa + i:* be'le'u', ne'd sb., vb., ne'dʔ, she't, ste'p.

6. ME. *ẹ̄* < OE. *ē* < *e* before lengthening cons.: fe'ld-fár, se'ld, se'ldọm, we'ld, ᵹe'ld.

7. ME. *ẹ̄* < OE. *ē* of various provenience: fifte'n, Gre'k, he', ke'p, ke'pọr, she', sixte'n, the', we', ᵹe'.

8. ME. *ẹ̄*? < OE. or ME. *ĭ:* e'u'l̦, e'u'ɴ ('even'), ge'u, ge'u'ɴ, ge'n, ge'u'ọr, gre'p sb. (< OE. *gripe*), he'l (ME. *hule hile*, cf. 'hill' vb., NED.).

9. OE. *ī:* le'k vb. (~ i, ẏ), misle'k*i*ng (~ ẏ), misle'kẹd, misle'kt.

10. ME. *ẹ̄* < East Saxon *ę̄* < *ȳ:* de'u', de'u'ẹd,

---

[1] Early Latin loan-words are also given here.

11. ME. $\bar{e}$ of uncertain origin: swe'porż (perhaps *swēpe : swept* on the analogy of *crēpe : crept*), cre'k ($<$ Du. *krēke?*, see NED.), ŋe'man (ME. *ȝiman, ȝeman,* cf. NED.).

In some of the words under **8.** *e'* may be a symbol for (i). Cf. p. 14 f.

If e' really denotes length in *even,* $\bar{e}$ may have arisen from an early ME. form *iven* with $\check{i} < \check{e}$. Note that Hart has *i* short in 'even', and that Bullokar also gives a form with *e* short: eu'en.

With le'k, misle'king, where $\bar{e}$ is well evidenced in e. NE. (cf. Zachrisson, p. 76) we may compare the following forms: *ditch, dike* with (i:) in English dialects (Wright EDD.)[1], Bullok-ar's cræp, by the side of cre'p, spón by the side of spoonż, Butler's rev' (*gerēfa*) (Eichler 22), and e. NE. *great* with (e:) for (i:). In all these words an old pronunciation (i:), (o:), (e:) for (ai), (u:), (i:) has seemingly been kept. This may be due to the analogy of related forms·or words with a short vowel: *leek,* adj., because of *lik, licke* Verney Memoirs I 240, 241, 330, II 27, *licker, likker* 5, *lickest* 4, *likkest* 4—6 (NED.), Smith's [lik] (with *i* short, Deibel 28); le'k, vb., on the analogy of *leek,* adj., or because of ME. or e. NE. variants with short $\check{i}$ (ME. *lĭkede, dislick* Verney Memoirs II, p. 57); *deek, deetch,* because of *ditch, dik* (dial., see Wright, EDD.); cræp, because of *crept,* spón because of ME. *sponful,* e. NE. *sponne* 5, 6 NED.[2]; rev' because of *shirĕv, great* because of *gretter, grettest* (cf. Jespersen 11, 75). Perhaps the forms *hame* ('home'), *stane* ('stone') (but cf. below) are to be accounted for in the same way, i. e. by the analogy of compounds, such as *hamfare, hamlinesse, hamsocne, hamward* etc., *Stanstead, Stanfield* etc.[3] Consequently words of this kind

---

[1] The pronunciation (di:k) I have heard myself in Norfolk. Sir Fer-umbras has *eke : deke* ('dike') 5008 (cf. Anglia 45, 374).

[2] As spón occurs only once and by the side of spoonż, it may be a mere error.

[3] That related forms can alter the quality of a vowel is clearly seen in e. NE. *cotch* for *catch* on the analogy of *caught.*

had three different pronunciations in e. NE.: (lik), (li:k), (leik); (dik), (di:k), (deik); (gre:t), (gret), (gri:t); (crep), (cre:p), (cri:p) etc. There is also the theoretical possibility that *līc, dīc* etc. were shortened in e. ME. and afterwards lengthened, cf. above p. 33.

In words of French or Latin origin Bullokar's e' corresponds to:

1. ME. *ẹ̄* < Anglo-French *ẹ*, Central French *ie:* bre'f, be'-se'g'*d*, che'f, gre'u'*e*d, Gre'c', gre'u'ǫos, mische'f, pe'c'e ʒ, rele'f.

2. ME. *ẹ̄* < Anglo French *ẹ* < Latin free *a:* degre', decre' sb. (< OFr. *decre,* variant of *decret,* see NED.).

3. ME. *ẹ̄* < Anglo French *ẹ* < *ue* < Latin free *ǫ:* pe'pl̦, be'u' ʒ ('beeves').

4. ME. *ẹ̄* < Latin *e* in early loan-words: discre't, exc'e'd-*i*ng, me'tʀ, proc'e'd, proc'e'd*i*ng ʒ.

5. French *i* in late loan-words: este'm.

6. ME. *ẹ̃?* < OFr. *i:* che'rý ż, che'ʒl̦, pe'ty.

As for the words under 4. see p. 47.

In the words under 6. e' may be a symbol for *ĭ,* see p. 14. Jones (1704) has (i:) in *chisel* (Ekwall, § 197).

I will now proceed to deal with Bullokar's e', æ before *r.*

Bullokars æ before *r* corresponds to:

1. ME. *ẹ̃* < OE. *ēa:* ær ('ear' = *auris*), eer ż ('ear' = *spica*), nær, nér, nær*e*r, nær*e*st.

2. ME. *ẹ̃* < OE. *æ* < WG. *ā:* fær, hær ('hair'), hær*i,* thér, thær-for, thær-in, thær-of, whær, whær-a ʒ, whær-by, whær-of.

3. ME. *ẹ̃* < OE. *æ* < G. *ai + i:* ærly, ærst.

4. ME. *ẹ̃* < OE. *e* etc. in open syllables: bær, pær ż, spær̦, tær, weer*i*ng.

5. OE. *ēo, ē* before *rd, rn:* hærd, lærn, lærɴor.

6. OE. *ē:* hær-ᵧnto, hær-after, hær-in, wæry.

7. OFr. e: pærl ż, pérc'-*a*bl̦, rehærc'ętħ, særch*i*ng, v'érs.

8. ME. $\ce{e}$ < OFr. e < earlier *ai:* hærɴ ('heron').
9. Anglo-French e, Central French *ie:* færc'ɴes.
10. OFr. *a:* særc'ęd (see NED.: *searce*).

Bullokar's e' corresponds to:

1. ME. $\bar{e}$ < OE. *ēo:* de'r ('dear'), de'r ('deer'), ste'r (*taurus*).
2. ME. $\bar{e}$ < Anglian and late WS. $\bar{e}$ < WG. $\bar{a}:$ þe'r.
3. ME. $\bar{e}$ < OE. *ēa:* te'rȝ sb.
4. ME. $\bar{e}$ < OE. $\bar{e}$ < $\bar{o}+i:$ we'ry.
5. ME. $\bar{e}$ < OE. $\bar{e}$ < *ēa+i:* hæ'r, vb., hæ'rorż, ne'r, ne'rer, ne'rest.
6. ME. $\bar{e}$ < OE. $\bar{e}:$ he'r, he'r-after, he'r-in, he'r-yntoo.
7. ME, $\bar{e}?$ < e. ME. $\check{i}:$ whe'ryman (from 'whir', vb.?; cf. NED.).
8. ME. $\ce{e}$ < Scand, *e:* bed-ge'r (ON. *gervi*).
9. ME. $\bar{e}$ < Anglo-French e, Central-French *ie:* fe'rc', ferc'er, fe'rc'ɴes, re'rward.
10. ME. $\bar{e}$ < Anglo-French e < Latin free *a:* appe'r, cle'r.
11. ME. $\bar{e}$ < Lat. $\bar{e}$ in early loan-words: me'r; cf. Ekwall, Jones § 204.

A transition of $\bar{e}r$ to $\bar{e}r$ has taken place in hærd, lærn, wæry, færc'nes and certain compounds with 'here'. Examples illustrating the change of $\bar{e}r$ to $\bar{e}r$ are adduced by Luick, Untersuchungen § 330 ff., Kluge in Paul's Gr. 1040, Horn § 85, Eichler, Butler 21, van der Gaaf (*heare, hearof, fearse(-nesse)* etc.) p. 153 f. We have obviously to do with a case of vowel lowering in front of *r* and *r* + cons. Kluge connects this with the change of ME. $\check{e}r$ to $\check{a}r$, but a more satisfactory parallel is the change of e. NE. $\bar{u}$ + cons. to $\bar{o}r$, as in *coarse* for *course* etc. (Luick), although here the lowering seems to take place mainly before *r* + cons. The change of ME. $\check{e}r$ to *ar* goes farthe back than is generally supposed. According to Luick § 430 n 1, the earliest *a*-spellings are found in Northern MSS. from the middle and end of the 14th cent., but Wyld (p. 213) has shown that isolated spellings with *a* occur in some Southern texts as early as the 13th century. In order to fix the date of the change I have gone through a great number of early spellings of place-names containing *ĕr*. The result is that *er* is by far the most usual spelling even as late as the 15th cent. At that date there is a small percentage of *a*-forms. Occasional spellings with *a* begin to crop up as early as the 13th century: *Harthal* 1227 Ass. = Hartall, Sal. (OE. *heort*); *Hartinton* 1253 IPM = Hartington, Derb.; *Barton* 1274—9 HR = Barton Steeple, Oxf. (OE. *beretūn*); *Charletone* Edw. II IPM. = Charlton, Ke., (Gevenich 51); *Quarndon* 1391 IPM = Quarndon, Derb. (OE. *cweorn*).

To judge by the somewhat scanty material the change of *er* to *ar* began in the 13th century and took place both in the North and South of England.[1]

Bullokar also has a few instances of [e'] for [æ] before *r*, such as ge'r (from ON. *gervi*) and te'rȝ sb. (OE. *tēar*).[2] Such forms are fairly common in Hodges, who has (i:) in *pearl, verse, pierce, hearse, perch, beard* etc. Other instances are adduced by Horn, p. 76. No satisfactory explanation has been given of this sound-change. Perhaps *ęr* passed into *ēr* in certain ME. dialects in the neighbourhood of the capital.

Whe'ry (cf. *wherye* 5—6, *whirie, whyrrye* 6 NED.) may be derived from 'whir', vb. (5—7 *whirre*, 7 *whurre*, from Danish *hvirre* NED.). Probably e' is a symbol for *ĭ*.

OE. *ĕa, ĕ* before *x* appears as *e* and *a*: wex~wax sb., and wex, vb. (~ a). Such forms were usual in the early London language. See Lekebusch, p. 57. Cf. also Smith's uäx, Zachrisson, p. 186 f., and Englische Studien 52, 324.

A similar old-fashioned form is swerd (< OE. *swēord*). The same form with *ăr* < *ĕr* occurs in Machin's Diary: *swarde*, 76.

In a few French loan-words Bullokar has 'er' for modern

---

[1] Place-names containing French words, such as *Armthewayt* 1254 Pi R. = Armathait Cumb. (OFr. *ermite*), are not conclusive, *er* and *ar* being interchangeable in Anglo-Norman French (Behrens, p. 91). Occasional spellings with *ar* for *er, ir* in Domesday Book are due to French influence.

[2] The base can hardly be Northb. *tehher* > *tēr;* neither is influence from Angl. **tēran* (cf. WS. *tīran*) likely.

English (a:) < *ăr:* meru'el (~ ar) (cf. 4—6 *mervell,* NED.) and
Serg'ant). In v'erlat) *e* is due to a French variant *verlet* for
varlet. Cf. 6 *verlet,* NED., and Zachrisson, pp. 57, 60.

Earlier *ĕ* is kept in prety and tet) ('tits') < OF. *tete.*

In pek-axe) (cf. 5 *pek-ax,* NED.) *e* is due to the labial, rather than to the usual transition of *ĭ* to *ĕ,* which is very well
exemplified in e. NE., but does not seem to be known to Bullokar. Lady Wentworth writes *e* for almost every *ĭ'*, and (e) for
(i) is often heard in the Present London pronunciation[2], e. g. in
if, till, different, difficult etc. Machyn has numerous forms with
e from *ĭ*, e. g. *sester,* 38, *Necolas,* 104, *Trenete,* 105, *emages,*
109 etc.

Bullokar has East Saxon *e* in shert (OE. *scyrte*).

Owing to the labial influence of the preceding consonant
ir has become *er, ur* in wherl, whurl by the side of whirl (cf.
whyrle, wherle, whurle 6 NED. from ON. *hvirfill*), and *er* or *ir*
has become *ur* in churl, (cf. *chirl* 5, *churle* 4—7 NED., *Churltone* Henr. III IPM., *Churltone* Edw. I IPM., Gevenich 51 f.).

Bullokar has no instance of the common change of *ir* to
er, ur and *er* to *ur*, which is generally considered to have taken
place at a comparatively late date[3]. From the material adduced
in the sequel we can conclude, however, that these changes had
begun in late ME. or early NE. times.

Spellings indicating the change of *ir* to *er, ur* and of
er to *ur*.

13th cent.: — *Scherly* 1296 IPM. = Shirley, Derb. (OE. *scīr*).

14th cent.: — *Shurle* 1306 Abbr. Plac. (MS. later) = Shirley,
Derb.; *Sherbourn* 1333 CR. = Sherborne Dors. (OE. *scīr*); *Shur-
mandbury* 1349 IPM. = Shermanbury, Suss. (OE. *scīrmann*).

15th cent.: — *durt, thurtene* NED.; *Shurland* 1451 IPM =
Shirland Derb.; *Thersday, bergeys, herte* ('hurt'), *reterned, werd*

---

[1] See Wyld in Mod. Lang. Teaching, 1915.

[2] See Jones, Pron. of English, 35, Zachrisson, Engelska Stilarter, p. 96.

[3] Cf. Horn, p. 25, Jespersen 11, 12 ff., Jordan § 271.

('word'), Paston Letters, (Dibelius p. 357, 360) *urk, ibid.* (Neumann 29, 66), *perse* ('purse') *ibid.* (Zachrisson 46), *sorepe* ('syrup') 689 *ibid.; furkin* Cely Papers (Süssbier 35); *kyrlewe* ('curlew'), *quirtayn* ('curtain') and *u*-spellings of *dirdum, dirge, mirror, myrmidon* NED. (Gabrielson 69); *perdge* ('purge'), Stonor Ls. 156.

16th cent.: — *thurd, thurty* NED.; *Shurcomb* 1548 Som. Rec. Soc., vol. 27, p. 268; *Shurton* 1569 Musters, Som. Rec. Soc., vol. 20 = Shurton, Som., *Shirueton* 1419—20 PF., *Sherueton, Sherreveton* FA. (OE. *scīrgerēfa*); *Shurland* 1585 Musters = Shirland, Derb.; *forvent* 1525 Tyndale (Sopp, in Anglia XII, p. 288); *orbese* ('herbs') 264, *forne* ('fern') 21, *surmon*(!) 112, *purjure* sb. 245, *durge* 112 Machyn.

From the material that has been adduced, we may conclude that the change of *ir* to *er, ur* began in the 14th, and that of *er* to *ur* in the 15th century. Of individual writers Machyn[1] in the 16th and the Verneys in the first half of the 17th century pronounced *ir, er* as *ur*.[2]

As usual the grammarians are very slow in registering this sound-change. The first authorities for the change of *er* to *ur* are Wallis 1650 (Ellis, p. 172) and Price 1665 (Zachrisson 46 n. 1). A common pronunciation for *ir, er, ur* does not seem to be taught until 1757 by Arnold (van der Gaaf, 158) and Johnston 1764 (Gabrielson, 106), consequently 200 years after the levelling had taken place in colloquial speech.

The early common sound for *ir, er, ur* in *dirge, sermon, urn* may have been different both as regards quantity and quality from that which resulted from the delabializing of *u* in *up*. One was the result of an isolative, the other of a combinative sound-change.

---

[1] Cf. *surmon, durge* Machyn 112. Considering such a safe instance as *surmon, o* in *fern, herbs* etc. is more likely to be a symbol for (u) than for (ɔ:)? from *ar.*

[2] Cf. *thorty, dort, stor* (= 'thirty', 'dirt', 'stir') 1639 Verney Memoirs I 153, 158, *hurd* ('heard'), *purle* ('pearl') 1657, 1654 Verney Memoirs II 70, 134, 206. Cf. also *Surlby* c 1650, map in Camden = Serlby, Notts (OE. *Serlo*); *Burnston, ibid.* = Barnston, Notts (OE. *Beorn*).

In my opinion the distinction kept up by the grammarians
between *ir, er,* on the one hand, and *ur,* on the other, was to
a great extent artificial and similar to the one made by some
modern speakers.[1] Whereas *ur* may have been commonly pronounced with the new colloquial sound, many refined speakers
tried to pronounce *ir* and *er* with a different sound, which is
commonly identified with that of ĕ short, but which, as has been
suggested by Gabrielson, probably was a mixed variety of ĕ.[2]

Some grammarians know the colloquial sound also in a few
very usual words containing ME. *ir,* viz. *bird, birth, third, thirty,
thirteen.* Gabrielson thinks that *ir* in these words is a spelling
for ME. *ur,* and that the distinction made by the grammarians
between *ir* (*er*) and *ur* consequently was not artificial but a real
one. The front vowel (ë) was assigned to ME. *er, ir,* the back
variety to ME. *ur.* This is far from certain. Spellings with *u*
do not occur for *birth, bird* and *third* at an earlier date than
for other words containing ME. *ir* (cf. my lists). The grammarians who first made the distinction between *ir* in *bird* etc.
and other words containing ME. *ir,* were not Englishmen. Miege
was a Frenchman and Sheridan an Irishman. Moreover the
pronunciation *ur* is not always assigned to the same words by
the different authorities. All this strongly savours of artificiality.

As Bullokar would not alter the existing spelling, we are
unable to decide in what way he pronounced *ir, ĕr, ur* in such
words as *bird, certain, burn* etc.

ME. ī in write.

That ī in 'write' was pronounced as a diphthong as early
as the 15th century is evident from spellings with *ei, ai,*

---

[1] Cf. Jones Pronunciation of English p. 45: — 'Some speakers endeavour artificially to make a difference between words spelt with *ur* and those
spelt with *ir, er, ear* by using a lowered variety of (ə:) in the former case,
and a raised variety in the latter.'

[2] The French grammarians do not identify it with *e* pure and simple,
and often transcribe it with *eur,* by the side of *er.*

oi, (*leik, whrayt, joist(e), vayage* etc.) and rhymes with ME.
ī and ME. *ei.* Nearly all the early grammarians teach a diphthongic pronunciation of *ī.* To define the exact quality of the
first element of this diphthong is extremely difficult. Spellings
with *ei* and the evidence of some grammarians (Salesbury, Hart,
Bellot, Mason) point to the stage (ei), spellings with *ay* and *oi,*
rhymes with *ī* and *oi* (Spenser, Shakespeare etc.), and the evidence of other grammarians (Lambeth Fragment 1528, Wallis
1650, Mauger 1679, and probably Gill 1632) point to more advanced stages: (əi) or (ai). At Shakespeare's time all these stages
may have been represented as in the modern vulgar pronunciation of such words as *be* and *feel*[1].

Bullokar's [i, ý].

In my opinion Bullokar as well as Smith looked upon *ī* in
write as a long *vowel* only for orthograpical reasons (cf. p. 36,
45), an error which is found in many orthoëpistical works of
a much later date; cf. Zachrisson, p. 205 and n.

That Smith actually pronounced *ī* in *write* as a diphthong
seems also to appear from a statement of his that the Normans
pronounced *moy, toy* etc. as *my, ty* etc. (i. e. with *ei*). This is
pointed out by Deibel, 21*, who nevertheless adheres to the
old theory that Smith's *ī* was a monophthong.

Under such circumstances Bullokar would be the only early
grammarian who teaches a monophthongic pronunciation of *i* in
write. The existence of such a pronunciation at Shakespeare's
time is improbable. The contemporary evidence also makes
one inclined to interpret Bullokar's [ý] in *write* as (ei) rather
than (ij).

In v'yag' *ī* goes back to Old French *viage.* See Horn,
101, Zachrisson, 89 n.

In shrých-owl (= 'shritch-owl') the length of the vowel is

---

[1] Cf. on these questions, Zachrisson, pp. 71 ff., Engl. Stud. 52, p.
310, Wyld, p. 223 ff., Rhymes, p. 75, Jordan, § 279.

due to the influence of *shrike*, sb., also found in *shrike-cock* etc. (see NED.).

Etymological (?) *ĭ* (see NED.) still appears in pirwincĺ. The earliest references have *i* and *e;* e may be due to weak stress.

In bul-rish *i* stands for PE. (ʌ) from (u).

Before *v,* *ĕ* has been raised to *i* in di'v'l. Cf. 6—7 *divel* NED.

ME. *ŭ* in gun, come, *ọ̄* in do, and *ū* in house.

The exact pronunciation of ME. *u* in *gun* at Shakespeare's time is one of the most difficult problems of the early NE. sound-history.[1] We know for certain that *u* in *gun* was pronounced as (u) by some speakers (Smith, Hart, Mason, Sherwood), by others (the majority of the French grammarians, Hodges, Wallis etc.) with a more open and perhaps sometimes delabialized sound. This modified sound is by several writers considered to have been (o). In my previous writings (e. g. E. Stud. 52, 318 ff.) I have tried to show that the identification of the English *u* in *gun* with the French and German *o* by the grammarians need not be interpreted literally, at the same time calling attention to evidence which tends to prove that the English *u* was sometimes pronounced with a sound approximating to the modern unrounded one (ʌ).

Some of this evidence may not be quite conclusive. Erondelle's and Cotgrave's directions to pronounce the French *e feminine* as 'the common do sound this English phrase: '*Is he come*' (Zachrisson 21, 133) probably refers to 'he' pronounced as 'a' not to *o* in *come* (Ekwall, Engl. Stud. 55, 400). Erondelle's identification of the French (y) with *u* in *murderer* is more likely to indicate a pronunciation of this word with (ə), (ʌ) or (ə:) than

---

[1] For recent literature on the subject, cf. Zachrisson, pp. 72, 81, 106, 133 f., 152, 202, 210 f., Anglia, 1914, p. 423 f., Anglia, Beibl: 1917, p. 78, Engl. Stud. 52, 318 ff., Engl. Stud. 60, 352; Wyld, p. 232 f.; Ekwall, Engl. Stud. 55, 399; Horn, Engl. Stud. 60, 121 ff.

with (u) or (y). The development of (u) to (ə) or (ạ) in the diphthong (ui) (cf. such 15th and 16th century spellings as *boil* for OE. *b̄yle,* Zachrisson 72) may, or may not, have been different from that of (u) in *come.* It has been suggested[1] that occasional spellings with *a* for *u* of *gun, come,* etc. are errors in which *a* has been miswritten for *o,* but several arguments can be adduced against this suggestion. In the facsimiles of letters and papers from the 15th and 16th centuries which I have been able to examine, *a* and *o* are often distinct in shape, and confusion has taken place mainly in very careless or rapid writing. Quite safe instances of *a* for (u) in *gun, come* etc. occur at least in documents of the 16th century, e. g. in Machyn's Diary.[2] That there must have been an acoustic similarity between *u* in *gun* and *a* in *man* appears from rhymes in Shakespeare, such as *adder : shudder* (Vietor 207), and from the pun upon the words *Anne* and '*un*done' which Shakespeare's contemporary John Donne indulged in after his clandestine marriage.[3] The old nursery-rhyme, 'There was a little man, And he had a little gun' etc. also deserves to be mentioned.

Moreover, some evidence remains which undoubtedly points to (ʌ), not to (o), e. g. French transcriptions of *u* as *eu*[4], Wallis' identification of *u* in *cut* with (œ) in *serviteur,* and Wilkins' identification of *u* in *cut* with the unstressed *e* in *rudder.*[5]

---

[1] Cf. Ekwall, Engl. Stud. 59, 399; Jordan § 274; Horn, Engl. Stud. 60, 122, nn. 1, 2.

[2] The following is a list of such spellings:

15th century: — *gannes* ('guns) 2× Marg. P., Paston Letters, no. 620, *sadanly,* Fortescue, p. 126; *camyth* ('cometh') William C., Cely Papers, no. 120. These are not quite safe, cf. below.

16th century: — *Chamley* ('Cholmondley'), *Samersett,* Machyn, pp. 38, 182; *wan* ('one') (*a* for *ŭ*?), *dall* ('dull') Verney Memoirs I 111, 150; *farniture, Saveraigne* (1601) Diehl 154, 158).

[3] On writing to his wife from prison, Donne subscribed his letter: 'John Donne, Anne Donne, Un-done!', Compton Rickett, A History of English Literature, p. 182.

[4] The earliest authorities (Bellot, Mason) have such transcriptions only before *r,* as in *church,* and *shirt* (Zachrisson 134).

[5] Cf. Ellis, p. 177.

An anonymous Dutch grammarian of 1568 identifies the English short *u* in *gun* with the Dutch *ŭ,* which is pronounced in about the same way as the German *ö* in *Götter.* Barnow (p. 27) correctly remarks that the grammarian's equation of Dutch and English *u* can only mean that the English *ŭ* at that early date had come very near to its present stage of (ʌ).

My chief objection[1] to the occurrence of (o) for (u) in early Standard English was the fact that according to Wright (EDD. § 101, 163), *ŏ* from *ŭ* is extremely rare in modern dialects, and does not occur in the neighbourhood of the capital. During some recent visits to England I have ascertained, however, that (o) is much more usual than is assumed by Wright. It is common in the Dorsetshire dialect, even among educated people. It is moreover characteristic of all the East Anglian dialects, Norfolk, Suffolk and Essex, and may therefore at an earlier date also have occurred in Middlesex and in the capital.[2]

Under such circumstances this dialectal sound, which varies from (u) to (o), may actually be indicated by the early French and some other foreign grammarians, although their identification of English *u* and French *o per se* does not fix *ŭ* as (o). Lediard's statement that the English *ŭ* was 'ein obskurer Laut oder Mittel-klang zwischen dem Teutschen kurtzen *u* und kurtzen *o*', also speaks in favour of *o,* whereas Cooper's *o labialis* short in *full* is, after all, most likely to have been (u). Cooper's general pronunciation of *ŭ* was (ʌ), or a near approach to it, and practically all his words containing *o labialis* are pronounced with (u) in Present English. Moreover, as far as my observations go, the dialects which have (o) for *ŭ* in *gun, come,* do not make any distinction between such words as *come* and *full,* but use the vernacular sound for all words containing ME. *ŭ.*

The result arrived at may be summed up as follows. In the 16th and 17th centuries ME. *u* was pronounced as

---

[1] Cf. Zachrisson, p. 202, Anglia 1914, p. 424.
[2] Cf. Engl. Stud., 60, 352 ff.

(u), (o)[1], and at least from the middle of the 16th century, also with a sound identical, or very nearly so, with (ʌ). This sound may date considerably farther back. The distinction between (u) in *full,* and (o) or (ʌ) in *come* is observed by some of the earliest grammarians (Bellot etc.), although the distribution of (u) and (o) or (ʌ) was not the same as it is now.

To ascertain the e. NE. pronunciation of ME. *ō* in *do,* does not meet with any difficulties. All the available evidence points to a common pronunciation of *ō* as (u:).[2]

From rhymes with *ọu* : *ū* (*avowe: flowe,* Palladius c. 1420) and a few phonetic spellings (*hew* for *how* in the, Paston Letters, *aur* for *our,* Cel. Papers[3]), we may conclude that ME. *ū* in *house could* have a diphthongic pronunciation as early as the 15th century. A diphthong is likewise testified by practically all the early orthoepists. Only Northerners, such as Richardson and possibly Mulcaster, pronounced *ū* as a simple vowel (u:).[4] It is difficult to fix the exact quality of the first element in the diphthong. The evidence of the earliest English grammarians points

---

[1] Horn, Engl. Stud. 60, 125, draws attention to several loan-words (*drug* from *drogue, stuff* from *estofe, tuck* from *etoc*) in which French (o) has been rendered with the English sound corresponding to ME. *u,* but these do not necessarily fix the English (u) as (o), for *u* in *stuf* etc. may go back to French variants with *u, ou* (cf. OF. *estufe,* Godefroi and *trutting* ('trotting') in the Paston Letters). The development of ME. *ul*+cons. to *o(u)l*+cons. (Horn, *ib.* 129) points, however, to an early transition of (u) to (o).

[2] Cf. Zachrisson, pp. 83 f., 90, 131, 142, 143, 155, 213, 223; Wyld, p. 234; Jordan § 278 etc. From the spellings with *ou* for *ō* adduced by Wyld from ME. MSS. of the 14th cent., it is probable that the change of *ō* to (u:) and *ū* to (uw) had already begun in the middle of the 14th century. The majority of spellings, with *au* for *ou* are not conclusive; cf. below.

[3] Cf. Zachrisson, p. 79, Engl. Stud. 52, p. 309; Wyld, p. 230 ff.; Jordan § 280.

[4] Cf. Zachrisson, pp. 102, 133, 154, 209, 223. Mulcaster's directions are far from clear. His remark 'Why might not *houl, coul, skoul* as well be spelled with *oo*' (Zachrisson, p. 208) may simply reflect wonder at the vagaries of the contemporary orthography not a direction as to the correct pronunciation of these words.

to (ou), the directions (*ou = au*) of the French grammarians from
Bellot 1580 onward, in conjunction with phonetic spellings such
as *hew* and *aur* for *how* and *our* may indicate a diphthong not
differing much from the present one. As in the case of *ī* in
like it is possible that all the different stages of (ou), (əu), (au)
were represented in the English pronunciation of the 16th century. We may compare the modern vulgar pronunciation of *o*
in *do* as (ou) and (əu).

Bullokar's [oy, ǫw, ǫ, y, ụ, oo].

In this place it will be convenient to deal with Bullokar's
pronunciation of ME. *ǭ, ŭ,* and *ū* in *do, gun,* and *house.* He
looks upon *o, u < ŭ* and *ou < ū* as vowels and diphthongs of
one sound. Consequently (see his definition of a diphthong,
above pp. 9 f.) the only difference he heard between ME. *ŭ* in
gun and *ū* in *house* was that the latter was pronounced with a
longer sound. This leaves [oo] < *ǭ* in *do* as a long vowel
without any short correspondent. As before in the case of *ȩ̄* in
be, his definition of *ǭ* in *do* does not permit us to draw any
safe conclusions as to its pronunciation. Bullokar's statements
have been looked upon as gospel truth by all his interpreters.
Sweet distinguishes the three sounds as (ù), (u:), and (o:), Luick
as (ù), (u:) or (ùw), and (o:) (very close *ǭ*), Vietor as (ù), (u:), (ù:).
Of these Sweet and Vietor leave too little distance between *ǭ*
and *ū.* Bullokar may have pronounced these two sounds as
(u:) and (ùw), but this also would be rather remarkable, as all
contemporary and later orthoepists (Richardson's (u:) is, of course,
a Scotch dialectal pronunciation) testify a fully developed diphthong. The Frenchman Bellot's evidence (1580) even points to
a diphthong, pronounced with a sound not differing much from
the present pronunciation i. e. (əu) or (au). However, if Bullokar
pronounced *ǭ* as (u:) and *ū* as (ou) or (əu), why did he not
couple *ǭ* with *ŭ* as vowels of one sound? We have now come
to the very nucleus of the matter, where Ellis, in my opinion,

has led all subsequent writers astray. Bullokar exemplifies his
'u flat' by the words *button, rush, full, lust* etc. Of these *full*
is identical with one of Smith's examples, which, according to
Ellis (p. 169), 'fixes the sound of Bullokar's u as (u)'! This
reasoning is not sound. It is wrong in principle to 'fix' the
pronunciation of one author by comparison with another.[1] The
combined evidence of a great many authors may be used as a
testimony against a pronunciation opposed to theirs, but it is
impossible to infer from the pronunciation of one author what
sounds were used by another. Such a procedure would highly
simplify the solution of all difficult problems in connection with
early English sound-history. Considering the fact that Bullokar
actually used in his amended orthography a considerable number
of dialectal or colloquial forms (cf. above, p. 22), it is highly
probable that in *most words belonging here* he pronounced ME.
ŭ as (o), a sound which is recognized as a current pronunciation
by Bullokar's contemporary Bellot. This may be the reason
why Bullokar did not couple *ō* in *do* with *ŭ* in *gun*. The
sounds (o) and (u:) are, of course, qualitatively, perfectly distinct.
The most probable explanation of how Bullokar could make
pairs of *ŭ* and *ū* is that he pronounced also the latter with the
more advanced sound (ou). Now at least the first element of
the diphthong was *similar in sound* to *ŭ*, and this was sufficient
ground for Bullokar to assume perfect identity. A phonetician
who considered (ei) or (əi) to be the long of (i), had certainly
no scruples in identifying (o) and (ou) from a qualitative point
of view.

Some transcriptions where Bullokar writes oụ for etymological *ō* (roụf ~ oo, boụth, broụȝd ~ bruȝẹth) or for *ou* pronounced
with a vowel corresponding to ME. *ọ̄, ŭ* (coụrs ~ coorc' moụrN ~
moorN, coụrt, goụrd, noụrc', poụp, rọwsh, rooM [oM = ouM] ~
room, boụrN, etc.) might be taken as an indication that in his

---

[1] In a similar manner Ellis 'fixes' Smith's pronunciation with the
assistance of Salesbury (see Ellis, p. 35, 113 etc.). Besides a pronunciation
(ʌ) in *full* occurs in many dialects. Cf. Wright, EDG. p. 456.

pronunciation both *ū, ǭ* and *ū* were qualitatively identical, i. e. pronounced as (u), (u:) respectively. Bullokar's oų in the above-mentioned words is, however, most likely to be due to the traditional spelling, which he did not care to alter. As to the origin of *ou* as a symbol for (u:), (u), see English Vowels, p. 54, p. 208.

To assume the existence of the pronunciation (u:) for ME. *ū* in *house* on the sole evidence of an authority whose sound-descriptions are extremely vague and who continually mixes up spellings and sounds, would not be advisable or even justified. An easy way of getting out of the difficulties is, of course, to assume that Bullokar's *ý* in *like* and oų in *house* was (ij), (uw), as opposed to (i:) in *be* and (u:) in *do,* but the combined evidence at our disposal goes against such an interpretation. We have every reason for assuming that the stages (ij), (uw) belong to a considerably earlier period in the development of the spoken language.

The fragmentary evidence of our earliest English authorities does not warrant us to conclude that the Continental pronunciation of the vowels still existed in the English of the 16th century. The supposed Continental pronunciations recorded by Smith and Bullokar are due to a desire of these authors to equate the English and the Latin vowel-systems, i. e. to find English equivalents to the five Latin long and short vowels: *a, e, i, o, u.* In choosing equivalents, our authorities were at the same time influenced by the traditional orthography. The long and short *a, o, e* do not offer any difficulties, but our authorities disagree, when the case is to find English equivalents to Latin *ĭ, ī* and *ŭ, ū.* Only Hart fixes upon the right English vowels, Smith wrongly equates the English and the Latin long *ī,* and Bullokar, who worked out his sound-system independently of his predecessors, not only couples *i short* in *if,* with *i* long in *like,* but also *u* short in *luck* with *u* long in *house.* We are presented with a multicoloured mosaic, not with a set piece of evidence, we are landed in a slough of despond dotted with will-o'-the-wisps, whose fallacious lights may lead the philological wanderer astray.

Boụth is evidently due to ME. *bǭþe* < O. Da. **bōd̄*, not to Icel. *búþ*, which word would have given ME. (buːþ) with voiceless (þ).

In broụ3d oụ might be taken to represent ME. (uː) for AF. (yː) (cf. AF. *bruser*) supposed to be characteristic of the North and North Midland[1], but also found in East Midland.[2] Considering such ME. and e. NE. spellings as *broose, brouse*[3], it is more probable that Bullokar's oụ in broụ3d is written for oo = (uː), due to the reduction of (iuː) to (uː) after *r*. The same combinative sound-change may have taken place after (d3), to judge by such spellings as *ioupe* 4, *iowpe* 5 (NED.) for French *jupe,* although *ou* may here also be a symbol for ME. (uː).

In rǫwsh from AF. *russher* ǫw is either a spelling for (uː), or what is more probable, for ME. *ŭ*. A short (u) rather than a long one, is graphically represented with oụ in such forms aş noụrc', noụrished (~ụ), noụrishment (~ǫ).[4]

In shoụlderż Bullokar's oụ would have given Modern English (au). This pronunciation is evidenced by Writing Scholar's Companion (1695); cf. also Horn, Engl. Stud., 60, 129.

A shortened form with *ŭ* from *ū* is represented by Machyn's *shuder* 134. Cf. *puterer* (= 'poulterer'), *ibid.* 136.

In boụl (< Fr. *boule*) and probably also in poụʀ, oụ stands for the sound corresponding to PE. (au), a diphthong being well evidenced in these two words. See Horn, § 68. On *pour,* see also Gabrielson, p. 167.

On the other hand, I think it improbable that a diphthongic sound is indicated by Bullokar's oụ in yoụ, yoụr, coụld, woụld,

---

[1] Behrens p. 118, Luick § 412.

[2] Zachrisson in Luick Cel. Vol., p. 146. Additional instances are *contenow* Will. Cely, Cely Papers, no. 171, *Touesday* J. Paston the Younger, Paston Letters, no. 745 (not quite safe, cf. below).

[3] Cf. 4—6 *broose,* 5—6 *brouse* NED., *brooseid* J. Paston the Youngest, Paston Letters, no. 708.

[4] Cf. such analogous forms as *soubgettes, soufissant, mourmour* noted and discussed in English Vowels, p. 87; cf. also pp. 84, 208 *ibid.*

shoųld.[1] Evidence from other sources (Gill etc.) renders it likely
that oų here stands for either (u) or (u:).

In woųnd, sb., oų may stand either for a diphthong or for
(u:). Both these pronunciations are well evidenced. See Jespersen, MEG. 8, 26. Horn § 113.

In 'couch', 'crouch' (and a few other words, see above, 61)
oų interchanges with oo. Jones gives (u:) for couch, crouch.
See Ekwall, Jones, 342.

Before *r* (u:) has not undergone any *r*-modification: floor,
whoorż, moorɴ, coorc', poor etc. As for dór ~ door, see Luick,
Anglia, 16, 455 ff.

Bullokar writes forth < *forþ* both with ǫ and oo; ǫ has
originated either by the influence of the lip consonant (see
Jespersen, MEG., 3, 43) or by the analogy of *further* < OE.
furðor. Here OE. ŭ could be lengthened befor (*rð*) (cf. 6
fourther, NED.), and the long vowel may then have been transferred to *furth*. Gill also has (u:) in this word.

In strook, sb., and goo oo may reflect a dialectal sound-
development of ǭ to ǭ. See English Vowels 84, n. and Engl.
Stud. 52, 322.

In cǫnyż (~o), grǫu'lɪ́ng, and wǫnt the etymological pronunciation has been kept.

In pookṭ oo may be due to the labial consonant.

In pǫu'erty (~o) and in pųlish*e*d, pǫlish*e*d (cf. 5—7 *pul-
lish(e),* NED.), ǫ, ų go back to French variants with ⸜*ou* by the
side of *o*. Cf. early French *pouvre* and pretonic *oul* for *ol*
evidenced in many words by early French orthoëpists. See
Thurot I 256, 430.

Hauck's (21) *son, filius* is an error; all the editions I have
examined have sǫn.

The short ŭ in amǫng (~o), ǫu'ɴ and shǫu'l has been accounted for in many various manners (labial influence; OE.
variants with ŭ *[oven, shovel]*; influence from *shove [shovel]*;
dialectal development *[among]*).

---

[1] As for the loss of *l* in these forms, see Horn § 68.

A very remarkable form is bǫstiǫs, where ǫ goes back to earlier (ui). According to NED., the monophthongic form is Scotch. As I have shown in English Vowels (p. 191) *oi* was certainly sometimes monophthongized in Northern English, but such forms also occur in the South of England.[1]

If stu̱ff is identical with *stifle,* u̱ may be due to the labialisation of ĭ < ī. Cf. *tumerous* for *timerous* in Caxton (Faltenbacher, 213). In point of fact *stuffle* for 'stifle' is given by Wright (EDD.) as a dialectal form (Cornwall).

ME. *au* in all and law and ŏ in not.

In English Vowels (pp. 81 f.) and Englische Studien (52, pp. 312 ff.) I have adduced a number of spellings with *o* for *au* in *all* and *law* and with *au* for ME. *o* before *f* + consonant, which, according to my views, show that in the fifteenth century ME. *au* had been monophthongized to (ɔ:), and in some instances shortened to (ɔ).

Prof. Ekwall (Engl. Stud., 49, 279—85, and Engl. Stud., 55, 401) has tried to show that the majority of these spellings are not conclusive. Some of his remarks are to the point, but I do not consider he has been able to invalidate my general conclusions. In the meantime new forms have come to light from other sources. It will therefore be appropriate to give a general survey of the whole material which is available at present.

Ekwall is undoubtedly correct in his assumption that a combinative sound-change has taken place in certain dialects, chiefly in the West Midland, according to which ME. ă passed into ŏ before *l* + consonant. Illustrative examples of this sound-change, which dates as far back as the 13th century, are *olr*, c. 1300, for OE. *alor* = 'alder-tree', and numerous forms with *ol* for *al* of place-names situated in SW. Yorkshire, Lancashire, Shropshire, Staffordshire, Gloucestershire etc. To Ekwall's mat-

---

[1] Cf. Zachrisson, Luick Celebration Volume p. 148.

erial may be added *holte* (*þe holte gon*), OE. Misc., p. 39, from the Jesus College MS, probably written in the second half of the 13th century, and perhaps Present English *oaf*, which may be a Western dialectal form perhaps first introduced into literary English by Shakespeare (cf. the earliest references in NED.). I have found traces of this sound-change in modern dialects also. In the Lorton dialect (Cumb.) the vernacular forms of ME. *galt, hals* are **gaut, auz,** which go back to ME. **golt, *hols*. The regular representative of ME. *ol* + consonant in the dialect is **au¹,** as in **baustər** ('bolster'), **kaut** ('colt'), **baut** ('bolt'), whereas ME. *al* + consonant gives **ō,** as in **mōt** ('malt'), **sōt** ('salt') etc. Brilioth's explanation of **au** in *halse* and *galt* (pp. 134, 144) is erroneous.

The following spellings should be eliminated, being errors, or not quite conclusive (cf. below: Palæographic Notes).

Cely Papers No. 149, *Dolton* (twice); read: *Colton; hanker-stolkes* No. 185 = 'anchorstocks' (Ekwall).

Paston Letters No. 75, *awnly;* read: *alonly; pawntements* No. 629, read: *pow(n)tements*.

Stonor Letters No. 68, a 1462, by H. Unton: *and I told Hampden withoute we dro to an end that ye wold execute your exigent ayeynest yong Wykes: and so I trowe we shall draw to an end*. Such a careful writer as Unton — a London lawyer — is not likely to have written *dro* for *drowe*.² Consequently, *dro* is either a phonetic spelling for the past tense *drewe* or for the present tense *draw*. Spellings with *o(o)* for *eu* being extremely rare (cf. p. 63), the second alternative is the more probable one.

Avowing of Arthur, c. 1420, S. Lancashire, *so* (ed. Robson p. 77, quoted by Jordan § 286), is undoubtedly an error for *se,* the usual form for 'saw' in this text (cf. pp. 77, 84 ff.).

---

¹ This is also the case in the dialect of Byers Green, Durham (Orton).

² The following variants of 'drew' are noted by Price, p. 152, and Dibelius p. 240: *drouh, drow(e), drue, drewe*. The archaic form *drogh* only occurs once in an early London deed (Morsbach, p. 139). Besides, Morsbach gives *drewe* (once).

Nevertheless other instances remain which, as far as I can judge, prove that in the course of the 15th cent. ME. *au* had passed into (ɔː).

15th century: — *on beholue*[1] 1425 London (Morsbach, Schriftsprache p. 50); *to the beholve of* 1482? Stonor Letters 312; *auffer* (= 'offer') 1475 (twice) London, Cely Papers 50; *y-fole* (= 'fallen') 1420 Wilts., S. Editha 522 (Wyld, 252); *loful* 1480, Newcastle Merchant Adventurers, pp. 3, 4 (cf. *lofulle* 1553, *ibid.*, p. 67)[2] (Publications of the Surtees Society, vol. 93).

16th century: — *saufte* (= 'soft') c. 1525 Tyndale (Sopp, 25); *oll* (= 'all') *my goodes* 1505, *olle tythe* 1552, *oggest* (= 'August'), *defolte, ofull,* recorded after 1500, Suffolk Records (Binzel 14, 49); *caumplet*[3] Machyn 12, and numerous other instances adduced in English Vowels (p. 82) and Engl. Stud. (52, p. 314) by the present writer. Add: *Hawpe* 1541 (orig.?) = Hope, Derbyshire (Walker 265); *ontt* ('aunt'), *monde* ('maundy'),[4] Machyn 61, 230.

These 15th and early 16th century spellings seem to warrant the conclusion that (au) had passed into (ɔː) as early as the second half of the 15th century. The spellings from the former half of the 15th century are not quite conclusive, for *ol* may be a graphic representation of a diphtong (ɔu), and *y-fole* in S. Editha may also instance the ME. dialectal transition of *al* to *ol* in *olr* (= 'alder-tree') etc. At least in some of the

---

[1] The labial may possibly have accelerated the process of rounding.

[2] These forms have been pointed out to me by Mr. H. Orton. To judge by the editor's note (p. 1), the text of the ordinances is printed from an original manuscript. Rounding being not characteristic of the Durham dialect, the form *loful* is due to the standard pronunciation.

[3] When commenting on this form (Engl. Stud. 52), I remarked that the vulgar lengthening of (ɔ), as in *gord, wrorng,* may be of great antiquity. This passage has been misunderstood by Jordan (§ 273, n.), who erroneously quotes *gord, wrorng* as early spellings from the Paston Letters. Wyld (p. 253) adduces the spelling *Gaud* for *God* from Otway, 1681.

[4] As Machyn also writes *o* for *al* in French words (*cardenoll, a nobe = an albe*) it is not probable that *o* in *ontt, monde* etc. is due to ME. *o* by the side of *au* in French loan-words.

examples *o* may also indicate a shortening of (ɔ:) from *au* to (ɔ).[1]

A monophthongic pronunciation of *au* in *all* and *law* is taught by practically all the French grammarians[2], whereas some early English orthoepists, such as Smith, Hart and Bullokar, direct *au* to be pronounced as a diphthong (au).

Salesbury pronounced *au* as a monophthong at the end of words. The English grammarians of the 17th cent. as a rule directed *au* to be pronounced as a simple vowel, but also testified a diphthong, at least in some words[3], especially such as are derived from French or classical sources.

After all it is not improbable that (au) in *all* and *law*, favoured by some of our earliest English authorities, is either due to a wrong analysis of (ɔ:) as a mixed sound of *a* and *u*[4] or a learned or archaic pronunciation in imitation of Greek and Latin, where αυ and *au* were actually pronounced as (au) by many English and French scholars in the 16th and 17th centuries.[5] This pronunciation has survived in the vernacular *owdacious* for *audacious,* a poor rustic relic of ancient learning, to be compared with *hume* for *hymn* in other dialects, which commemorates the early English pronunciation of the Greek υ as *u, ew* in *due* and *new*[6].

---

[1] Such spellings as *dauhter, baughte* etc. may possibly be due to a levelling of ME. *ọu* in *douhter* and *au* in *law* under the same sound. The levelling may have taken place when *au* had reached the stage of (ɔu). Spellings such as *daughter* do not seem to occur until the end of the 14th and beginning of the 15th cent. (Jordan § 287) when *au* in *law* may have developed into (ɔu).

[2] Zachrisson, pp. 138 ff.

[3] Cf. Zachrisson, pp. 211 ff. Wallis (æu) is undoubtedly a theoretical pronunciation, Gill's and Cooper's (ɔ:u) is either a stage in the development of (au) to (ɔ:) or a compromise between the learned (au), used in the reading of Latin, and the colloquial (ɔ:).

[4] Some of the early grammarians (Hart, Barclay, Meigret, Sylvius etc.) analysed (o) and (ø) in the French words *aucun, peu* etc. as a diphthong consisting of *a+u* and *e+u*. Cf. Ellis, pp. 806, n. 3, 819 ff., below pp. 79 ff.

[5] Cf. Ellis, pp. 819 ff., Deibel, Smith p. 49*, Jones, Cooper 69*, and below pp. 88 ff.

[6] Cf. Zachrisson, Luick Celebration Volume, p. 142.

The numerous identifications of English *au* in *all* and *law* with French and German *a* only indicate that *au* was pronounced with a somewhat more open and less rounded sound than in Present English.[1] In several dialects near London (Bucks, Bedf, Essex, etc.) *au* in *law* is pronounced as (a:)[2], and this sound-change may also have taken place in London itself, as will appear from the following spellings in the Diary of Machyn, the Londoner: *facon* ('falcon') 12, *dran(e)* ('drawn') 91, 106, 258, *drahyns* 142, *sarter* 226 (? 'salter')[3], *unlafull*[4] ('unlawful') 253, *laer* ('lawyer') 309, *draebryge* 52. Additional instances from the Verney Memoirs are: *drane* 156, 263; *laful* 26, 261; *naty* ('naughty') 287; *case* (= 'cause') 263; *lay* ('law') 261 etc.[5]

It is doubtful if the spellings with *a* for *au* represent (a:) or (æ:). In the modern dialects Wright (EDGr. § 49) gives (æ:) only for Norfolk, Wilts, Devon, Dorset and Hants, but it is possible that (a:), which has a much wider distribution, sometimes, has developed from (æ:). At Shakespeare's time both (a:) and (æ:) may have occurred. The isolated spelling *lay* ('law') speaks in favour of (æ:), likewise *hears* for *horse* 1665 (Krapp 144).

The following remark by Aubrey (1626—97) reads like a commentary upon the spellings with *a, ay*: »The Westerne people cannot open their mouthes to speak *ore rotundo*. We pronounce *paal, pale* etc., and especially in Devonshire. The Exeter Coll. men in disputations when they allege *Causa Causæ est Causa Causati*, they pronounce it, *Caza Cazæ est Caza*

---

[1] Zachrisson, p. 139, Shakespeare's Uttal, p. 40.

[2] Wright, E. D. Gr. § 49.

[3] Cf. such 16th and 17th century spellings as *Harton* (= 'Haughton'), *harser* (= 'hawser') noted by Horn, Untersuchungen 23. Horn maintains that (a:) for (ɔ:) had been introduced into London English from the dialects, whereas I assume that the sound-change of *au* to (a:) took place in London itself among certain classes of speakers.

[4] These spellings make it doubtful if *a* in *laful* is due to the reduction of *au* to *a* before *f*, as is assumed by Flasdieck (p. 39) and Jordan, § 286.

[5] A few additional instances are noted by Diehl, 178, and Wyld, 142.

Cazati very ungracefully» (Halliwell, Dict. of Archaic Words, p. XIV).

In early New English the short English *o* in *not* was also pronounced more open and with less lip-rounding than at present.[1] Here again unrounding has taken place in many dialects, especially in the south of England.[2] Early spellings with *a* for *o* of place-names in Bedford,[3] Bucks,[4] Essex,[5] and Middlesex[6] show that this sound-change took place as early as in ME. times.

As occasional spellings with *a* for *o* also occur in the early forms of place-names from Essex and Middlesex, as well as in documents hailing from London, e. g. the Cely Papers, Machyns' Diary, and letters written by Queen Elizabeth etc., the change of *ŏ* to *ă* cannot have been foreign to the speech of the capital. This way of pronouncing *o* is classed by Gill among *Fictitiæ Mopsarum*, i. e. certain pronunciations which the somewhat pedantic Gill looked upon as less correct, but which in point of fact were quite usual in the current speech of the capital. A few words, such as *nap, ratchet, sprat* (Horn), exhibit *a* in Present English.[7]

---

[1] Zachrisson, 135.

[2] Cf. Wright EDGr. § 83, and the material adduced by Dr. A. Kihlbom, Fifteenth Century English, p. 143.

[3] Mawer and Stenton, Place-Names of Bedfordshire and Huntingdon, p. XXIV.

[4] Mawer and Stenton, Place-Names of Buckinghamshire, p. XXIII.

[5] Zachrisson, Luick Celebration Volume, p. 145. Several other instances have been kindly pointed out to me by Mr. Reany, Director of the English Place-Name Survey of Essex.

[6] Gover, Place-Names of Middlesex, pp. 43, 69.

[7] Illustrative examples are adduced by Horn, Untersuchungen, p. 28, Diehl, p. 154, Wyld, pp. 142, 165, 240, Kihlbom, pp. 142 ff. I no longer adhere to my suggestion in English Vowels that the pronunciation of *o* as *a* was made fashionable by Devonshire men, such as Raleigh and Drake — compare Prof. Wyld's able criticism in his Colloquial English, p. 240 — but think it much more probable that the unrounding both of (ɔ:) in *law*, and (ɔ) in *not* took place among certain classes of speakers in London itself. Dr. Kihlbom (p. 144) suggest that the *a*-forms represent 'the sporadic extremes of a general tendency to reduce the degree of lip-rounding — — a tendency which seems especially pronounced in the Southern districts'.

In a recently published paper by Luick (Sievers Celebration Volume, pp. 341—352) it is maintained that ME. *au* in *awe* and *o* in *not,* were pronounced in early NE. with the Continental *a,* which in the second half of the 18th century was changed into the modern sound (ɔ:). Luick also assumes that ME. *a* in *name* was pronounced both with (æ:) and (a:) in the 16th century, and that the present pronunciation of ME. *a* in *man* (with æ) only dates back to the 16th century. These views are not borne out by the available orthographical and orthoepistical evidence. The raising of ME. *a* in man to (æ) had begun as early as the 15th century[1] (cf. above, p. 36), and it is extremely improbable that the Continental (a:) in *name* was still heard at Shakespeares time, as it is not mentioned by any foreign grammarians.[2]

Luick, moreover, is of the opinion that early Continental loan-words, such as *potato* (evidenced in 1565), *pomade* (1562) etc., which now have (eⁱ), were in the 16th century pronounced with the sound in *name* — according to Luick (a:) — whereas in later borrowings, such as *spa* (1590), *vase* (1629), *tomato* (1604), *hurrah* (1686), the English sound in *awe,* or (æ:) > (a:), as in *far,* was used to render the Continental (a:). It is impossible, however, to determine the early phonetic value of *a* in loanwords of this kind. Krapp (pp. 45 ff.)[3] has shown that there was a great vacillation between (e:), (æ), (æ:) and (ɔ:) in the early American pronunciation of words containing the Continental

---

The correctness of this theory can only be proved by individual observation of the way in which words containing short *o* are pronounced in the dialects. That the pronunciation of a vernacular sound can vary considerably within the same dialectal area, is proved by the many variants that exist for the short *u* in *come,* which as I know from personal observation, often vacillates between (u) and (o), as in the dialects of Dorset and Norfolk.

[1] Cf. also *sakkes* 1531 NED. = 'sack' where French (e) is rendered with English (æ) (Zachrisson, Engl. Stud. 52, 317).

[2] Cf. Lambeth Fragment 1528, Tory 1529, Wes 1532 (Zachrisson, p. 120).

[3] Krapp gives (ɔ:) and (æ) for *canal,* (a:) and (ɔ:) for *spa,* (e:), (a:) and (ɔ:) for *hurrah* etc.

a. Both in England and America *vase* still appears with (e^i), (a:), (ɔ:), in English *bravo, hurrah* and *tomato* sometimes have (e^i), not to mention numerous other dual forms. Often the Continental *a* may have been rendered with the English sound in *name* only on account of the spelling. It is only from spellings with *au* that we can learn something definite about the sound-value of e. NE. *a* in *name*. Luick's first spellings with *au* date from 1590 (*spaw*) and 1629 (*vause*). It has already been pointed out (p. 37) that such spellings occur in the 15th century, which proves that at this early date some speakers did not pronounce *a* in *name* in the Continental manner.

With regard to *o* in *not* and *au* in *law* etc., Luick has apparently overlooked some important evidence which renders a general e. NE. pronunciation of these words with the Continental *a* improbable. The short *o* in *not* is equated with the French short *o* by Erondelle (1605) and Gres (1636) and by the Italian open *o* by Florio (1611) (Zachrisson 134 ff.). Miege (1691) denies the identity of the English short *o* with the French *a* (Zachrisson, 135). Some English grammarians, e. g. Smith, Hart, Butler, and Gill, consider *o* in *bone* to be the long equivalent to *o* in *not* (Zachrisson, 211). These statements will suffice to prove that the short *o* cannot have been *generally* pronounced as (a) in early New English. Occasional identifications of *o* in *not* with the French *a* only indicate similarity, not identity of sound. This being so, we are hardly justified in placing more confidence in the numerous equations of the English sound in *law* with the Continental *a,* especially as several English orthoëpists, such as Wallis, Price, and Cooper, expressly tell us that *au* in *law* and *o* in *not* were qualitatively identical (Zachrisson 212). The early English grammarians identified (ɔ:) in *law* with (a:), simply because there was no English equivalent to the Continental *a*. Even at the present day an Englishman often pronounces the French *pas* as *paw,* and in the second half of the 18th century, when, according to Luick, *all* and *law* had their present pronunciation, many English grammarians¹ still equate the English *aw* with the French *a*. Luick himself points out that Erondelle objects to Delamothe's identification of the French *a* and the English *aw*, and that a Welsh orthoëpist of 1670 directs the English *au* in *cause* to be pronounced as the long Welsh *o* (Jones, ed. Cooper, p. 165). A rounded vowel is also unambiguously indicated by the many phonetic spellings with *o* for *au* which have already been discussed (p. 67). So far as I can judge, the conflicting evidence can only be reconciled on the assumption that in early NE. the vowel in *not* and *law* was somewhat more open or less rounded than in present English. The modern tendency towards increased rounding and narrowing is best seen in the London pronunciation where (ɔ:) is sometimes raised to (o:) (cf. Jones, Pronunciation of English, p. 41). Early New English (a) in *not* and (a:) or (æ:) in *all, law* was merely a dialectal or occasional pronunciation.

In the above-mentioned paper, Luick also discusses the early pronunciation of (a:) in *far, dance* etc. To trace the early history of this sound does not fall within the scope of the present investigation. We have good reasons, however, for assuming that at an early date this sound was not only pronounced as (æ:) but also as (a:).²

Bullokar's [aṷ].

As Bullokar had no clear notion of the true nature of a diphthong, we cannot determine how he pronounced *au* in *law*. I am inclined to think that he either pronounced *au* as (ɔ:), which he analysed as a diphthong, i. e. a mixed sound of *a* and *u*, or used a theoretical or archaic pronunciation (au). Length in the first element of the diphthong may be indicated by Smith's notations uäl ('wall') and läu ('law')³, and possibly by

---

¹ Johnston 1764, British Grammar 1762, 1784, Bachmair 1750, 1788, Walker 1791 (Zachrisson 139, Krapp 42).

² Cf. Zachrisson 62, 139 and references.

³ Cf. Zachrisson 211, Engl. Stud. 52, 324 n. 2.

Bullokar's hám (= ʿhaulm³), which, however, may stand for *hám (cf. 6—7 *hawme, ham(e)* NED.) with reduction of *au* to *ā*.

Little is to be learned from Bullokar's notations of *au* in French words. He writes almost invariably aм, aн (= aum, aun): chaмber, chaнg', haуnteth, graнt etc. (more seldom an, am: chamber etc.). Hauck is wrong in giving á for *change, changed, chamber* (p. 31).

Bullokar's [o].

Short *ŏ* in *not* was probably pronounced by Bullokar as it is now, though somewhat more open and less rounded. He couples it with *ē̜* long in *bone*.

The forms word (~ wǫrd), worĺd go back to OE. *word, worold,* which deserves to be pointed out against Luick's assumption (Hist. Gr. § 286, 3) that *wŏr-* was almost always pron. *wŭr* in ME.

Before *nd o* still lingers on in Bullokar's bond and brond-ýʀн. For instances of *o* before *nd* in early London English, see Lekebusch pp. 53 ff. Cf. also Present English ʿbond' sb.

In the following words Bullokar has *ŏ* for etymological (u): comfort, comfort*a*bĺ, lou' sb., stomak (~ ǫ), wǫǫd-dou', үn-worthy, wort7. In some of these words, e. g. *stomach* and *comfort, ŏ* may be due to spelling pronunciation (cf. Horn, § 64), but in the native words the diacritic mark may have been omitted, especially as it often appears in other forms. Gill has (u) in *wort;* his *ŏ* in *love* (once) is certainly an error.

In gou'erн, góu'erн ~ gǫu'erн o, ó ~ ǫ reflects the usual interchange between pretonic *o* and *ou* in French words of this type instanced by many French orthoëpists. Cf. Thurot I 244 n. (Palsgrave: *governail ~ gouverneur*). Gill has *ŏ* in *govern.* The same explanation will hold good for *poppet* (cf. early French *popelin ~ poupelin,* Thurot I 266).

Boȝǫm ~ bǫȝom represents different stages in the shortening of OE. *ō*.

In dolt and dolt*i*sh *o* has not been diphthongized before *l* + consonant. They may be errors of the same kind as sold and holpN, but it is also conceivable that in words of this kind (opprobrious terms) the pronunciation does not always follow the etymology. Influence from OE. *dol* is also possible, if this form survived in ME. and early NE., which is not quite certain. Moreover the diphthong in *dolt* may have been shortened to (ɔ) as in the early American pronunciation of *colt* (cf. Krapp 134).

ME. ǫu in blow and ę̄ in go.

Phonetic spellings with *ow* for ę̄ in *go* and with *o* for ǫu in *know* in numerous original 15th century letters[1] as well as rhymes with words originally containing ǫu and ę̄ in the works of Shakespeare[2] and Spenser[3] indicate that *go* and *blow* were commonly pronounced with the same sound in the 15th and 16th centuries. The French grammarians identify the vowel in *go* and *blow* with the French long ō.[4] Some of the English orthoëpists, e. g. Smith and Gill, teach a diphthongic pronunciation for ǫu in *blow* and *old* as distinct from the long *o* in *go*. The fact that the sound in *old, hold, cold* etc. — in spite of the historical spelling with *o*, not *ow* — is also looked upon as a diphthong, renders it improbable that this distinction is altogether due to the spelling.

According to Salesbury, *u* was mute at the end of such words as *bow* (= *arcus*), whereas *o* before *ld* or *ll* was to be pronounced 'as though *u* was inserted between them'. Some later grammarians, such as Price and Cooper, who, on the whole, equate the sound in *blow* and *go*, nevertheless insist on a diphthongic pronunciation of *o* in *old, cold* etc.[5] Lastly it should be pointed out that some orthoëpists, who assign a diphthong to ǫu in *blow* and a simple vowel to ę̄ in *go*, confuse these two sounds in a few isolated instances.[6]

---

[1] Zachrisson, pp. 83 ff., Jordan § 287.
[2] Vietor, pp. 235 ff.
[3] Gabrielsson, p. 41.
[4] Zachrisson, pp. 142 ff.
[5] Zachrisson, p. 215.
[6] In his Orthographie (1569) Hart renders ǫu in *blow* with [oˑ], whereas in A Methode to read English (1570) he writes both [oˑ] and [oˑu] for ǫu.

I suggest the following interpretation of the conflicting evidence. In colloquial speech *ǫu* in *blow* and *ǭ* in *go* were pronounced as a rule with a common sound ever since the second half of the 15th century. This common sound is most likely to have been a half-open or half-close long (o:), possibly a faintly diphthongized (oᵘ), as has been suggested by Jespersen.[1] Some speakers, probably those belonging to the refined or learned classes, favoured a full diphthongic pronunciation of *ǫu* in *blow*. The last authority for this archaic mode of speech is Cooper.[2]

In *old, cold* etc. monophthongisation may not have taken place at all, or the old diphthong may have remained longer in these words than in *blow*. The correctness of the one or other of these views depends upon the degree of confidence we are willing to place in the conflicting evidence of the various early authorities.[3]

The rule in Alphabet Anglois (1625) according to which *o* before *ld* and *lt* is pronounced as *aou*[4] (the same sound as in 'flower') I now take to be due to confusion between ME. *ū* in *flower*, pronounced as (ou), and ME. *ǫu* in *old* pronounced with a half-long *o* for ist first element. A very similar rule is given

---

Mulcaster describes *ǫu* as a diphtong but writes *shro* for *shrew* from OE. *scrēawa*. Butler writes *slow* for *sloe* and *sloth* for *slowth* (Zachrisson 214, Eichler, Butler 38, 46).

[1] What to a certain extent speaks against Jespersen's theory is the clear distinction some of the early English grammarians make between the diphthong *ǫu* in *blow* and *old*, on the one hand, and the simple vowel in *go*, on the other. At the same time the diphthong favoured by the early orthoëpists may have been a fully developed (o:u) not the faint gliding diphthong (oᵘ) of present English speech. The chief objection to Jespersen's views that ME. *ai* in *day*, and *ou* in *blow* remained diphthongs in early Standard English is that a monophthongic pronunciation of words containing these sounds actually exists not only in many dialects (cf. Wright, EDG. §§ 48, 127), but also in the American pronunciation, which on the whole is based on that of Standard English in the 17th century, and retains many archaic features of pronunciation.

[2] Jones, Cooper, p. 69*, Zachrisson, Engl. Stud. 52, 324 n. 1.

[3] Zachrisson, p. 216, where the evidence is summed up.

[4] Zachrisson, p. 142.

by Cooper (1685), according to which some speakers use the same sound for *ow* in *how* as for *o* before *l*+consonant.[1] In certain dialects ME. *o* before *l*+consonant has developed into (au) (SE. Kent and the North of England) and (ʌu) (Norfolk, Wilts, Yorks etc., cf. Wright, EDGr. § 86), but it seems less probable that the e. NE. diphthong should be due to such vernacular forms.

Bullokar's [ó, ou, ow].

Bullokar describes *ǫu* in *blow* as a diphthong composed of *ŏ* short and *u*. That the first element was long seems, however, to appear from occasional spellings, such as cóld, hólm, tól etc.

Theoretically he keeps *ǭ* in *go* and *ǫu* in *blow* strictly apart, but in his notations they are sometimes confused before *r* and *l*+consonant. Cf. owerż ('oars')[2], fólkȝ, cóld, hóld, hólding, hóldᴎ, hólm, óld by the side of hołd, ołd[3] etc.

From the previous discussion we can assume that Bullokar pronounced *ǭ* in *go* as a·long half-close (o:), *ǫu* in *blow* and *old* as (o:u).

Butler has the same vacillation between *o* long and *ow* (o:u) in his quasi-phonetic notations of words containing *ol*+consonant: bowl, enrowl, gold' etc. Such forms as gold (Butler) and hold (Bullokar) are influenced by the traditional orthography.

In Bullokar's fowʀ, fowʀ*t*h, slowth̦, slowth̦ful and th̦rowż the old ME. diphthong is still kept. According to NED. the spelling 'throes' is not earlier than the 17th century. On *sloth, troth,* see Zachrisson 83.

Present English *roam* appears as rowm in Bullokar (cf. 4—6

---

[1] Jones, Cooper, p. 69*. When late English and American orthoëpists describe the first element in the diphthong (au) in house as (ɔ), they are not to be implicitly trusted (cf. Zachrisson, Anglia Beiblatt 1918, p. 176, Krapp, p. 51), but I have heard (ou) or (ɔu) for (au) used by provincial speakers, e. g. from Wales and from the North of England.

[2] An analogous spelling is *sowyr* (= 'sore') Paston Letters, 701.

[3] Smith's notations exhibit a similar vacillation. See Deibel, 55*.

rowme, NED.). The word is of uncertain etymology. Some forms point to ME. ǭ, others to ǭ. Thus Gower rhymes *roam : home,* but Shakespeare rhymes *roaming : coming,* Twelfth Night II, 3. 39, 40 and has a pun on *Rome, roam,* Henry VI, 3. 1. 11 (Ellis 925).

In astón*e*d (∼ ǫ) ó is in my opinion due to folk-etymological association with 'stone'; astóned was considered to mean 'petrified, turned into a stone'. In early spellings, quoted by NED., such as 5—6 *astoyned, oy* is evidently a symbol for *o* long. Cf. Zachrisson 65, and Engl. Stud. 52, 308, n.[1]

Unetymological ó in tók (∼ oo) and in ɥndertók (cf. the spelling *toake* in Ellis, Letters III, 3. 165, quoted by Price 149) may be due to the analogy of *brake* (this infinitive was not unusual in e. NE., cf. Zachrisson, 58, and references), *broke, spakc* (inf.), *spoke.* Cf. also Present English 'wake', 'woke', which may be accounted for in the same way.

Long ó in lóȝ goes back to OE. *losian* (cf. the present spelling 'lose'), and oo (= uː) is due to the influence of *loose,* vb. (NED.). On the other hand, *loose,* vb. and adj., have been influenced by lóȝ ('lose') with ó, and therefore appear as lóȝ*i*ng, lóȝęd (∼ looȝ*i*ng etc.), and lós (adj.). In Spense rboth *lose, loose,* vb., and *loose* adj., often rhyme with words containing ME. ǭ. See Gabrielson, p. 84. Cf. also such spellings as *loast* (= 'loosed'), Spenser (Gabrielson, *ibid.*), and 6 *loase* (= 'loose', vb.), NED.[2]

On sponȝ (∼ oo), cf. above p. 48.

---

[1] The learned editors of NED. are evidently not aware of the fact that *i* could be used as a length-mark after *o, u* in the South of England also, and are therefore much baffled by such spellings: *astoyned* is said to be unexplained.

[2] This interchange supports NED.'s suggestion that (uː) in *lose,* vb., is due to the analogy of the verb *loose* (not to OE. *lēosan*). At the same time we must also reckon with the possibility that the Scandinavian diphthong *au, ou* could sometimes result into ME. ǭ. This is shown by the early and modern forms of certain place-names containing Scandinavian *raupr, haukr* etc. (cf. *Hokesworth* 1295—1428 = Hawksworth, Notts, *Moreholme* 14 c. = Morholm, Lancs, *Rotheclyue* 1280—1323 = Roecliffe, Yorks etc., Lindkvist 145, 148, 159).

ME. *u*, *ẹ̄u*, *ẹu* in **use, new, few.**

The early New English pronunciation of (ju:) in *use, new,* and *few* is a very difficult and much debated problem. It was generally assumed by most early writers on the subject that *use* and *new* were pronounced both with a diphthong (iu) or (ju:) and with the French *u* (y:). This theory was severely criticised by Professor Jespersen, who by a careful examination of all the orthoëpistical evidence tried to show that the supposed pronunciation with (y:) is due to an erroneous analysis of (iu) or (ju:). The same result was arrived at by the present writer. Statements by English grammarians, according to which the English *u*, *ẹu* in *use* and *new* was identical in sound with *u* in French seem to speak in favour of (y:). That such statements are due to an erroneous analysis of (iu), (ju:), seems to be proved by the following facts. Some grammarians who look upon, or transcribe, *u*, *ẹu* in *use* and *new* as a diphthong, nevertheless, identify this diphthong with the French (y:). The grammarians who identify the sound in *new* and *use* with the French (y:), as a rule, also identify the sound in *few* (e:u) with the sound in *neuf, neutre,* which in the 16th century was certainly generally pronounced as (œ), (ø), at least in Parisian French. None or few of the early grammarians were able to analyse correctly the rounded front vowels, which did not exist in the classical vowel-system. They seem to have looked upon (y:) and (ø:) as made up of (i:) and (e:)+(u), they did not understand that the labial action ('rounding') takes place simultaneously with the raising of the tongue to *i*- and *e*- position. It is for this reason they continually confuse (y:) and (ø:) with (iu) and (e:u). If (y:) was common in such English words as *use* and *new*, how is it then that our *French* authorities, Desainliens, Bellot, Maupas etc., continually pointed out what a difficult sound the French (y) was for the English to learn, at the same time cautioning them against pronouncing it as a diphthong? In the whole long list of French orthoëpists there is not one who teaches a general pronunciation for the English

u in *use* and *ẽu* in *new* as (y:). It is true some of them direct
this English sound to be pronounced as the French (y:), but, as
a rule, this is only in words spelt with *u*, such as *use* and *blue*,
where they are led astray by the orthography. The theory that
use and *new* were pronounced with a diphthong, not with (y:),
has been gaining ground rapidly. Spira (p. 249) admits that
'von unseren französischen gewährsmännern könnte kein einziger,
wenn man ihn für sich allein betrachtete als einwandfreier *ū*-
zeuge gelten', and authors of recently published handbooks on
the early New English pronunciation, such as Ekwall and
Wright, do not seem to believe in the existence of a general
pronunciation of *use* and *new* with (y:).[1]

In a paper in Anglia, vol. 45, pp. 132—181, Luick has
recently re-examined the evidence, and the results he has arrived at, coincide to a certain extent with mine. He agrees
with me that 'a Frenchman was certainly the best person to
decide whether English possessed a French sound or not'
(p. 133). He also seems inclined to assume that occasional
identifications of the English sound in *use, true, blue* with the
French (y:) are to be considered as errors (p. 159), and that
some English grammarians, e. g. Smith, Gill, and Hart,[2] may

---

[1] Cf. Jespersen, Hart pp. 44—63, Gr. 3, 819, Zachrisson, pp. 146, 158,
217—220, and Shakespeare's Uttal p. 41 f., Ekwall, Hist. Lautl., p. 46,
Wright, H. N. E. Gr., § 86.

[2] I will again draw attention to a few facts which render this very
likely. Smith's description of [v] in *use* and *new* is a mere paraphrase of
Dionysius Halicarnasseus' description of the Greek υ (which Smith had
copied in his book on the Greek pronunciation). Both of them say that
the sound is very narrow and pronounced with the lips pressed together.
Smith did not know French, and he erroneously identifies not only the
sound in *new* (iu) with French *u*, but also the sound in *few* (e : u) with
French *eu*. Cf. Zachrisson, pp. 163, 218.

Hart's evidence on *u* reads as follows:

»Now to come to the *u*. I sayde the French, Spanish & Brutes,
I maye adde the Scottish, doe abuse it with vs in sounde and for
consonant, except the Brutes as is sayd: the French doe neuer sound
it right, but vsurpe *ou*, for it, the Spanyard doth often vse it right
as we doe, but often also abuse it with vs; the French and the

have erroneously looked upon the English diphthong in *use* and *new* as identical with the French (y) in *user* etc. (p. 160).

Luick also assumes the existence of the pronunciation (iu), (juː). The former is in his opinion not evidenced until the 17th century by Mason (1622), Alphabet Anglois (1625 not 1635), Hodges (1644), Wallis (1653), Wilkins (1668), and Cooper (1685). This pronunciation, which was originally dialectal (Kent, East Midland), is supposed to have become general at about the same time as (eːu) in *few* passed into (iu), (juː). A pronunciation with *j* in the first element of the diphthong is, according to Luick, indicated by early spellings such as *shewet* 1615 for *suet* etc. (p. 157) and certain directions and transcriptions in the grammars by Butler (1631) (cf. Zachrisson 219), Mauger, Miège etc.

On this I will make the following preliminary remarks. To judge by rhymes and some orthographical and orthoëpistical

---

Scottish in the sounde of a Diphthong; which keeping the vowels in their due sounds, commeth of *i*, & *u*, (or very neare it) is made and put togither vnder one breath, confounding the sounds of *i*, & *u*, togither; which you may perceyue in shaping thereof, if you take away the inner part of the tongue from the vpper teeth or Gummes, then shall you sound the *u* right, or in sounding the French and Scottish *u*, holding still your tongue to the vpper teeth or gums, & opening your lippes somewhat, you shall perceyue the right sound of *i*.»

Here Hart gives a fairly accurate description of the French and the Scotch (y), but he does not describe the corresponding English sound, and if he pronounced the English *u* in the same way as the French, he ought, as Jespersen remarks, also to have pronounced the English *ew* in *few* as the French *eu*. When Hart says that *u* is abused 'with us' as well as with the French and the Scotch, he only wants to point out that *u* has not its proper sound (*u*) either in French, Scotch or English, not that *u* was pronounced in the same way in these three languages. Like many other Englishmen, Hart may have thought that the English diphthong in *use* was pronounced in the same way as in the French *user*, but, as Luick himself admits (p. 140), this does not prove the identity of the two sounds.

Gill classes [ei] for [j] in *like* and [iu] for [v] in *use* among *Fictitiæ Mopsarum* simply because he erroneously looked upon the diphthongs in *like* and *use* as simple vowels (Zachrisson 175 f.).

evidence[1] a common pronunciation of *ẹu* and *ę̣u* in *new* and *few,* evidently (iu) or (ju:), must have existed at least as early as the 16th and the beginning of the 17th centuries.

According to my views, the pronunciation (ju:) is also indicated by such spellings as *shue, shooter* (= 'sue', 'suitor') in Shakespeare's Love's Labour Lost, *sheute* for *suit* in the Alleyn Papers (c. 1590), puns on the words *suitor* and *shooter* in Elizabethan dramas, and probably also by such early spellings as *shue, shute,* for *shoe, shoot*[2]. A different view maintained by Luick (p. 179) is based on the assumption that *u* and *ẹu* were not generally pronounced as *iu* in the 16th century.

Luick assumes the existence of the following e. NE. pronunciations of *u, ẹu* in *use* and *new:* (yu), (y:), and (iy). Note that (iy) in my phonetic notation corresponds to Luick's (iü). In my notation (ü:) stands for the vowel in the Swedish word 'hus' = 'house'.

If the arguments which are marshalled by Professor Luick are not always convincing, this is not for want of accuracy or scholarly methods. There is not a more painstaking or conscientious writer than Professor Luick, who has rendered the greatest services to the historical study of the English language. Prof. Luick carefully weighs and sifts all the available evidence. True scholar that he is, he does not even hesitate to adduce fresh evidence of a kind which, at least apparently, does not favour

---

[1] Cf. rhymes with *ẹu* and *ę̣u* in Spenser, Shakespeare etc. (Vietor, p. 194, Gabrielson, p. 42 f.), and spellings such as *lude* ('lewd') Cely Papers no. 28, *lude* 6, *due* ('dew') 1508, *butyful* 6 (NED.) (*beauty* is not pronounced with the sound corresponding to ME. *ẹu, u* by any of the early English grammarians, Gill, Hart, Butler, Daines etc.). But ME. *schued, shued* ('showed') is due to the change of *ẹu* to *ę̣u* owing to the patalal influence of *sh* (cf. Zachrisson, Engl. Stud., 52, p. 319, n. 2), and *lude* may go back to ME. *ẹu* by the side of *ę̣u*. Cf. ME. *leouwede, laude, lowde,* which seem to presuppose an OE. form *lēowed* > ME. *lude, lowde, laude.* The first orthoëpistical evidence for a common diphthongic pronunciation of *ew* in *new* and *few* is that of Alphabet Anglois (1625).

[2] Cf. Ellis I, 215, III, 922, Jespersen 12, 26, Zachrisson, p. 85, Wyld, p. 293.

his own conclusions. But he does not always seem to pay sufficient regard to the errors and inaccuracies which are likely to abound in early works of this kind, to the many weaknesses and frailties which, phonetically speaking, the flesh of all the early orthoepists is heir to. To interpret them correctly it is necessary to be like one of themselves, unburdened for the time being by any theoretical knowledge of phonetics.

Luick's assumption that there existed an early pronunciation (yu) in *use* and *new* is based solely on Salesbury's and other Welshmen's identification of the English sound in *new* with the Welsh *uw*. We are, however, justified in interpreting Welsh *u* as English *i*, in which case the intended sound is (iu) not (yu).[1] I have recently had the opportunity of consulting Professor T. Glyn Davies on the pronunciation of the Welsh *u*. In the south of Wales it is pronounced as (i:) and in the north of Wales as a mixed close vowel (ï:) without any trace of rounding. This distinction existed at the time of Salesbury, who hailed from the north of Wales (cf. Salesbury's Welsh pronunciation in Ellis III, 761). The Northern Welsh (ï:) cannot very well be confused with (y:); acoustically it comes much closer to (i:), and it is often used as a substitute for the English (i), e. g. in English loan-words in Welsh and in the Hymn to the Virgin. Professor Glyn Davies suggests that Salesbury wrote *uw* for the English *u* in order to indicate that the correct or best pronunciation was ('i : u) or (i'u:), not (ju:), for in northern Welsh *uw*, as in *duw*, 'god', is always pronounced as (ï : u), whereas *iw* and *yw* can also be pronounced as (ju:) in Present English *use*, *new* etc. In the Hymn to the Virgin and other Welsh transliterations of English texts *uw*, *iw*, and *yw* are

---

[1] Cf. Ellis, pp. 164, 760, 785, Zachrisson, pp. 104 n., 217, Jones, Cooper, 24*, 68*, Flasdieck II, p. 43, Jordan § 109. Shillingford's *knyw* I interpret as (iu) (cf. Zachrisson 85, Jordan § 289) not with Wyld, p. 242, as (jy:). Note also that Wallis (see the passage quoted by Luick p. 148) identifies the English sound in *new* with the Welsh *uw*, whereas a Welsh Dictionary from about the same time (Jones, Cooper, 68*) renders English *ew* with Welsh *iw*.

used promiscuously to render the English diphthong. Consequently there is no evidence whatever for the supposed early
New English pronunciation of the present diphthong in *new*
and *use* as (y:u).

Luick (p. 160) reckons only with Holder and perhaps
Wallis as *safe* authorities for the pronunciation (y:). It would
be very astonishing if a general pronunciation (y:) were taught
only by Englishmen as opposed to the many French writers
of English grammars, who ought to be better judges of the
existence of a French sound in English.

Holder says: (Elements of Speech 1669, p. 88):

> »And in this, *ʊ* and *u* are peculiar, that they are framed
> by a *double motion* of Organs, that of the Lip, added to that
> of the Tong; and yet either of them is a single Letter, and
> not two, because the motions are at the same time, and not
> successive, as are *eu. pla.* etc. Yet for this reason they seem
> *not* to be *absolutely so simple* Vowels as the rest, because the
> voice passeth *successively* from the Throat to the Lips in *ʊ*,
> and from the Palat to the Lips in *u*, being there *first* moulded
> into the figures of *oo* and *i*, *before* it be fully Articulated by
> the Lips . . . . . I have been inclin'd to think, there is no
> Labial Vowel, but that the same affection from the Lips may,
> *somewhat in the nature of a Consonant*, be added to every of
> the Vowels, but most subtleley, and aptly to two of them,
> whose Figures are in the extreames in respect of Aperture and
> Situation», i. e. to *oo* and *i*. — (Jespersen 54 f.)

I hold with Jespersen (p. 55) that the lip action which,
according to Holder, takes place when *u* is pronounced need
not have been simultaneous with the raising of the tongue to
i-position (cf. above p. 79); and that we consequently are justified in interpretating Holder's *u* as a diphthong.

If Holder meant to describe (ju:) not (iu:) it is easier to
understand why he looked upon it as a single letter, (not made
up of i + u:) formed by the simultaneous action of the lips and
the tongue.

The most important statement in the passage quoted by
Luick (p. 152) is:

Thus *u* will be only *i* labial, and *ʊ* will be *oo* labial, that is, by adding that motion of the under lip, *i* will become *u*, and *oo* will become *ʊ*.

This description applies both to (juː) and to (yː), for what constitutes the main difference between (iː) and (juː) is exactly 'the motion of the *under* lip', which takes place when the tongue passes from (iː) to (uː) position.

Against the interpretation of Wallis' *u* in *use* etc. as (yː) the following arguments can be adduced. Wallis (p. 10) states that 'foreigners would obtain the pronunciation of the English *u*, *ew* (in *use, new* etc.), if they endeavoured to pronounce the diphthong *iu*, namely by putting the slender *i* before the letter *u* or *w*, as in the Spanish word *cindad;* but this is not entirely the same sound, for *iu* (sc. in Spanish *cindad*) is a compound sound, but the French and English *u* is a simple sound' (quoted from Greenwood's translation). In my opinion this means that the English *u* was pronounced not as ('iu) but as (i'uː) or (juː). Later on (p. 58) he states that the English *u*, is 'compos'd so to speak of *ĭ* and *u*', which undoubtedly points to a diphthong. For 'yew' (< OE. *ēow, iw*) a diphthongic pronunciation is unambiguously implied by the direction (p. 34) that *yew* obtains the sound of 'chew' if a *t* is prefixed. We arrive at the same result when examining Wallis' rule on the pronunciation of the diphthong *ew* in *new* (stated previously to be identical in sound with *u* in *use*) and *few* etc. The theoretically correct pronunciation of *ew* in these words is (eːu) ('*e* clarum & *w*'), which was in actual use only for ME. *ęu* (in *few, beauty* etc.). Especially *new, knew, snew* (i. e. *ew* < ME. *ęu*) are said to be pronounced by some speakers more sharply, as if they were written *niw* or *niew* (pp. 32, 60). I cannot find there is any reason whatever for interpreting the spelling *ie* as indicating a sound between (eː) and (iː) (thus Müller after Vietor, Shakespeare Phonology, § 32). Wallis makes no distinction between *ie* and *i*, but simply says that *ew* is pronounced 'as if written *iew* or *iw*'. Hence *iew* and *iw* are spelling devices indicating a diphthongic pronunciation (i'uː) (with a short or half-long first element) or

(ju:). The fact that *iew* was altered to *iw* speaks in favour of
(ju:). The result of the above examination is that Wallis pronounced *u* < French (y:) and *ęu* with a *diphthong* (ju:); for *ęu*
he knew two pronunciations, 'iu' and (e:u), of which he only
considered the latter to be correct. Sweet's argument (HES.
§ 878) that 'when a competent phonetician like W. plainly says
that his *u* long, is a monophthong identical with French *u*, we
are bound to believe him', loses much in weight by the fact
that Wallis not only teaches a host of theoretical pronunciations
due to the spelling, but also commits some grave errors in his
analysis of the consonants. Thus French (ʒ) in *age* and English
(ʃ) in *shame* are said to be composed of *z+y* and *s+y*, English
(dʒ) and (tʃ) in *jaw* and *orchard* of *d+y* and *t+y* (p. 33). In
Wallis' day the existence of (y:) in England was denied by
Wilkins, his friend and fellow-collegian (see Jespersen, Hart's
Pronunciation, p. 59), and in the next generation by Lediard
(see Müller, p. 55). It was *left unnoticed* by careful analysers
of the English pronunciation of the 18th cent., such as Johnston,
Elphinstone, and Nares. The latter even interprets *Wallis'* *u*
as a diphthong. Cf. Zachrisson, p. 220 n. Wallis would hardly
have identified the English *u* with the Welsh *uw, iw, yw* (cf.
the passage quoted by Luick, p. 148) if he had not pronounced
it as a diphthong.

Luick is anxious to prove that the diphthongic pronunciation of *u* and *ęu* in *use* and *new* which is taught by English
orthoëpists, such as Hart, Baret, Bullokar, Butler and Price
should be interpreted as (iy) or (jy:), not (iu) or (ju:). I cannot
find he has given any conclusive proofs of this. It is possible
to give almost any interpretation to the vague descriptions these
authorities make of the sound in question. But nearly all of
them denote the diphthong with [iu]' or [iw], which certainly
speaks in favour of (iu) (ju:), rather than (iy) (jy:). Hart writes
iu for *new, use* etc., and the phonetic value of his [u] is (u), as
in [sukses], [upon], [iung] etc. I quite fail to see how it is

---

' Sherwood's [iu] should be interpreted in the same way as the [iu]
of the French grammarians; cf. below, p. 89.

possible to construe the following description of the diphthong by Butler as anything else than (iu): 'ee and i short with w have the very sound of u long' (English Grammar, ed. Eichler, p. 9).

As phoneticians and analysers of the spoken sounds all the early English grammarians before Cooper have to 'hide their diminished heads', and even Cooper himself is far from infallible. The fact that the diphthong in early NE. may have been pronounced not only as (iu:), (ju:), but also as (iü:), (jü:) (cf. below) renders a correct interpretation of their evidence still more difficult.

Nevertheless the pronunciation (iu) or (ju:) is obviously taught at least by Baret 1573 (Jespersen, Hart 53, Zachrisson 39), who says that 'u (in Scotch)' is rather a diphthong than a vowel, 'being compounded of our English e and u, as in deede we may partly perceyue in pronouncing it, our tongue at the beginning lying flat in our mouth, & at the ende rising up withe the lippes also therewithall somewhat more drawen together'. This description does not apply either to (iy:) or (iü:), which are both front-vowels,[2] only to (iu), (ju:), for we are bound to raise the back of the tongue when we pronounce (iu), (ju:), not when we pronounce (iy:) or (iü:).

According to Luick, all the French grammarians of the 16th and 17th centuries, with the exception of Mason 1622 and the author of Alphabet Anglois 1625, teach a pronunciation (iy), graphically represented with [iu, iü, ieu]. The pronunciation (iu) is taught only for the letters of the alphabet u, q, w (iou, qiou, double iou).

When we examine the evidence we shall find that things are not quite as simple as that. Our first authority Bellot (1580) calls the letters u, w, q, yu, qiu, and double yu respectively (Zachrisson 13, 14). That u need not be interpreted as (y)

---

[1] B. evidently thought that the Scotch and the English u were pronounced in the same way.

[2] For a description of (ü:) see Zachrisson, Engl. Stud. 60, p. 351. It is a *mid front* vowel with inner rounding.

appears from Bellot's rule that *ou* in *thou* is pronounced as
French *au*, which I take to be a mere spelling device for the
diphthong (au) (Zachrisson, 131 n. 1). A similar direction is
given by Mauger 1685: 'La Diphthongue Angloise *ou* se prononce comme *au* en Latin ou *au* en François: *thou* [thau]'
(Spira, 120). As the illustrative example *thou* is the same in
Bellot's grammar, Mauger has undoubtedly borrowed the rule
from his predecessor, but to make it clearer he has added '*au*
en Latin', which we know was pronounced as (au) (Zachrisson,
131 n. 1). We should also note that in an earlier edition of
the grammar (1679) (Zachrisson, 26) Mauger only says that *ou*
in *thou* is pronounced as *au* in the Latin word *autem*. This
shows that we must not interpret the evidence with Spira
(p. 120) as referring to a pronunciation of *au* in *French* words.
That *au* is merely a spelling device to denote a pronunciation
(au) is also evident from the direction in Mauger-Festeau 1693
that '*ou* se prononce separement comme *au*'[1] (Spira 186), corresponding to a rule in Festeau 1672 that '*ou* se prononce separement *o, ou*' (Spira, 102).

Contrary to what is maintained by Spira and Luick, we
are consequently fully justified in concluding that Bellot's *yu*
for *u* is simply a clumsy orthographical device to indicate the
pronunciation (ju:). This is the more plausible as the majority
of the French orthoëpists call the English *u* 'you' not 'yu'.
Evidently in order to prevent his French pupils from pronouncing the English *u* as (iy), the author of Alphabet Anglois (1625)
directs the letters *u, q, w* to be pronounced as *iou, qiou*, and
double iou, and directs both *u, ęu* and *ęu* in *use, new, few* etc.
to be pronounced as *iou* (Zachrisson, 14, n. 1, 16).

Mason 1622 (Spira 70) calls *q, u, w, kyou, you, douliou*,
and in his notations writes both *iu* and *iou* (*iou* in *new, news,
iu* in *muse, refuse* etc.). Contrary to Luick, I consider it very
unlikely that Mason pronounced (iu) in *new* and in the names
of the letters, but (iy) in other words. I look upon *iu* as an

---

[1] In my reprint of Mauger-Festeau 1693 (Zachrisson, 32) the rule is
worded as follows: — '*o* se prononce presque comme *a* & *u* se prononce'.

imperfect notation for (iu), perhaps to a certain extent influenced by the conventional spelling. In the same way we should interpret Maupas' (1607) [iü] for the English pronunciation of *u* (Zachrisson, 144) and Sterpin's (1660—70) (Spira 91) direction that the English *u* is to be pronounced as *i-u* (whereas the exemple *due* is transcribed *deu*), so much the more as Sterpin transcribes the letters *q*, *u* with *ki-u*, *i-u*, but *w* with *double i-ou*.

This survey shows that our earliest French authorities do not consistently write [iou] for the letter and [iu] for the examples. They write *iu* and *iou* promiscuously both for the letters and in their transcriptions of words.

Later authorities, such as Mauger, Festeau, and Miège, on the other hand, always call the letters *iou,* *quiou, double iou,* but write *iu,* and *ieu* in their transcriptions. But they also teach a pronunciation (y:) for English words which are spelt with *u* and *ue* (*blue, true* etc.), and all the French authorities teach the same diphthongic pronunciation for *ẹu* in *few* as for *ẹu* in *new*. As *ẹu* is not likely to have been generally pronounced with (iy), we are again forced to the conclusion that *iu* and *ieu* are only spelling devices for the pronunciation (iu), (ju:), which is clearly testified as a general pronunciation of *u* by the author of the Lambeth Fragment in the 15th cent.[1], by Baret[2], and Desainliens[3] in the 16th cent., and by Mason[4] and the author of Alphabet Anglois in the 17th cent.

Luick fails to give any convincing reason for the fact that *u* as the name of the letter was pronounced differently from *u* and *ew* in separate words, and the passage he quotes from Desainliens, according to which Englishmen pronounced *u* in Latin words as *iou*, is an additional proof of the existence of a general 16th century pronunciation of the English *u* in *use* as (iu),

---

[1] '*V* (in French ought to be pronounced) . . . . as *ou* and not *you*' (Zachrisson 143).

[2] Cf. above, p. 87.

[3] 'When englishmen do profer *u*, they say *you*' (Zachrisson 144). That this only refers to the pronunciation of the *letter u* is unthinkable.

[4] Cf. above, p. 88.

for it is utterly inconceivable that Englishmen should have
pronounced *u* in Latin words differently from *u* in English
words.

It is also highly improbable that (iy) should have been
replaced with (iu) on the analogy of the few words containing
ęu, for which Luick, in spite of the unanimous evidence of the
French grammarians, does not seem to claim a general pronunciation with (iy). In the 18th century the elusive evidence
for (iy) and (y) disappears with the progress of phonetic analysis and the improvement of the handbooks in which English
was taught to foreigners. Very characteristic in this respect
is the treatment of the rules on the pronunciation of English
ęu, ęu in the later editions of Miège's grammar. The notation
iu is kept as late as 1728 (very long after *iu* for *ęu* had become generally accepted), in 1750 *iou* had taken the place of
iu but not in all the examples, and even in 1756 a few faulty
notations with *iu* still linger on (Spira 196, 202, 206), whereas
in Rogissard's grammar (1738) and Siret-Parquet's (1796) the
notation *iou* is general (Spira 200, 223).

If (jy:) in *use* and *new* was an intermediate stage in the
development of ME. *ęu* to (ju:), we should expect (jy:) to have
been preserved at least in *some* modern dialects, as is the case
with (iu), which is a usual vernacular variant of (ju:) (cf. Wright,
EDGr. § 193). In a similar manner the early pronunciations of
ou in *house* (u:), *ę* in *speak* (e:), *u* in *come* (u, o), *ī* in *like* (ei),
ū in *house* (u:, ou etc.) have invariably been kept in some modern dialects. According to Wright (EDGr., § 193) (iy) for *u,*
ew is found in certain Eastern dialects, but this (iy) is an erroneous analysis of (ü:), the vowel-sound in the Swedish word
'hus''[1], and this is also the case with Wright's (iy) in W. Somerset, Devon, and Cornwall, as I have been able recently to ascertain (cf. below: Additions). Moreover, the vernacular forms
characteristic of the extreme South-West are not likely to have
been generally current in early Standard English.

---

[1] Cf. Zachrisson, Engl. Stud., 60, p. 351.

Spellings with *ou* for ME. *ǭ* in place-names containing common words such as *broom, hook, ford, brook* (cf. Ekwall, Engl. Stud. 55, pp. 403 f.) are most likely to indicate the change of *ō* to (u:), but as they are all derived from the Feudal Aids which mainly exist in copies of the 15th and 16th centuries, they are not conclusive for the date of the change. Contrary to Ekwall, I believe that Rowde, Wilts, which nearly always exhibits *u* in the early spellings, does not contain ME. *ō* but either *ū* (OE. *rūde*) or *ēo* (OE. *hrēod*). In *Suthbrun, -brum* 1227 Ch. R., 1231 Pat. R., *u* is due to weak stress and the influence of the labial consonant. Consequently none of these instances are conclusive for an early dialectal change of *ō* to (y:) or (ü:). In some of Ekwall's instances *ou* may of course represent Standard English (u:) used as a substitute for the dialectal sound. I have, however, noticed a few instances of *ou* for *o* in contemporary MSS., and from areas where the change of *ō* to (ü:) (cf. Wright, EDGr., § 163) is rare or not evidenced at all.: *Milbrouke* 1363 IPMR. = Millbrook, Bedf., *Mourton* 1281 IPM. = Maids Moreton, Bucks, *Spoundon* 1335, 1391 IPM. = Spondon, Derby (OE. *spōn*). At least in *Milbrouke* labial influence seems to be excluded. These instances should be compared with the 14th century *ou*-forms adduced by Wyld (p. 234) from Robert Brunne (*touper, doun*) and Shoreham (*roude, doup* etc.), and may be looked upon as the first indications of the change of ME. *ǭ* to (u:).[1]

The evidence of late German and Dutch grammars (Luick 139 f.) is not of sufficient importance or independent enough to settle the quality of this much debated sound. The direction to pronounce *u* as *iü* or *ü* given by some German grammarians (Nicolai 1693, Tiessen 1705) is undoubtedly a borrowing from

---

[1] In his place-name material for Devonshire Mr. Blomé has safe spellings with *u* only for OE. *bōcland* (*Ekebukelond* 1297 Pat. R., *Bukland* 1316 Cl. R. etc.), where *ō* may have been raised to (u:) because of the labial consonant and subsequently shortened to *ŭ*. *Suthbrouk* 29 E I IPM. = Southbrook, is to be explained as *Milbrouke* above.

French sources[1], and this is also very likely the case with similar rules in Dutch grammars (Hillenius 1664: English $u =$ Dutch *ju*, Hexham-Manley 1672/75: English $u =$ Dutch *yu*, Richardson 1677: $u = yu$, *u*, but $ew = ieuw$), especially as some of them (Sewel 1705 etc.) make the same artificial distinction between the name of the letter u ($= joew$) and the general pronunciation of u ($= uu$, uw) as the Frenchmen do.

If any real importance is to be attached to the notations *iu* and *yu* in French and Dutch grammars, they are best interpreted as due to a mispronunciation of (iu), (ju:) as (iy) (jy:)[2], which could take place the more easily as the English sound in *use* and *new* is pronounced by many speakers not only as (ju:) but also as (jü:) ([ü:] $= u$ in the Swedish word 'hus'),[3] and this pronunciation is likely to have been current in early New English also. The Dutch and French grammarians who direct *u, eu* to be pronounced as (y:), substitute (y:) for the English diphthong, and a similar sound-substitution accounts for the graphic rendering of English *u, eu* with Dutch *u* and *uw* in Dutch records from the beginning of the 17th cent. Here the Dutch scribe writes *Nubere, Hendruw, Stuert, Stuwert* for the English personal names *Newbury, Andrew*(?), *Stewart*. These spellings do not prove that Present English (ju:) was pronounced as (y:) and (y:u) in the early 17th century, as is maintained by Barnouw (p. 38), they only prove that the Dutch as well as the French replaced the unfamiliar English diphthong (i'u:, i'ü:) or (ju:, jü:) with (y:) or (y:u), which is exactly what has happened in the present Dutch pronunciation of the English personal name *Stuart* (stjuət) as (sty : art.). Barnouw is much puzzled by the Dutch rendering of the English name *Brewster* as *Bruyster* (brəuster?). The enigma is solved by the simple as-

---

[1] Podensteiner's (1685) *u* in *use* sicut *iû*, on the other hand, ought to mean (iu) not (iy) from a German point of view.

[2] Notice that (ju:) is rare in Dutch words, whereas (y:) — spelled *u, uu* — and ('iu) — spelled *ieuw* — are common.

[3] Cf. Jespersen, Lehrbuch der Phonetik § 157, Jones, Pronunciation of English, p. 43.

sumption that the Dutch transliterations of the English names do not always reflect the accurate English pronunciation, but rather the substitution of Dutch for English sounds. In *Bruyster* (əu) was substituted for (iu), exactly as (y:) was substituted for (iu) in *Nubere*.[1]

In the previous discussion it has often been assumed that (y:) could be substituted for the English diphthong in *use*, or, in other words, that the sounds (y:) (ü) and (iu) or (iu:) (ju:) could easily be mistaken for one another. Attention will now be drawn to a few indisputable cases of such a confusion. In Domesday Book, as early as 1086, the OE. diphthong in *nīwe* is occasionally rendered with *u*, i. e. the French (y:) was substituted for the English (i:u). It has already been pointed out that Ellis in his analysis of the phonology of the Eastern dialects consistently mistakes (ü:) in *blue, do,* etc. for (y:) or (y:u). I have also heard Englishmen, when speaking Swedish, substitute the present diphthong in *new,* for the long Swedish (ü:) in *hus, kula* etc. All this tends to make us more sceptical than ever towards the equating of the English diphthong in *new,* and *use* with the Continental (y:).

Among minor evidence for (ju:) at Shakespeare's time we may quote the Londoner Robinson's (1617) transcriptions of *u* in Latin words with *iw* (iu) and *yiw* (ju:), e. g. *diwsit = ducit, tenyiwis = tenuis* (H. G. Fielder), and perhaps the Italian Gondola's (1590) rendering of *your* with *youhor* (ju:ər) (A. C. Paues). Many early English grammarians used the transcription *iu* both for English *u, ew* and for *you, your*.

Lastly I will adduce some orthographical evidence which conclusively proves that the present pronunciation (ju:) in *use* and *new* was common towards the end of the 16th and beginning of the 17th century among educated people living in or near the capital. The majority of these spellings are from

---

[1] It may also be asked if *Nubere* and *Stuert* are not *English* orthographical variants of *Newbery* and *Stewart*. The latter name was often spelt with *u* from about 1250, and at the present time both *Nubery* and *Stuart* occur as personal names (cf. Bardsley, Dictionary, 555, 717).

letters written by members or friends of the Verney family
'men and women belonging to the class of country gentry, some
of them living pretty continuously in the country — at Claydon
on the borders of Oxfordshire and Buckinghamshire — others
living principally in London' (Wyld, 162). The writers as a
rule use the conventional spelling *ew, u* for words such as *use,
sure* etc., but as will appear from the following survey, *you* is
occasionally written for *u* in *use* etc., and *o* for *u* in *sure*.

> Mary Verney's Will: *yousefull* 1638, I, 224.
> Lady Sussex: *youse* 1643, I, 293; *shorly* 1639, I, 149;
> *youse*, I, 293.
> Lady Denton: *yoused* 1639, I, 170, *shore* 1639, I, 217.
> Lady Elmes: *yoused* 1647, I, 436.
> Mrs. Sherard: *yousful* 1653, II, 89.
> Mall Verney: *youst* 1639, I, 172.

I do not think Luick (p. 180) is right in interpreting this
you as (jy:), on the doubtful supposition that the same sound
occurred in *you* and *youth*.[1] I interpret them as denoting the
pronunciation (ju:). We know that *ou* by the side of *oo* was a
common symbol for (u:) in the 16th and 17th centuries (Zachrisson, 78), and *choused* in the Verney Memoirs, II, 186, is a
clear instance of *ou* written for (u:). This spelling also makes
it improbable that the Verneys pronounced *choose, youth* etc.
with (jy:), as is assumed by Luick. Moreover the same writers
who favour *yous* for *use,* also write *shc e)* for *sure,* and I think
Professor Luick will agree with me that a sound-development
(y:r) to (o:r) is against the law of continuity, whereas (jo : r) for
(ju : r) is the normal development. Spellings such as *yumor,
uemored, yuemored, yus, yumer* (II, 3, II, 203, 207, II, 208) as
well as *shur* (I, 246, 139) used by other members of the family
have naturally the same phonetic value as *youse, youmor* and
shore. We should also notice that ME. *ęu* in *few* was pronounced in the same way as *ęu* in *new,* at least by the younger
members of the family (cf. *fu = few,* Verney Memoirs I, 244).

---

[1] Cf. below pp. 97 ff.

This also speaks in favour of (juː) as a common pronunciation for ME. ẹu, u, ęu. The pronunciation of *use* etc. as (juːz) must go back to the end of the 16th century, as it was used as early as 1639 by the elder members of the family. I have also found the spelling *youse* for *use* in the Luckin Letters, Essex, late 17th century (Trans. Dial. Soc., VI, 217), and *ashoure* in a letter written by Mrs. Basire from Shropshire (1653) indisputably indicates a pronunciation (əʃuːr) not (əsjyːr) for *assure* (Wyld, 244). Additional instances of *you* for *u* are adduced by Wyld (*ibid.*) from the Wentworth Papers (early 18th cent.).

The combined evidence of such 17th century spellings as *youse, shore, chouse, fu* for *use, sure, choose, few* used by one well defined group of writers living in London and Oxfordshire, enables us to conclude that these writers, the Verneys and their friends and social equals, pronounced such words as *new, use, few* in the modern manner with (juː), not with (yː) or (iyː). Moreover, when similar spellings are used not only by correspondents from the east (Essex) but also from the west of England (Shropshire), we can be sure that this modern pronunciation was established in colloquial speech everywhere in England in the 17th century.

The local distribution of the early spellings with *you, o, ou* for ME. *u* in *use, sure*, etc. gives no support to Luick's theory that early NE. (juː) was characteristic of the eastern parts of England.

The results obtained from the previous investigation may be summed up as follows. In the 16th and 17th centuries ME. *u, ęu* in *use* and *new* was commonly pronounced as ('iu), (i'uː), (juː), possibly also as (i'üː) and (jüː). There is no conclusive evidence for (yː), (yuː) or (iyː). Some writers of foreign grammars (especially French) recommend the sound-substitution (yː), and possibly (iyː), (jyː) for the English diphthong. ME. *ęu* in *few* was pronounced either in the same way as *u, ęu* in *use, new* or with (eːu) as in the Swedish pronunciation of *Europa*.

Bullokar's [eu, e'w, v, u].

I fail to see how Ellis and most other writers on the subject have been able to interpret Bullokar's evidence as to the
pronunciation of ME. ẹu, u in *use, new* as indicating (y:). Bullokar is not very clear, but the information he gives decidedly
points to a diphthongic pronunciation. In his amended spelling he uses for ẹu in *new* the symbols e' (< ẹ̄) and w, which
in diphthongs is written for 'u flat' (p. 259). The sound consequently was made up of i+u. He moreover informs the reader
(p. 286) that when 'w: is in diphthong with any vowell before
it, then is the vowell perfectly sounded, and: w: is lightly touched,
except in :e'w: where bothe are like sounded', i. e. in e'w,
w (=u) is more distinctly heard than in aụ, ow etc. This
obviously reads like a description of a diphthong (iu) or (ju:).
English 'u sharpe' (< French [y]) is pronounced with the same
sound (p. 314). The sound of ẹu is different.

After a consonant + l and (dʒ) Bullokar has the diphthong
corresponding to ME. ẹu, at least in the spelling: rul, cruel,
brut*i*sh, Jun etc.

On bruʒẹth (~oụ), see above p. 63, on bury, busy, che'wʒ
~u~oo, below pp. 97.

Bullokar has the old-fashioned form shew, sb., vb., the
only one noted by Lekebusch (p. 48) in early London documents.

A very remarkable form is pewtrelż (<O. Fr. *peitrel, petrel*
etc.) likewise evidenced in 16th century spellings, such as
pewtrell, peutrall, NED. To judge by certain forms adduced
by Godefroi, it appears as if pretonic e (and i?) could pass into
eu after *p* (labialisation). Cf. the following spellings: *peuçoer* for
peçoier, pieçoyer (= 'mettre en pièces'), *peunos* for *penos* (= 'pe-
nible'), *peurrier* for *perrier, peusson* for *poisson, peulleul* for *pail-
leul, peugnore* for *pignore*. In A. F. texts I have found no
equivalents to these forms.

The Pronunciation of you, youth, choose, buy, bury, busy etc.

Present English *you, your, youth* often rhyme in ME. with words containing ME. *ū* (cf. Marcus, pp. 15 ff.). The reason why ME. *ū* did not develop into a diphthong in *you* and *your* is possibly the influence of weakly stressed form; in *youth* (u:) may have been kept on the analogy of *young* and shortened forms with *ŭ*.[1] There is, however, another explanation which may account for (u:) in all these words. It is conceivable that (ju:) in *you, your, youth* was levelled under (ju:) from *ēu* in *new* etc., and consequently not diphthongized. What speaks in favour of this suggestion is 15th century spellings, such as *u, yw, ʒew* (= 'you'), *vthe* (= 'youth')[2], and rhymes with *you, youth* and words containing ME. *ēu, u,* in the works of Shakespeare and Spenser[3]. Hart uses the same transcriptions [iu] and [iu·] for *you* and words containing ME. *ēu, u* (Jespersen, Hart, 48, 75), and Butler (ed. Eichler, p. 91) seems to assign the same pronunciation to *you* and *yew(-tree)*. Early NE. *shewer* for *shower* is due either to the levelling of *sure* and *shower* under a common 15th century form (ʃu:r) or (ʃur), or to the fact that ME. *ū* was sometimes not diphthongized in front of *r*. For additional instances see Zachrisson, Anglia Beiblatt 1918, p. 173. Illustrative instances are:

shower transcribed as [chōer] by Peyton (1756) (cf. 7 *shore* NED.); *alff a nore* (= 'half an hour') Machyn's Diary 29; 4—6 *pore, poore* (= 'power') NED. The forms with (u:) originated in connected speech (*a shour pat*) and in inflected forms when a consonant followed (*shours* < *shoures*), wherupon (u:) could be analogically transferred to other forms.

When some English orthoepists transcribe *youth* as (jiuþ) we probably have to do with a wrong analysis of (ju:þ) as (jiu:þ)

---

[1] Bullokar and Jones (p. 114) have *ŭ* short in *youth*.

[2] Cf. Dibelius 347, and NED.

[3] Cf. Vietor 31, Gabrielson 43. The levelling must have taken place at a stage when (u:) in *you* was only slightly diphthongized.

— especially as these transcriptions occur at a time when *ēu* was generally pronounced as (ju:) — rather than with a combinative sound-change of (ju:) to (jy:) (jiy:) as has been assumed by Luick (Anglia 45, pp. 171 ff.).

The rules given by Cooper afford an excellent illustration of this confusion.

Cooper (ed. Jones, p. 50) says —: ʿ*ou* ponitur pro *eu* in *you, your, youth*ʾ, but nevertheless directs *in your* to be pronounced in the same way as *inure* (p. 83) and *your* to be pronounced as *ewer* (p. 85). This proves that the sound meant by Cooper is (ju:) not (jiu:), and that he ought to have written: — ʿ*you* ponitur pro *eu*ʾ, instead of ʿ*ou* ponitur pro *eu*ʾ.

Similarly Price's rule: ʿ*ou* sounds like *iw* in *youth*ʾ should probably have been more accurately formulated as ʿ*you* sounds like *iw* in *youth*ʾ, for Price adduces *ewe* and *you* among words pronounced alike.

Gill's notations [yʋ, yʋrz] (once) are errors for [yü, yürz] (more than twenty times) (cf. Zachrisson, 222), and Gill's [yvth] may due to wrong analysis of (ju : þ) as (jiu : þ). Cf. also below.

Hence I interpret Bullokar's ꞩoy, ꞩoyr ꞩuth as indicating the Present English pronunciation (ju:), (ju : r), (ju : þ). In ꞩuth (u:) has been shortened to *ŭ* (cf. above, p. 97 n.).

Bullokar's che'wȝ, chuȝ[1] (~ chooȝ) is based on spellings such as *chuse, chewse* for *choose*. They are to be compared with *shute, shewte, sute, shue* etc. for *shoot, shoe* — *chu, chew* and *su, shu, shew* being originally graphic representations of the sounds (tʃu:) and (ʃu:), on the analogy of such spellings as *eschue, chew, sure, sugar, shure, shew, shue* (= ʿshowʾ, cf. p. 82 n.) in which *chu, chew, su, shu, shew* could be symbols for (tʃu:) and (ʃu:), because of the change of (iu:) to (ju:), as in (ʃu : r) from (sju : r), and the reduction of (iu:) to (u:) after a sibilant, as in (tʃu:) from (tʃiu:). To put it more simply, *chewse (chuse)* is an inverted spelling for (tʃu:z) on the analogy of *chew* (tʃu:),

---

[1] Cf. Zachrisson, pp. 85 ff., and above, p. 18.

and *shewte* (*shute*) is an inverted spelling for (ʃuː t) on the analogy of *shew* (ʃuː).

At the same time I will not deny that *choose* may occasionally have been pronounced as (tʃiuː z) — and even perhaps *youth* as (jiuː þ) — but this is hardly the result of a sound-change but a mere spelling pronunciation caused by the orthography (cf. *chewse, chuse* 5—6, *yewth* 7 NED.) or by analogical transference of the interchange between (uː) and (iuː) which is likely to have occurred in such words as *chew, jew, brew* etc.

In numerous original letters of the 15th century *bury* and *busy* are almost invariably written *besy, bisy, bery*. Dr. Kihlbom (p. 23) only gives one instance of *busy*, and no instances of *bury*. The form *busy* does not occur in the official language of London, and in the early London deeds (1387—1420) *bery* is by far the most usual form (cf. Morsbach, pp. 39 f., Lekebusch, p. 15). In English Vowels (p. 88) I have already pointed out that *uy* in *buy* and *build* was a rare and, on the whole, late spelling, possibly due to the analogy of *ui* in *guide, juice* (cf. below, p. 101) etc. The fact that the forms *busy, build*, and *buy* are missing, and *bury* extremely rare in the Standard language of the 15th century renders it impossible to uphold the old theory that these forms are survivals of the ME. (y), (yː) in early Standard speech. They are to be looked upon as spellings for $\bar{\imath}$ and *e*, which did not become established until after the 16th century[2].

---

[1] In the original letters examined by Dr. Kihlbom (cf. pp. 23, 39) there are no instances of *buy* or *build;* neither in the material investigated by Flasdieck, p. 22.

[2] As has already been suggested, *uy* is due to the analogy of *ui* in *guide, juice*, pronounced (dʒəis) etc. In *bury*, pronounced (bʌri) by Wilkins 1668 and some early 18th century orthoëpists, (cf. Zachrisson, Anglia Beiblatt 1917, p. 79) and in *busy u* is most likely to have indicated an occasional early NE. pronunciation with (u) from (i) or from ME. *y*, owing to the labial effect of *b* (cf. early NE. *bushop* for *bishop*). When *u* in *bury* and *busy* is sometimes pronounced with (iu) in early NE. (cf. Zachrisson, 87 n., and spellings such as 6 *bewry* = 'bury' NED.) this is entirely due to the spelling.

According to Salesbury (cf. Ellis III, 760) *u* in a similar manner was to be pronounced as the Welsh *u*, i. e. as (i), not only in *busy,* but also in *trust* (cf. *trist* 4—6 NED.), *bury* (cf. *byry* 4—6 NED.) and *Huberden,* and in certain southern place-names *u* is sometimes a symbol for *i*, as in Puddletown and Marnhull in Dorsetshire, which as I was informed when staying in Dorchester, are pronounced ('pidltən) and (ma : nil).

Bullokar's [oi, ooi, uy].

Bullokar knows two diphthongs, one composed of *o* + *i*, another composed of *oo* + *i*. According to my views we need not necessarily interpret Bullokar's ooi as (u : i). It is worthy of note that Bullokar uses e' (=i:) in the first element of the diphthong (iu) < *ẹu*, *u* although we have good reasons for assuming that *e* here was always pronounced with a short vowel (cf. Butler, 1633). Bullokar's pronunciation of oi, ooi in *joy* and *boil* may have been (ɔi), (ui) respectively.

Bullokar's pronunciation of ui in anguish, languish, ịuic', ịuyst is not clear. Bullokar expresses himself very vaguely: 'we sounde the same :v: (rather: y)' etc., see p. 274. The restriction 'rather y' (=u) tells against a literal interpretation of ui as (iui). It may indicate that the first element was (u) or even (ə). Possibly ui may stand for (wi) in anguish, languish, for (əi) in ịuic' and ịuyst. For ui = (wi) in anguish and languish speaks the following notation: consangụinatiu'7 ~ consanguinatiu'7, and the fact that langụag' is given together with anguish, languish (p. 274).

The ME. basis for Bullokar's uy in ịuyst is *ī* (Fr. *giste*), so in this word (əi) is the most likely pronunciation. Early spellings, such as 5—6 *joist*, 6 *moynes* (= 'mines')[1], 6 *royetous* (= 'riotous') etc. (see Zachrisson 72 f., E. St. 52, Wyld 224) presuppose that ME. (ui) in *boil* and (i:) in *like* had been levelled under a common sound (əi). Spenser frequently rhymes

---

[1] Here belongs also *moining,* Butler, not explained by Eichler, 44.

words containing ME. (ui) with ME. *ī*-words. See Gabrielson, p. 115 ff. This pronunciation of (ui) was, as a rule, not recognised by the early English orthoëpists, possibly because it was considered as vulgar.

Juice < OF. *jus* appears in early spellings as 6—7 *iuyce*, *iuice*, 6—7 *ioyse*. How are we to account for the spelling with *oy?* That (y:) should have been diphthongised to (əy) or something of the kind (cf. Western, Engl. Stud. 42, p. 269) is in my opinion less probable. There are hardly any *safe* instances of such a sound-development.

To · account for the *oi*-diphthong in *juice* it seems safer to start from a variant with ME. *ī*[1] for OF. (y:). We may compare such spellings as *yistice* Paston Letters 140, *syte* ('suit') (error?) *ibid.* 4, and ME. *rybe* ('ruby') *kyryous* ('curious'), *fryte* ('fruit'), *nye* ('annoy'), *destrye* ('destroy'), Behrens 119, 159 f. *fysoun* ('foison'), *feyne*, *fyn* (OF. *foine*), Zachrisson 89, n. 1, *inion* ('onion'), Peyton etc. where *i* is either due to the occasional substitution of ME. *i* for OF. (y)[2], or to the reduction of *ui* to *i* in AF. itself[3]. In point of fact ME. *i* has remained in Miserden, Glouc., from earlier *Musardere*, *Miserdine* (OF. *Musard*, pers. n.). Note also that *ui*, *uy* in *iuice*, *iuyce*, may very well be a spelling for ME. *ī* (cf. above p. 99).

It appears from the previous discussion that Bullokar pronounced *joist* and *juice* with a diphthong — (əi)? — which in *joist* and in all probability also in *juice* goes back to ME. *ī*. This proves that Bullokar at any rate knew of an advanced pronunciation of ME. *ī* in *like*, and at the same time renders it less likely that he used such an old-fashioned pronunciation as (i:) or (ij) for ME. *ī* in general.

---

[1] Butler (pp. 30, 75) pronounced *juice* with the same sound as *buy* and *build* (i. e. ME. *ī*), and couples *juice* with *joice* (= *joist* < OF. *giste*).

[2] Considering these forms Luick's HEG. § 427, explanation of *i* in *rybe*, *restytyschon* etc. as due to the reduction of *iu* to *i* before *b* and *sch* is doubtful.

[3] Cf. Stimming, Boeue, p. 210.

The following is a complete list of Bullokar's forms arranged according to etymological principles:

1. *oi* < Latin *ō, ŭ + i* :(a.) appooint, boystiọs (< Fr. *boisteus?*), booil*i*ng, cooynẹd, destrooyᵛ¹, dis-ịooin*i*ng, ịooin ~ ịoin, ịoint, looynż, ointment, pooint ~ point?, pooiʒnż, tooil; (b.) coif, v'oic'.

2. *oi* < Latin *ŏ* before *l mouillé:* oyl̦, soyl, spooil ~ spoil.

3. *oi* < Latin *ŏ + i:* au'oyd, noysọm.

4. *oi* < Latin *au + i:* choic', ịoy, ịoily, ịoyd̦, noiʒ.

5. *o* < Central French *oi + ei:* imploy*e*d, royal.

6. *oi* in words from Dutch: loiter*i*ng.

7. *oi* of uncertain provenience: boy, booy ('buoy').

Bullokar's forms seem, on the whole, to corroborate, the conclusions arrived at by Luick² (Anglia XIV, 294 ff.).

Nevertheless Luick's explanation of (ɔi) in 'vòice', 'moist' and in words belonging to group 3. is hardly convincing. Bullokar's many forms with (ɔi) in group 2. go also against Luick's theories (*ui in buiste* ~ *o, oi* may be due to *b*).

The question of the distribution of (ɔi) and (ui) has been recently dealt with by Dr. E. Slettengren (On ME., early NE. *oi, ui* in French loan-words containing pop. Lat. stressed ọ, ọ, Från Filologiska Föreningen i Lund IV, 1915), whose results considerably differ from those obtained by earlier writers.

According to Slettengren (ui) appears regularly only for ọ + *l mouillé, ọ + l mouillé* and *n mouillé, ọ + i* in originally unstressed position (*poison* etc.) and in the two verbs *annoy, destroy*. In all these cases English (ui) is due O. Fr. (ui), except in the verbs *annoy, destroy,* where early NE. (ui) goes back to ME.

---

¹ Here ooy is due to the analogy of *anue ~ anoie;* cf. Slettengren, p. 174, But cf. Jordan, § 237.

² Hanck's (p. 92) criticism of Luick is not to the point. Luick's examples are derived not only from BL. but also from other works of Bullokar. I have not however found any instances of *rejoice* and *moistness* in Bullokar's amended spelling.

(y:) or (i:). In my opinion, the latter alternative is the most probable one. Cf. ME. *anie, destrie,* and above p. 101.

I all other cases the rule is ME. and NE. (ɔi) < OFr. *ǫi* and *ǫi,* which in a stressed position were levelled under the same sound (see *op. cit.,* p. 176). For *oil,* where early NE. (ɔi) is well evidenced, a special explanation is given (*op. cit.,* p. 178).

The appearance of (ɔi) in (ui)-words is, according to Slettengren, due to dialectal development in Norman French, Continental French or Anglo French itself.

With the exception of words belonging to group 2. (*soil* sb., *spoil* etc.) where both (ɔi) and (ui) seem to be well evidenced by the early orthoëpists (cf. Slettengren's lists, p. 172), the material I have adduced from Bullokar tallies well with the results obtained by Slettengren. The many instances where we find oi for more regular ooi (coin, joint, point?, ointment etc.) are, however, very remarkable. That such forms are not only errors appears from the fact that the diphthong in early NE. was reduced not only to *ū̆,* but also to *ō̆,* as in *adjoneinge* etc. (cf. Zachrisson, Luick Celebration Volume, p. 149, n. 1) and *johnture* Verney Memoirs I, 120. Such forms with (ɔi) for (ui) are perhaps due to the influence of the spelling, rather than to AF. or OF. variants, as is suggested by Slettengren. To distinguish between (oi) and (ui) in ME. and OF. is extremely difficult, as *oi* may sometimes be a graphic representation of (ui). Moreover, we know that the ultimate victory of the (ɔi)-diphthong is due to spelling pronunciation.

Sometimes *ui* appears in words which always have *oi* in OF., e. g. in *employ* and *rejoice : emplyed* 15 c. (Zachrisson 89, Engl. Stud. 52, 310), *implyment* 1670 Verney Memoirs, *regis* 1654 Mrs. Basire (Wyld, 224). I account for these forms in the following way. In such words as *join, boil* etc. (ui) was the usual early NE. pronunciation, and (ɔi) was looked upon as less correct. This distinction between (ɔi) and (ui) may have induced some speakers to use the refined (ui)-diphthong in words where only (ɔi) was etymologically justified. A similar notion may have helped to establish the pronunciation of (ai) in *like* as (ɔi) in vulgar English (cf. Standard E. *boil* sb., *joist*), although (ɔi) may also be due to the sound-change of (ai) to (ɔi) which has taken place in many regional dialects (cf. Wright EDGr. § 154).

Notes on the Unstressed Vowels.

The lists of occasional spellings adduced by Wyld (267—282) go far to prove that the reduction of the unstressed vowels which is characteristic of present English speech had to a great extent already taken place at Shakespeare's time or earlier, although such colloquial forms are as a rule not taken much notice of by the early orthoëpists. One of the first grammarians who teaches very much the same pronunciation for the unstressed vowels as in Present English is Lediard (1725). Cf. Zachrisson, Anglia Beiblatt 1917, pp. 78 f.

In rendering the unstressed vowels Bullokar generally follows the historical spelling, with such few alterations as his system admits of. His spellings do therefore not always reflect the actual pronunciation, which undoubtedly in many instances was more advanced and less dependent on the spelling than is suggested by his forms. As will be seen from the brief account given below, a few phonetic spellings, after the manner of the time, ocasionally crop up among the host of traditional forms.

The prefix com- occasionally appears as cǫm-: cǫmplain*i*ng (otherwise: com-, con-).

Sometimes *en-* interchanges with *in,* as in interteinment etc.

The almost constant spelling be'- (be'fór, be'gin etc.) probably indicates a pronunciation which was confined to reading and solemn speech. Cf. Zachrisson, 141 n.[2] For similar reasons

---

[1] Cf. also the rhymes with *oi : ī* adduced by Gabrielson, p. 117. On the other hand early NE. (ɔi) in *royal, voyage, loyal,* (Ekwall, Jones, CXCVI) goes back to ME. *rial, viage, lial* (NED.).

[2] But e' may also be a symbol for (i).

we once find ó in cómpoṣ̣ṭionż. The popular form appears in bicayӡ, bycayӡ.

Pretonic *a-* has been dropped in lǫw (~alǫw), ray (~array). Cf. Slettengren, 125, 127, Wyld, 281.

In middle syllables *ăr* once appears as *er* (ə), and *ĕ* as *ĭ* after the manner of the present pronunciation: seperát*e*d, enimy (~enemy).

The ending *-ei(e)* has been levelled under *-y* in chimny and v'alyż.

The long *ý* in cǫntrýż (~cǫntry) and bodýӡ is evidently due to spelling pronunciation (cf. be'-); perhaps also in che'rýż (~-yż). Cf. pu̧rpóӡ, sb.

Short *ŏ* always appears in words of the type naṭion, passion.

The endings *-our*, *-ous* are as a rule rendered as -ǫr, -ǫs, ǫos (= [ur], [us]): fau'ǫr, labǫr, graṭiǫs, gloriǫos, prec'iǫs. In emperou̧r the length of the vowel may be due to extra stress, harbou̧r*e*d (~harbǫr͜) and prec'iou̧s are influenced by the orthography.

For nomina agentis in *-or*, *-er* Bullokar consistently[1] writes *-or*: au̧tor, fundor, fou̧lor etc. (also fingorż etc.), but this is probably a mere orthographic device. The actual pronunciation of B's -or, -ǫr is most likely to have been (ər). Cf. the phonetic spellings cawdernż (~cau̧dorɴ), and sau'ery (~sau'or).

The endings *-al*, *-able* are mostly written with a short, more seldom with a long, vowel or with a diphthong: g'eneral ~ g'eneral, mortaɭ, seu'eral*l*y ~ seu'eral; ab-ŏminábɭ, cápábɭ ~ cápabɭ, riht-ŏnor*á*bɭ etc.

Whether a diphthong was actually pronounced in the following forms is doubtful: carain, battailż (~ battelż), c'ertain (~ c'erten), Britain. They may all be reminiscences of the historical spelling.

---

[1] Cf., however, soldu̧ǫr ~ soldu̧or.

In the endings *-age, -ate* Bullokar has a for Present English (i): cǫrag', langag', deʒolat; for Present English (e^i) Bullokar sometimes has á: seperáted, mag'istrát?. Cf. reg'enerat.

Unetymological *o* and *e* in caben and emot (< OE. *emete*) may indicate that the vocal murmur was not unknown in endings of this kind.

That *-ess* etc. could be colloquially pronounced as (is) appears from the isolated phonetic spelling óstis.

Bullokar's seu'ɴtiþ etc. reflects the early pronunciation of *-ieth* in the ordinals as (iþ). Cf. Horn, Gr. § 151, Jespersen, MEG. 9, 811.

Endings containing French (y) + consonant are given with a full [u] or a shortened [ù]-vowel: execùtorż, figur, figùred, meʒur ~meʒùr etc. The short vowel, which represents the colloquial pronunciation, is said to stand for [ṳ], but the actual pronunciation may have been (ə), at least before *r*. Cf. natʀal (= nateral) ~ natural ~ natùral.

For 'porcupine' Bullokar has the etymologically correct form porkepin. In the modern pronunciation (ju) is either hyper-literary for earlier (i) or due to Latin *porcus*.

Bullokar has an inorganic *i* in fashion (now vulgar) ~ fashon, whereas such an *i* is missing in be'hau'ǫor.

The forms goshop ('gossip'), wynddoor, wýndór (~ window) are due to popular etymology. Cf. Jespersen MEG., 13, 27.

Thou always appears as thṳ.

The remarkable forms ón, ón a tým, may, if not mere errors, be accounted for as due to lengthening in originally stressed position (Luick, HEG. § 390). Note *apoun* ('upon') in the Shillingford Papers, and dialectal *own't* 1755 ('on it') in the Hotham Letters (ed. Stirling, II, p. 267).

A long vowel in the last elements of compounds has been shortened in eftsons, wǫod-dou', wǫod-betl.

Consonants.

c

The French form alternates with the Latin one in perfet~ perfect.

d

The old Anglo-French forms with *d* for *t* are kept in Gilberd and Roberd.

d has been lost in wan, wanż (~ wand), and added in móld ('mole').

d for (đ) appears in farder, fardᴚ*i*ng.

h, gh

In words derived from French *h* is generally not pronounced: abŏr, disŏnest, ĕirż, erb, ŏnest, ones*t*i, ŏnor, riht-ŏnorábĺ, ŏrribĺ, ŏspital*i*ty, ŏst ~ óst ('host') ŏstis ('hostess'), ower (hour), ŭmbĺ, ŭmbĺẹth̩.

Although generally written, *gh* in *delight, bough* etc. appears to have been mute in colloquial speech to judge from numerous phonetic and inverted spellings. Cf. above p. 17.

k

ME. *k < gh* before *f* has survived in hekfer. Cf. 6 *hekfar* etc., NED.

kn, gn

According to most 16th and 17th century orthoëpists *k* and *g* were still pronounced before *n*. The Italian Gondola (1590) transcribes *knave* as *cheneve*, which also indicates that *k* was still pronounced at Shakespeare's time (Paues). The first grammarian who seems to recognise loss of *k, g* in this position is Daines (1640). See Horn, Gr. p. 185 f., Jespersen NEG., 12, 71 ff.

A weak pronunciation seems however to be implied by Coote's (1596) statement that *gnaw, gnat* were vulgarly pronounced *knaw, knat*. We may compare with this Bullokar's forms knawęth, knaw*n*.

That *k* could be dropped before *n* in colloquial. speech from the end of the 15th century is proved by the following phonetic spellings: *I cowd no* ('know') *none body to convey theme* (i. e. 'the letters'), Stonor Letters a. 1476, 165; *I now*[1] ('know') c. 1475 Cely Letters 15 (both these instances have been pointed out to me by Dr. Kihlbom), *Notingbarns* 1519, *Nuttingbars* 1544 Ped. Fin. = Notting in Kensington (London) from OE. *Cnotting(as)* (cf. *Knottinge Bernes* 1476 Escaet, Gover 64). Horn (p. 185) adduces a few similar spellings dating from the 16th century (*nuckle, knouches*). Add: *nott* ('knot'), 1657 Verney Memoirs II, p. 121.

Loss of *k* before *n* is also indicated by certain puns in Shakespeare's plays, which have previously been taken very little notice of: »Let not us that are squires of the *night's* body be called thieves of the *day's* beauty», Henry IV, Act 1, Sc. 2 (*night, knight,* Ellis 922); Wurth (p. 120) notes another pun on the words *knave, nave* from Henry IV B, Act 2, Sc. 4. Such puns would fall utterly flat if they only indicated similarity not identity of sound.

In my opinion the following passage from Much Ado, Act 4, Sc. 2, contains a pun on the words *none* (pronounced at Shakespeare's time as [*no:n*]) and *known:*

> *Dogb.* — Masters, it is proved already that you are little better than false knaves; and it will go near to be thought so shortly. How answer you for yourselves?
>
> *Con.* Marry, sir, we say we are *none.*
>
> *Dogb.* A marvellous witty fellow, I assure you; but I will go about with him. — Come you hither, sirrah; a word in your ear, sir; I say to you it is thought that you are false knaves.

---

[1] Such a careless writer as Richard Cely might possibly have omitted *k* in *know*, owing to a mere slip of the pen, but *no* in the Stonor Letters (I have had the reading verified) where *o* is also written for *ow* is a perfectly safe instance of early loss of *k* before *n*.

Bora. Sir, I say to you we are *none.*

Dogb. Well, stand aside. — *Fore God, they are both in a tale: have you writ down, that they are *none?*

The occurence of *are none* in no less than three places, as well as Dogberry's remarks 'A marvellous *witty* fellow', 'They are both in a tale' and 'have you writ down that they are none', seem to prove that Shakespeare here aimed at a play on the two words 'none', 'known'.[1]

Similar stories from trials are usual. Thus a man named *Knot* accused of murder could not be comdemned, because after having taken the oath he assured the court that he was *Knot* (*not*) the man.

We may also compare the well-known tale of the Swedish poet-adventurer Lars Wiwallius, who had falsely assumed the name of a Danish nobleman ('jeg Eriche [er ikke] Gyldenstiern').

1

Vault appears with or without an etymological *l:* v'aṳt, v'aṳt7 (~ v'aṳlt).

As for *l* in *soldier, half, walk* etc., see above p. 17.

m

Renown has *m,* probably on the analogy of *renomee,* now obsolete: renọwm (2×). Cf. 6—7 *renowme,* NED., and Jespersen MEG. 2, 413.

r

A vocal murmur appears before *r* after certain long vowels and diphthongs, e. g. ai, ow, ọw, i, u:ᴀ aiʀ, faier, paieṙ, fowʀ, fower, ọwer, fier, fiʀing, fiʀi, puer, suerly, suʀ. This seems to indicate a weak pronunciation of *r* (cf. below, p. 116).

In særc'ed (< ME. *sarse*) *r* is excrescent. See NED.

---

[1] This pun has so far as I know, not been previously noted. The pronunciation in question was probably vulgar and therefore very appropriate when used by Dogberry.

s, z

The distribution of these two sounds differs from the modern one in the following instances.

Bullokar has (s) for Mod. English (z) in the following words: a-pæc'ẹd (~ appæȝ), cau̯sẹth ~ ȝ, chástic'ed, c'itiṣen, dis-æȝe7, enterpryc', glasᴎ, (= 'glazen'), Hercules, hu̯sband, hǫwse7 (~ hǫw-ȝe7), Lesbos, lǫwsi, noic' (~ noiȝ), possesiu', Thales.

A-pæc'ẹd is influenced by *peace,* chástic'ed and enterpryc' may have been influenced by words in *-ice;* besides Elphinston seems to have pronounced *merchandise* with (s) (see Müller, p. 197). The only parallels I can find to noic', cau̯sẹth are certain transcriptions in Peyton, all of them rather doubtful (Stichel, p. 84), and possibly (s) in Elphinston's *usance* (Müller, p. 195); hence Bullokar's (s) in these words may be an error. Elphinston has (s) in *disease* (Müller, p. 197). Hu̯sband, hǫwse7 and Lesbos are probably errors; possesiu' has *ss* because of the traditional spelling (cf. Hart's *possessed*), lowsi, glasᴎ, and probably also c'itiṣen, because of the derivation mark. In Thales and Hercules, (s) may be due to an earlier pronunciation of such classical names.

In Boeţiu̯s *t* is pronounced as (s) in the French name.

As for aᴎc'etorż, see Zachrisson, Anglo-Norman Influence p. 74.

Bullokar has (z) for Present English (s): compáriȝon, Æsop7 (~ Æsop7), Epheṣus, gariȝon and gariṣonż, pu̯rpoȝ, pu̯rpóȝ, Thraṣo, promiȝẹth. In the classical names (z) may be due to an earlier pronunciation of intervocalic *s* in classical words as voiced (see Elphinston, Müller, p. 195), in *garison* and *comparison* to French (ȥ), and in *purpose* to the corresponding French verb. Hart has (z) in *comparison.* In promiȝẹth ȝ may be due to weak stress.

Bullokar has no assibilated forms of (s), (z) + ĭ.

t

Tyrant and *graft* have no excrescent *t:* graf, tyran. Cf. 5—7, *tyrane,* NED.; 4—7 *graffe,* NED.

In some learned words *th* is pronounced as *t:* autŏr, ortŏgraphy.

th

The distribution of (þ) and (đ) differs from the modern one in the following instances.

Bullokars (đ) corresponds to mod. English (þ): be'næth, bouth, bóth (~bóth̬), both, dooth (~dooth̬), fowr*t*h, hath (~hath̬), south (~south̬). In south and fowr*t*h the diacritic mark has been left out.

Bullokar's (þ) corresponds to mod. English (đ): clóth̬ʔ (~th), láth̬ᵗ, with̬ (~ with) ([ᵭ] is rare in Present English), with̬in (~ within).

Cf. on this question Ekwall, Zur Geschichte der stimmhaften interdentalen Spirans im Englischen (Lunds Universitets Årsskrift, 1906).

According to Bullokar, *th* was pronounced as (d) in East Sussex and Kent, e. g. in *dis, dat, dose, dumbe* ('thumb'), *dorne*. In the modern dialect of these districts (d) appears to have been kept only in pronouns and adverbs. Cf. hereon Zachrisson, Anglo-Norman Influence, p. 43 ff. and references.

Th is kept in th̬witł.

v

South-English dialectal *v* appears in vád̬eth̬, which form appears to have been common in the Standard English of that time. Cf. 5—6 *vade* NED.

Elphinston (Müller, p. 179) gives *vew* for *few* as characteristic of vulgar London English. Cf. also Horn Gr. § 137.

w

The modern spelling-pronunciation had not yet been carried through in banket and langag' (~ langu̬ag').

In the combination *wr*, *w* is always written: wrangłor, wrath̬, wrastł etc. Loss of *w* before *r* is however testified by Abraham

---

ᵗ According to Ekwall, *op. cit.*, th in láth̬ is an error for th.

Vander-Milii, Lingua Belgica (1612), p. 27: ʿWrong, quod Angli pronuntiant.... Rong, etsi w præscribant' (Barnouw, 19 n.), and goes at least as far back as Shakespeare's time. Cf. the following phonetic spelling: Roxwell Eliz. Chanc. P. = Roxhill, Bedf.< OE. Wroccesheale (other early spellings exhibit Wr-, cf. Mawer and Stenton, p. 80). Butler (p. 90) couples wrest and rest.

Bullokar's Rhymes.

The rhymes are quoted from Plessow's reprints of Bullokar's works. Rhymes from Brief Grammar, pp. 376 ff., have not been included here, as Bullokar does not seem to follow any distinct rules for his rhyming-usage.

Æsop's Fables.

praiʒ: al-waiʒ 1, trieþ: flieþ 1, lak: bak 38, thær: wær 40, tre': fre', 48, frut: sett 49, dy: ytterly 49, alas: past 49, agein: mór-c'ertein 62, fal: al 63.

Sentences of Cato.

be': dry 215, fayl: smal 215, be'gin: win 215, we'ld: þe'ld 215, first: such 215, hand: ynderstand 215, plæʒur: procur 215, prýc': gýʒ 216, mæn: rým 216, forc': cours 216, nón: any-ón 216, sák: mák 216, effectually: ty 216, fám: blám 216, mýnd: býnd 216, fámoos: ys 217, de'd: sayd 217, hy: clænly 217, spár: wel-fár 217, faier-spókn: scórn 217, he'd: ne'd 217, thu: toó 218, contry: sáfly 218, fle': ly 218, spýt: riht 218, paţienţi: the' 218, wýʒ: anguish 218, dyż: adu'ýc' 218, despýʒ: iʒ 218, law: aw 218, stil: wil 218, say: al-way 218, sle'p: de'p 218, sæʒn: ræʒn 218, contrary: agre' 219, men: blám 219, they: al-way 219, claym: blám 219, complaynıng: joyth-in 219, warned: harmed 219, prátorż: fautorż 219, de'r: ne'r 219, autor: talkor 219, c'ertein: se'ldom 220, remember: consider 220, many: any

220, talk: ſpók 220, contrary: gre' 220, frayl: at-al 220, smal:
with-al 220, the': pǫu'erty 220, lýf: it-self 220, iụst: rest 221,
maiṣt: hast 221, promis: coụrtiſh 221, hart: art 221, spe'ch:
catch 221, bend: defend 221, this: niggish 221, sám: blám 221,
ŏnest: ærst 221, acqeintanc': chaɴc' 222, daɴg'erż: labǫrṣt 222,
ou'ercǫm: sǫm 222, smal: he'r-withal 222, iooyned: cooynęd
222, crým: thýn 222, sụffRing: lærNing 222, labǫr: eu'er 222,
neihbǫr: eu'er 222, thụ: hǫw 223, Carthag': rág' 223, go: doo
223, v'ýc': iʒ 223, may: al-way 223, hæu'ɴ: erthN 223, foolly:
ioylly 223, angRi: truly 223, deʒýr: reqýr 224, remember: riu'er
224, the': ónly 224, gain: plain 224, despýʒ: wýʒ 224, yn-eqal:
thral 224, acqeintanc': sụbstanc' 224, the': the' 224, fýnnes:
gre'u'ǫos 224, yn-iụstly: falsly 225, strýf: rýf 225, blám: shám
225, aboụnd: foụnd 225, it: wit 225, remember: eu'er 225,
týdingꝛ: thingꝛ 225, neu'er: drinkor 225, cǫmpanyon: phiʒic'ion
225, yn-worthy: qikly 226, borɴ: harM 226, contrarying: dying
226, the': hæri 226, ou'er: either 226, stronger: plæʒùr 226,
many: any 226, al: thral 226, ræp: sle'p 226, thrǫwly: fitty
227, stil: il 227, it: neglect 227, il: wil 227, may: al-way 227,
glóʒing: spæking 227, fle': body 227, ioyż: al-wayż 227, de'd:
derýd 228, hath: sayth 228, ág': pág' 228, coụnc'el: wel 228,
had: glad 228, dǫwer: too-sǫwer 228, discụs: ys 228, pain: v'ain
228, lest: wǫrst 228, yn-fitty: rihtly 229, iụstly: gilty 229,
thrǫwh-rædd: be'le'u'd 229, sóbR: bablor 229, angRi: crafti 229,
them: ṁen 229, fær-fụl: e'u'l 229, mǫther: maner 229, læd:
ypbrayḍ 230, ou'er: maister 230, happy: gre'dy 230, the': be'
230, ræʒɴ: sæʒɴ 230, smally: slyly 230, welthi: rihtly 230,
maister: anger 230, agein: pain 231, fre'ly: party 231, try-oụt:
hụrt 231, the': bely 231, creáted: færed 231, body: truly 231,
acqeintanc': assuranc' 231, the': foolly 231, cǫmpanyon: lookt-on
231, gre'dy: plenty 232, liu'ęst: fle'ęst 232, v'ádęth: forsákęth
232, ág': rág' 232, spækęth: be'wrayęth 232, cụning: vʒing 232,
mụch: sụch 232, yn-lærNed: spredd 232, soụndly: daily 232,
men: agein 233, contrary: adu'ersity 233, særching: far-pasing
233, alǫwęst: past 233, tauht: nawht 233, plæʒùr: eu'er 233,
remember: de'per 233, dis-plæʒ: thæʒ 233, owerż: waterż 233,

lewd*l*y: sharp*l*y 234, moụrn*i*ng: tḥing 234, los∫: mụst 234, neu'er: whær-soeu'er 234, plọw: cọw 234, miht*i*: welṭḥ*i* 234, after: pláster 234, tým: mýnd 234, mór-lọu'*e*d: ca*l*ed 234, harᴍ-fụl; fær-fụl 235, ne'd de'd 235, *c*aụht: nawht 235, ṁen: blám 235, decay*e*d: au'oyd*e*d 235, awht: *t*aụht 235, nák*e*d: dọb*l*ed 235.

Book at Large.

mankinde: minde 245, hée: agrée 245, made: vade 245, lesse: gesse 245, earth: breath 245, minde: behinde 245, knowʒ: ouerthrowʒ 245, deuiʒd: disgiʒd 245, still: vntill 245, case: grace 245, winde: vnkinde 245, gonne: vpon 245, knowe: fo 246, shot: not 246, points: ioints 246, A. B. C.: agrée 246, some: none 246, voice: choice 246, be: thrée 246, same: name 246, more: before 246, learne: turne 246, ortography: truly 246, lacke: vndertake 246, béene: séene 246, know: grow 246, out: doubt 246, fiue: riue 246, sound: ground 246, plaine: remaine 246, vse: excuse 247, hereto: knowe 247, too: lowe 247, language: age 247, enclinde: finde 247, wel: tell 247, sée: be 247, welth: stelth 247, maʒe: gaʒe 247, might: sight 247, also: knowe 247, suffice: wise 247, plainly: thereby 247, great: heat 247, also: snowe 247, néedes: déedes 247, show: below 247, will: still 247, degrée: high 248, finde: ende 248, then: Amen 248.

a*l*so: know 316, sillab*l*ż: v'ọwelż 316, alón: ón 316, along: diphtḥong 316, v: tru 316, vʒed: derýu'*e*d 317, last: mụst 317, be'fór: stór 317, be': tru*l*y 317, stand: band 317, ypon: alón 317, ịoin*d*: fýnd 317, word: accord 317, derýu'*e*d: deu'ýd*e*d 317, this: iʒ 317, too: go 317, r: toogether 317, g'eneral: a*l* 317, sillab*l*: v'ọwel 317, alón: on 317, ges: ∫ 317.

bre'd*d*: espýd 324, reu'ók*t*: lót 324, appe'rż: encræc' 324, kýnd: fýnd 324, ŋe'ldż: fe'ld∫ 324, kýnd: fýnd 324, be': se' 324, tụrɴ*d*: bụrɴ*d* 324, groụnd: foụnd 324, fórc': coụrc' 324, disc'erɴ*d*: coụch*e*d 324, digres: bæst 324, hand: foụnd 324, tám: dám 325, sow*n*: ypon 325, tre': be' 325, self: lýf 325, strech: ræch 325, smart: hụrt 325, wọrᴍ: rụn 325, be'ho*l*d:

móld 325, wýnd: rýnd 325, být: bliht 325, harм: warn 325, flǫwer: ǫwer 325, sǫbịct: direct 325, prýc': paradýc' 325, vc': iȝ 325, wǫrk*i*ng: seu'r*i*ŋg 325, disdain: v'ain 325, be': tre' 325, il: wil 326, ón: alón 326, mis: iȝ 326, rein: own 326, skil: wil 326, hærd: bre'd 326, bołd: fołd 326, warn: harм 326, lamb: dam 326, rýȝ: noic' 326, rul: tru 326, lýf: strýf 326, hand: band 326.

Brief Grammar.

thær: ne'r 333, a-riht: siht 333, cráu'ː: hau' 333, ón: món 333, frut: sut 333, kin: be'gin 333, pain: attain 333, chýld: fe'ld 334, mýnd: býnd 334, agein: pain 334, ałso: toó 334, alón: nón 334, tooyl: soyl 334, grow: só 334, fýnd: yn-kýnd 334, God: bad 334, in: be'gin 335, cǫm: sǫm 335, reinȝ: painȝ 335, rele'f: gre'f 335, train: pain 335, tʰing: bend*i*ng 335, mýnd: fýnd 335, lædḍ: spred*d* 335, renǫwn: tǫwn 335, me': degre' 336, toó: shew 336, ernest*l*y: me' 336, hýd*d*: ne'd 336, reqýr: deȝýr 336, skil: il 336, wæl: dæl 336, sway: day 336, ‚wry: try 336, degre'ː se' 337, gain: pain 337, fám: nám 337, sæt: græt 337, rest: too-pas 337, toó: mo 337, phráṣ: waȝ 337, tụng: long 337, offenc': dispenc' 337, trau'el: tel 338, compár*d*: erḍ 338, at-ał: cał 338, sór-oppres*t*: bæst 338, hau': sáu' 338, procur: plæȝ*u*r 338, hand: band 338, pain: agein 338.

In the following pages we shall only discuss rhymes which are imperfect or differ from the general standard of pronunciation adopted by Bullokar in his amended system of orthography. Rhymes in Book at Large and Brief Grammar have been marked with an asterisk, because the rhymes are better here, and more correct than in his other works.

A glance at the lists above at once reveals two important facts. In the first place it is evident that many of the rhymes are not based on the pronunciation which is taught by Bullokar, and this holds good not only for isolated words but for the sounds in general. Note such rhymes as ræp: sle'p, thụ: too, spýt: riht, go: doo, also: knowe, booil: spoyl etc.

Secondly, Bullokar is a very careless rhymer. Nevertheless his vagaries can nearly always be paralleled from other sources, e. g. in the useful survey Dibelius gives of the rhyming-usage in the 15th century (Anglia XXIII, pp. 166 ff.).

Before we proceed to a discussion of the phonetic value of Bullokar's rhymes, we should note the following peculiarities or deviations from a correct rhyming-usage.

I. Rhymes with consonants which are not identical in sound: *m: n* (crým: thýn, borN: harM, them: men, men: blám, *some: none etc.); *s: z* (vy'c: iȝ, prýc': gýȝ); *s, z: sh* (this: niggish, wýȝ: anguish, promis: courtish); *st: ch*[1] (first: such).

II. Rhymes exhibiting an excrescent consonant: *s: st* (alas: past, daNg'erż: laborst, [cf. alowest: past], los7: must, *digres: bæst); *m: nd* (tým: mýnd); *ct, kt: t* (*reu'ókt: lót, it: neglect); *lf: f* (*himself: lýf, lyf: itself); *iul: iu* (*rul: tru). Rhymes exhibiting an excrescent *r* are particularly usual, which tends to prove that *r* had a weak pronunciation at Bullokar's time[2] (ŏnest: ærst, lest: worst, *earth: breath, try-out: hurt, worM: run)ı

III. Rhymes confined to a mere ending or suffix: *-eth: -eth* (v'ádeth: forsáketh); *-est: -est* (liu'est: fle'est); *-ed: -ed* (creáted: færed, warNed: harMed, lou'ed: caled, rædd: be'le'u'd[3], bre'dd: espýd[3]); *-en: -en* (hæu'N: ertḫN, spókN: scórN); *-er: -er* of various provenience (remember: consider, labor: eu'er, remember: riu'er, prátorż: fautorż, autor: talkor) *-es: -es* of various provenience (fýnnes: gre'u'oos); *-en: -en* or *em* (certein: se'ldom); *-y: -ly* (fre'ly: party, welthi: rihtly).

In spite of these irregularities there are no rhymes which are only based on the identity of the consonants. The rhymes

---

[1] Cf. rhymes with *p: k, s: d, dg: d* etc. adduced by Dibelius, *l. c.*

[2] Note that *r* before a consonant is omitted in numerous spellings from Machyn's Diary and the Verney Memoirs.

[3] Such rhymes are evidently based on an earlier pronunciation, such as *red: beleved, bred: espyed.*

always indicate that the vowels preceding the consonants are either similar or identical in sound, although
the pronunciation reflected by one individual rhyme is often
entirely different from the one indicated by the spelling.

Starting from this principle of interpretation, which, according to my views, holds good for 16th cent. rhymes in general,
the various pronunciations indicated by Bullokar's rhymes may
be placed in one or other of the following three groups.

I. Rhymes based on an old-fashioned pronunciation, which probably no longer existed at Bullokar's
time. Here belong in the first place the following rhymes with
ME. $\bar{e}$ in *be* and $\bar{\imath}$ in *like,* based on the pronunciation (i:) for
$\bar{e}$ and (ij)[1] for $\bar{\imath}$, which was usual in the 15th century, but had
probably become obsolete at Shakespeare's time: de'd: derýd,
fle': ly, be': dry, *degree: high, *chýld: fe'ld, and probably
also finde: ende (ME. $\bar{e}nde$), mæn: rým (ME. $m\bar{e}n$). A long $\bar{\imath}$
in -*ly* (cf. above, p. 105) is the base of the rhymes dy: ytter*ly*,
hy: clæn*ly* etc. On the other hand, the pronunciation (i:) for $\bar{e}$
seems to be implied by such rhymes as *be': tru*ly*, ernest*ly*:
me', paţienţ*i*: the', contrary: agre', the': poу'erty, the': on*ly* etc.[2]
In a similar manner Bullokar couples ME. $\breve{u}$ and $\bar{o}$ in the rhyme
thu: toó. The rhyme joyż: aĺ-wayż may be based on l. ME.
ai for *oi* (cf. Zachrisson, Luick Celebr. Vol., pp. 143 ff.), which
probably was no longer heard in the London pronunciation of
the 16th cent.; hand: found seems to pre-suppose hond: fond
(cf. Dibelius, 230), of which the latter form may not have been
current at Bullokar's time (cf. 1—5 *fond* NED.).

II. Rhymes based on advanced forms of pronunciation which are not as a rule recognised by Bullokar,
but nevertheless were of common occurrence in contemporary colloquial speech.

A palatal pronunciation of *a* in· *man* and *name* can be

---

[1] Cf. Dibelius, Anglia XXIII, pp. 348 ff.

[2] Note, however, that Cooper heard a long $\bar{e}$ in *gravity* etc. (Zachrisson, 202).

inferred from the rhymes men: blám, *compárd: erd, *rest: pas, alǫwęst: past.

The levelling of *ā* in *name* and *ai* in *day* under·the same sound: claym: blám, maist: hast.

The pronunciation (əi) for *ī* in *like* (cf. above, p. 101): joind: fýnd.

The pronunciations. (o), (ʌ), or (ə) for *ŭ* in *come*: losʃ: mųst, *tung: long [(o) rhyming with (ɔ)], last: must, smart: hųrt.[1]

The levelling of *ir, er, ur* under the same sound (cf. above, pp. 52 f.): first: sųch, *learne: turne.

The pronunciation (ɔ:) for *au* in *law* and loss of *l* before *k*: talk: spók (ɔ: rhyming with o:).

The levelling of *ǭu* in *blow* and *ǭ* in *go* under the same sound: *grow: so, *also: knowe, *also: snowe, *knowe: fo, *hereto: knowe, *too: lowe (cf. above, p. 76).

The pronunciation (u:) for *ęu* in *new* after (ʃ) (cf. above, p. 98): *toó: shew (cf. Wyld, Rhymes, 131).

The loss of *gh* (cf. above, p. 17): spyt: riht, *být: bliht.

III. Rhymes based on phonetic variants of isolated words.

Shortened forms (cf. above, p. 30) are probably the base of the following rhymes: ŏnest: ærst, *digres: bæst, *opprest: bæst (for *bĕst*), *strech: ræch (for *rĕch*), inde'd: sayd (*indĕd: sĕd*), hýdd: ne'd (*hĭd: nĭd*), spe'ch: catch (*spĕch: kĕtch*), try-oųt: hųrt (*ŭt: hu(r)t*, cf. Zachrisson, p. 80), lýf: itself, *himself: lýf, (*lĭf: sĭlf*, cf. *sĭlf*, Lekebusch 114).

Variants with close or open vowels before *r*-combinations: *thær: ne'r, fær: ne'r (cf. Bullokar's nær), *appe'rż: encræc', fórc': courc', forc': cours (*foarce: coarse?*, although Bullokar has no instances of (o:) from (u:) before *r* + consonant).

Other phonetic variants: also: toó, *toó: mo, *too: go, go: doo may be based on early NE. *to* with (o:) (Cooper,

---

[1] Cf. on such rhymes, above p. 57. Dibelius (p. 168) adduces *thus: was* from S. Editha, 2635. They are probably originally based on such pronunciations as (a) for *ă* in *man* and (ʌ) for *ŭ* in *come*.

Lediard, cf. also Wyld, Rhymes 107 f.) and Bullokar's goo~go (cf. above, p. 22); *some: none may reflect the present pronunciation of *none;* it: neglect (for *neglict,* cf. *afflict: infect,* Spenser, noted by Gabrielson, p. 56); lest: wǫrst (for *werst*); men: agein (for *agen*); hath: sayth (for *heth, seth,* cf. Zachrisson 68); *God: bad, borɴ: harᴍ indicate unrounding of ŏ to ǎ, cf. above, p. 70); *tooyl: soyl, sb. [for *soil* with (ui), Gill etc.]; rýz: noic' points to analogical (əi) for (ɔi) cf. above, p. 103; thu: hǫw (for weakly stressed *ho,* cf. Kihlbom, 192) just: rest (cf. Vulg. Engl. *jest* for *just,* and Krapp, 165).

Several of the rhymes admit of more than one explanation: *lacke: undertake may be an instance of ǎ: ā but also of ǎ: ǎ (cf. above, p. 31) *ypon: alón, *sowɴ: ypon may reflect ŏ: ō, but also ō: ō (cf. Bullokar's ón for *on* and above, p. 106); læd: ypbrayd is either a case of ę̄: ai (cf. above, p. 39) or of ę̄: ę̄ (cf. 6—7 *breade* NED.), despýȝ: iȝ, výc': iȝ is either a case of ĭ: ĭ or of ME. ī: ĭ. Although there are various other possibilities to take into account, I am inclined to look upon frayl: at al, fayl: smal, *rein: own as instances of half-open long ē (from ME. *ai, ei,* cf. above, p. 42) rhyming with the variant (æ:), (a:) for ME. *au* which has already been discussed.[1]

It is very difficult to decide if the rhymes vc': iȝ, frut: sett, are based on ME. (i:) or (iu) in *fruit, use.*

I am well aware that many of my interpretations of Bullokar's rhymes can be improved upon, but I trust that the general principles which have been laid down are sound and will hold good for the elucidation of early New English rhymes in general. The most important lesson we learn from this brief analysis is that the rhymes used by a sixteenth century writer do not, or need not, reflect his own pronunciation any more than

---

[1] This suggestion gains in probability by the fact that Butler in his 'Index of Woords like and unlike' couples *aul* with *ale, tall* with *tale,* and *hall* with *hale, hail.* Butler's sound-identifications, after all, deserve more credit than I was inclined to assume in English Vowels, p. 173. Thus his equations of *tale, tail, teal* and of *sow,* vb., and *sow,* sb., etc. are supported by evidence from other sources. Cf. above, pp. 39, 76.

the spelling does in printed works from the same period. The spellings are on the whole due to the activity of the printer, and the rhymes are based upon almost any conceivable pronunciation used not only in the writer's own day but also by his predecessors for several generations. Moreover some of the rhymes do not indicate identity but merely similarity of sound. Anyhow the many advanced forms of pronunciation seen in Bullokar's rhymes tend to justify the scepticism I have expressed with regard to many of his rules. Like his more learned colleagues, Smith, Gill and Wallis, he sometimes endeavours to set up a standard of pronunciation which in many respects differs from the common colloquial speech of the capital reflected in rhymes and occasional phonetic spellings.

Bullokar's Vocabulary.

Although the meaning of the words and the phraseology differ in many respects from the present usage, Bullokar's vocabulary is, on the whole, that of modern English. Of the three thousand words recorded in our lists, only about forty are now obsolete or dialectal. The learned editors of the New English Dictionary have evidently not consulted Bullokar's works. We find here many remarkable forms which are not given in NED., e. g. flýc' for *fleece,* pewtrelż for *peitrels,* fųndẹd, fųndor for *founded, founder,* to mention no more. Some of Bullokar's words do not agree with the dates given in NED. The following forms will serve to illustrate this: hylu' for *helve* (cf. 4—5 *hilve* NED.); splekẹd, 'spotted' (not noted after 1422 in NED.); stųflẹd for *stifled* (not noted after the 14th century in NED.); rýu' for *rife* (not noted after the 15th century in NED.); ynfitty (not noted until 1613 in NED.); tḩwitḷ, vb. (not noted until 1593 in NED.).

Some of the words used by Bullokar are not noted either in the New English Dictionary or in Wright's English Dialect Dictionary.

1. — Which thing the fox be'hóld*i*ng, saięth too' the man, ḍoo not hau' this ægſ *a-gest*r*ed, aȝ be'fór tým, lest, aȝ she' catchęth the hár, she' catch the' lýk-wýs. Fables, p. 148. — I take a-gest*r*ed to be the past participle of a ME. verb **gestre(n)*, a variant with an *r*-suffix of ME. *gestne(n)*, 'to entertain, to lodge'. The derivation mark under *r* proves that the base is ME. *gest*, 'guest'. The prefix *a*- is probably a dialectal feature, *a*- being in many southern dialects added to the past participle.[1] It may also be due to the analogy of other verbs beginning with *a*-[2], in which case we have to start from a ME. form **agestre(n)*. ME. *gestnen* appears in early NE. as *gestene* (3—5 NED., cf. also *gestener* 1375 'a guest', *ibid.*), and has survived in Modern N. dialects as *g(u)esten* (EDD.). A cognate word *guesting* still occurs in the Kentish dialect (EDD.).

2. — A lók or pin-fóld, Book at Large, p. 297, i. e. 'an enclosure for goats, sheep or cattle'. — The base is OE. *loc*, 'enclosure, fold' as in *gata loc, in scipa loce = in ovile ovium* (B.-T., and NED.). The last reference to *loke*, 'pinfold', which I have been able to trace is: *in ane loken* = 'a pen for goats' in Lagamon (Mätzner, Wb., p. 260). The nearest modern equivalent is *loke* in East Anglian dialects, which means, however, 'a (private) lane' (NED. and EDD.).

3. — The sám lark by chanc' had goṇ aſso intoo ráthR*e*d sæȝnź of sow*i*ng, thær-for the córn wax*i*ng ḥelow of cọlọr, the ḥọng-ónź aſso ẉær then not flụsh', Fables, p. 76. — The context is not quite clear, and the word is very difficult to explain. I can only offer the conjecture that it is the past participle of a ME. verb **rathere(n)*, 'quicken, hasten' formed by means of an *r*-suffix from the ME. adverb *rape* 'quickly' or the OE. verb *hraðian*, 'quicken, hasten'. The expression would then mean 'the busy, or perhaps hurried sowing-season'.

4. — A litſ fish caſ*e*d a smarid, Fables, p. 144. This is a pure Latin word: *smaris, smaridis*, 'a small fish', and has

---

[1] Cf. Zachrisson, Engelska Stilarter § 61, 3.
[2] Cf. Slettengren, Apharetic Words, p. 88 f.

probably been taken over by Bullokar from the Latin version
he used of Æsop's Fables. In the Romance languages it is
found in colloquial use only in some Italian dialects (East
Venitian *smarida,* see Meyer-Lübke, Rom. Etym. Wb.).

5. — Thrọwh the rent*i*ngꟲ of the door, Fables, p. 26. —
This is a noun formed from the verb *rent,* 'tear', with the pas-
sive sense of 'something torn', i. e. 'opening or rift'. In the
references given by NED., *renting,* sb., has only the sense of
'action of tearing'. A noun 'rent' = 'a narrow breach in a wall',
also occurs, but is not evidenced until 1705.

Some of Bullokar's words are now confined to the dialects,
although the majority, or all of them, were undoubtedly current in early Standard speech. Several of them are noted by
Nares in his Elements of Orthoepy published two hundred years
after Bullokar's time.[1] Nevertheless the following survey of the
distribution of some words and forms in the modern dialects
will perhaps help to throw light on the difficult problem of the
original home of Bullokar and his family. Particular attention
will be paid to the question whether Bullokar could have been
a Northerner or not.

1. *brack,* 'breach': in northern English dialects.
2. *culver,* 'dove': Lancs, Lincoln, Sussex, Devon etc.
3. *deve,* 'dive': Suff., Norf., Sussex (cf. 3—6 *deve, deave*
   NED.).
4. *divel,* 'devil': chiefly in Northern dialects, but still
   current in London as late as 1794 (Nares).
5. *fardel,* 'burden': chiefly in Southern and Western dialects.
6. *fet,* 'fetch': in all dialects.
7. *gorbellied,* 'with a big stomach': Linc. and Devon, but
   was used by Shakespeare (I, Henr. IV, II, ii, 93).

_____

[1] Cf. 'coney' with *u* short (p. 32) 'puppet' with *o* short, 'perhaps cor-
ruptly' (p. 37), 'beard, falsely spoken *burd* on our stage' (p. 56), 'either' and
'neither' with *a* long (p. 59), 'pierce' with *u* 'very improperly' (p. 66), *glister*
for 'clyster' (p. 264), *hern* for 'heron' (p. 265), *divil* for 'devil' (p. 287) etc.,
Nares, Elements of Orthoepy, London 1794.

8. *hame,* 'horse-collar': in general dialectal use.
9. *hilve,* 'handle': in Wilts and Devon (*helve* also in Northern dialects, cf. 4—5 *hilve* NED.).
10. *hill,* 'cover': in Oxf., Wilts, and also in Yorks, Chesh, Leic., Worc. etc.; *hill,* 'cover up potatoes', in Sussex and Kent.
11. *kemb,* 'comb': Northern dialects and Cornw., but usual in early NE. (Caxton, Camden, Fletcher).
12. *kitling,* 'kitten': Northern dialects, but also in Bedf., Sussex, and Hants.
13. *lask,* 'diarrhoea': Northern dialects, but also in Worc, Somers, and Suff.
14. *lease,* 'pasture-ground': in all dialects.
15. *mow,* 'stack of hay': in general dialectal use.
16. *pill,* 'peel': sb., in Linc., Notts., Warwick, Suff., etc.
17. *pook,* 'gore' etc.: Kent, Hants, I. of Wight.
18. *shrape,* 'bait for birds': Eastern and Southern dialects.
19. *stuffle,* 'stifle': I. of Wight, Cornw. (not after 14 c. NED.).
20. *unvitty,* 'unfitted': Devon, Cornwall (1613 NED.).
21. *thwittle,* 'to cut': Northern dialects, but also used by Chaucer, Cotton 1664 etc.
22. *whittle,* 'white cloak': in most dialects.

The chief conclusion we can draw from our list is that Bullokar was not a Northerner or descended from a Northern family. Merely three of the words we have examined occur only or chiefly in the North (4, 11, 21), and all these were current in early Standard English.

Moreover, a third part of the words or forms noted are foreign to the Northern vernaculars (3, 5, 9, 17, 18, 19, 20). Three words (3, 17, 18) only occur in the East and the South, three others (9, 19, 20) are now confined to the south-western vernaculars. For reasons already stated it is probable that Bullokar had some connection with Kent or Sussex. He may have spent some part of his life in Sussex, or his family may originally have hailed from that part of England. This assumption is at least not contradicted by the material at hand. Scanty as the material is, it indicates a spot on the English map where East and West meet. Of our nineteen Southern vernacular words or forms only five are not recorded either for Sussex or Kent, but in dialects (Suffolk, Hants etc.) not very far removed from these counties. Most conclusive from a vernacular point of view are *deve,* which, though not unusual in early new English, now only seems to occur in the dialects of Norfolk, Suffolk and Sussex[1], and *hilve;* if *i* in this word goes back to OE. *ie* (*hielf*)[2], and is not due to the raising of *e* to *i* before *l,* we have here a dialectal form which is not likely to have occurred farther east than Sussex[3]. The quaint word *loke or pin-fold,* apparently not evidenced in English literature after the time of Lagamon, is only likely to have been preserved in a sheep-breeding county, and Sussex is famous for its downs and its sheep. The forms *goo* and *strook* for *go* and *stroke* do not bespeak Bullokar to be an East-Anglian, for easternisms of this kind were quite usual in early London speech.[4]

Bullokar's name not being of local origin, gives no clue to the early home of the family. It may be a worn-down

---

[1] But Kruisinga (p. 70) gives *dive* with (e:) < (i:) for W. Somerset.

[2] Bullokar's flýc' from WS. *flīes* speaks in favour of the first of these alternatives.

[3] ME. *i, u* for OE. *īe* occurs in Hants, Berks (cf. Kögel, *Ie und seine Parallelformen*) and occasionally in Sussex (cf. *Ifiwirde* DB. = Iford. from OE. **Ifigwyrþ, Durinton* H. III. IPM. = Durrington, from OE. **Dyrantun* (cf. also Ekwall, English Dialects, p. 49), but, to judge by the somewhat scanty material that has been examined hitherto, not in Surrey (cf. Wyld, English Studies, vol. III, no. 2, p. 3) or Middlesex (Ekwall, p. 56). The *y*-spellings quoted by Miss Serjeantson, Dialect Characters, p. 19, and Dölle, Zur Sprache Londons, p. 37, from some London charters of the 11th and early 12th centuries are not conclusive, as they may be survivals of the literary West Saxon language.

[4] Cf. *goo* for *go* evidenced by Price, *strooke* 5—8 NED., and numerous spellings with *ou* for ME. *ǭ* in early Standard English (Zachrisson, English Vowels, p. 84, Engl. Stud. 52, p. 322, Kihlbom, pp. 159 ff.). Besides *goo* (but not *strook*) also occurs in Sussex (Wright, EDGr., pp. 463, 625).

form of *Bullocherde* 'the keeper of a herd of bullocks', with loss
of *d* in the genitive case. Bardsley (Dictionary of Surnames,
p. 146) has an early entry of this name: *John le Bollochurde*,
1 Edw. III, Somerset, Kirby's Quest, p. 231. Surnames compounded with *-herd* are very usual, but the terminal appears
invariably as *-ert, -erd,* as in Calvert, Stoddart, Coultherd etc.'
The final *d* was, however, more likely to be dropped in a word
of originally four syllables, than in the trisyllabic ones, where *d*
has been regularly kept.

However this may be, the only safe conclusions we can
draw from the previous investigation is that Bullokar was a
Londoner, in all probability born and bred in the capital,
although certain words and forms of pronunciation used by him
are more southern in character, which renders it at least probable that the original home of his family was in a county south
or south-west of London, possibly Sussex.

Some Palæographic Notes.

I. Spellings with *a* for ME. *u* as in *gun*.

Paston Letters no. 620, a. 1469, British Mus. Add. MS.
34889 f. 88. See **facsimile,** opposite to p. I. — The letter
is written by Margaret Paston or a secretary, in a clear but
rapid handwriting: *they fayll gunnepowder and arrowes; thei
have sent for gannes; ther gret multitude of gannes.*

The letters *o* and *a,* as a rule, are quite distinct in shape,
o is a closed ring (cf. *sore, of, toder,* l. 3 in MS. etc.), and *a* is
made up of a semicircle very much overlapped by the minims
(cf. *lakke, Dawbeny* 2, *that, hasty* 3 etc.). Sometimes *o* is open
at the top, as in *brother, joperte* 1, *brokyn* 3 etc. It is this fact
that leads to confusion. Especially when *o* is followed by
minim letters (*u, n, t,* etc.), a stroke is added to the top of *o*

' Numerous early references are adduced by Bardsley, English Surnames, pp. 266 ff.

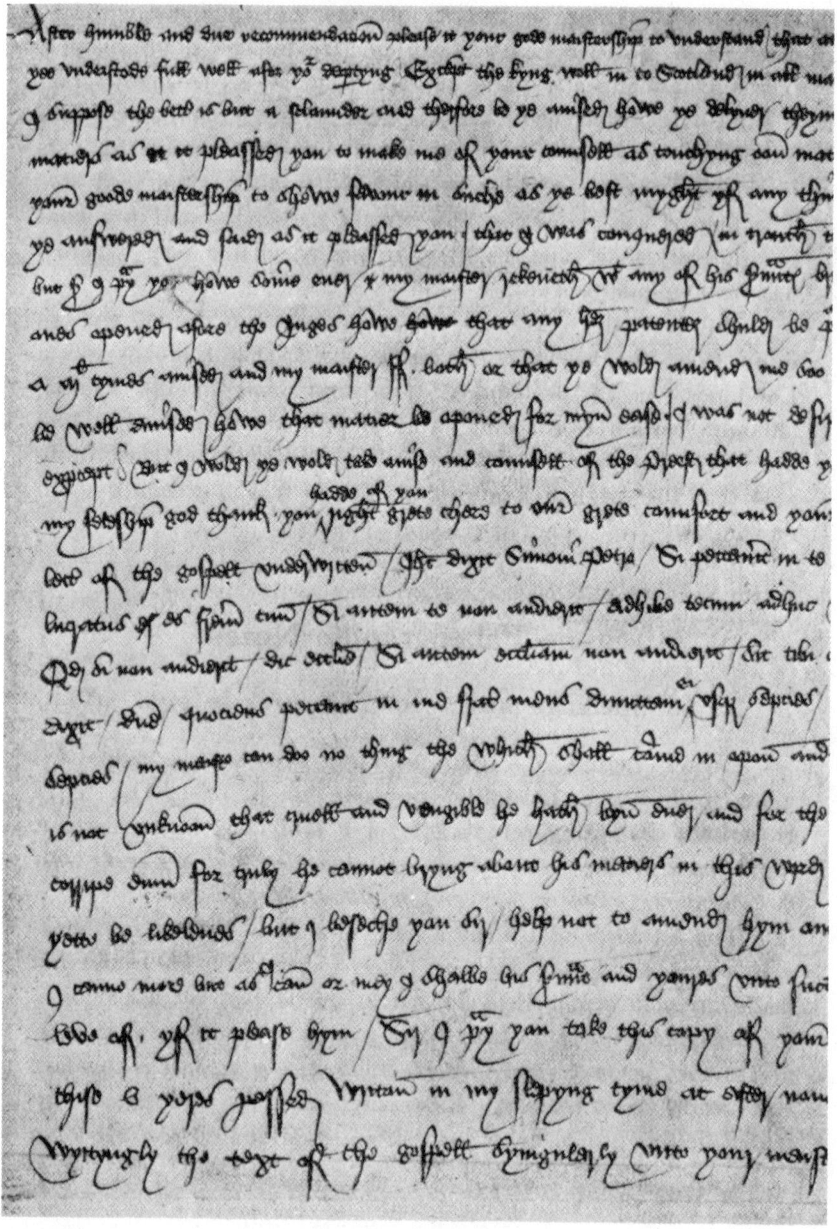

Facsimile of Paston Letter, No. 283,

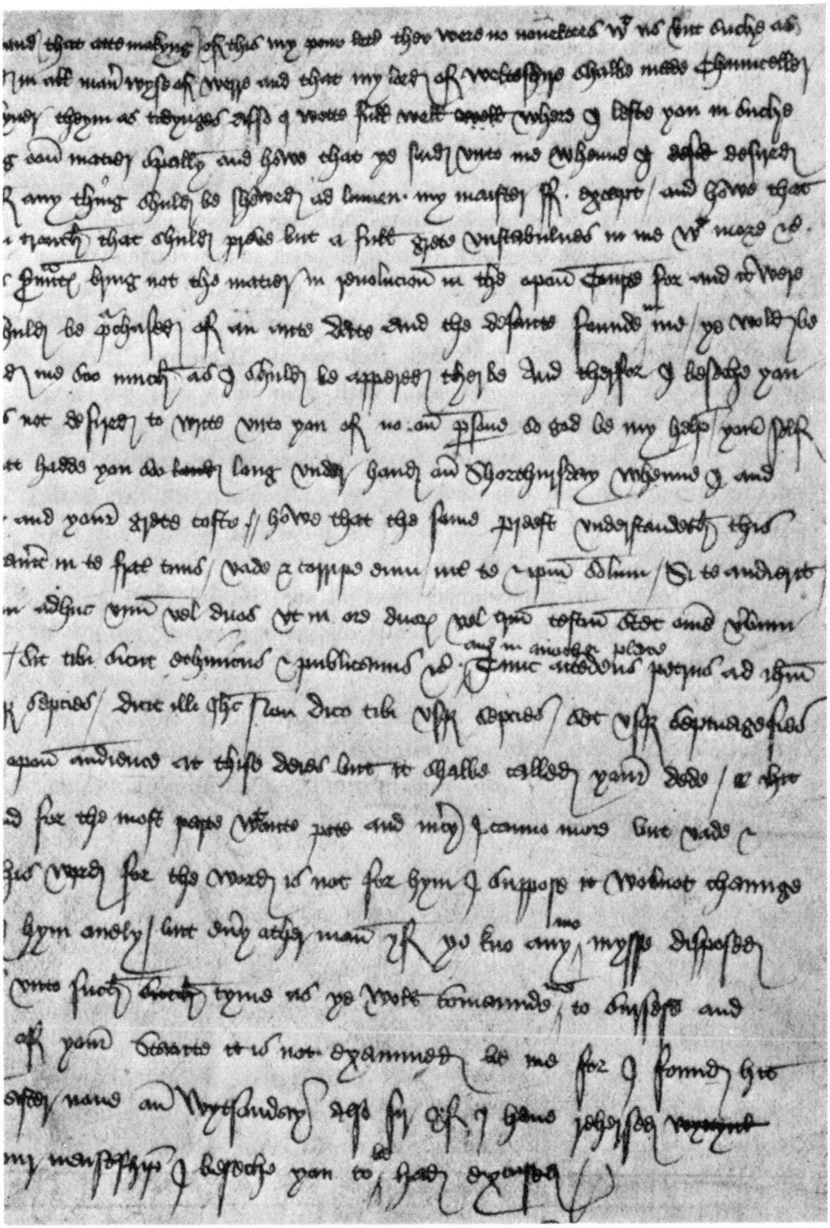

Br. Mus., Add. MSS. 34888 f. 130.

in order to close the ring (cf. *countre* 5, *withought* 6, *you* 14), and when this top-stroke overlaps the ring of which *o* is formed, it resembles the minim of *a,* and the whole letter *o* comes to bear a close resemblance to the letter *a* (cf. *gonnepowder* 2, *gonnes* 3, *gonnes* 10, *London* 21, and especially *upon* 8, 20, *gonnes* 11, *withought* 13). There are, however, as a rule, some small differences between *a* proper, and what we may call the deteriorated *o.* The second minim of *a* is more vertical than the top-stroke of *o;* moreover *a* is on the same level as the next letter (*u, n,* etc.), whereas *o* is on a somewhat lower level than the letter (*u, n,* etc.) that follows it. Compare the deteriorated *o's* (*gonnes, upon* etc.) with *a* in *haue sent* 10, *haue my blissing* 14, *cause* 20. In *stand* 1, *an* very much resembles *on* in *gonnes,* but the *minim* of *a* is joined closer to the body of the letter than the top-stroke is to *o.* Between the *a* in *shall,* 20, and the *o* in *other,* 2, there is, however, hardly any difference.

The result of this survey is that we should read *gonnepowder* 2, *gonnes* 10, 11 instead of *gunnepowder, gannes* in Fenn's reprint of the letter.

Cely Letters, No. 120, a 1484, Record Office, AC. 53, 166, written by William Cely: *any marchauntes that camyth heder.* — The second letter in *camyth* is probably *o,* although it much resembles *a,* the right semicircle of the letter being somewhat blurred.

Diary of Machyn, Brit. Mus., MS. Vitellius F. V.: *my lord cheyffe justes Chamley* ('Cholmley') 1553 (p. 38); *master*

1558 (Samersett) (p. 182). These spellings

whith *a* for *u* are quite safe, the two letters *o* and *a* never being confused in this manuscript: *o* is a semicircle, *a* is formed by two strokes at a pointed angle, which often gives the letter the shape of an inverted *v.*

The only remaining 15th century spelling with *a* for *ŭ* is

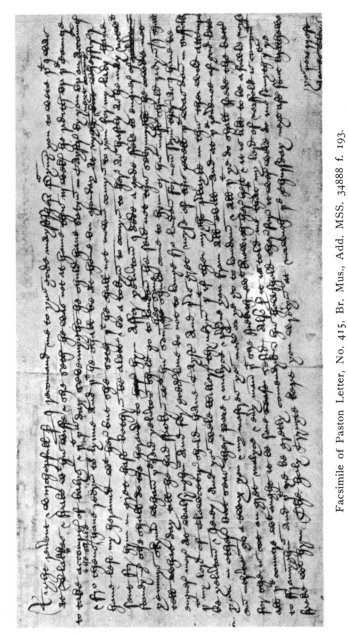

Facsimile of Paston Letter, No. 415, Br. Mus., Add. MSS. 34888 f. 193.

sadanly, Fortescue, p. 126, in which *a,* if genuine, may be due to anticipation of the following *a.* Consequently there do not seem to be any phonetic spellings with *a* for *ŭ* on record, until the 16th century.

II. Spellings with au for ME. *ū* as in our.

Paston Letters, No. 283, a. 1456?, Brit. Mus. Add. MSS. 34888 f. 130. See **facsimile,** pp. 126—127. The letter is written in a beautiful formal handwriting by Henry Wilson, who, to judge by various allusions to legal matters as well as the polished language of the letter, was a London lawyer: *the de- faute faunde in me; withaute pite and mercy.* — The letters *a* and *o* are often quite distinct, *o* having the shape of a ring, *a* that of a semicircle with two minims; sometimes the body of *a* is formed by two strokes at a pointed angle instead of a semicircle (cf. *recommendacion, such a,* l. 1 in MS. etc.). But here too we have to reckon with an *o* of *a*-type or a deterior- ated *o* made up of a semicircle and a down-stroke, which, when overlapping the ring, gives *o* a close resemblance to *a.* More or less typical instances of a deteriorated *o* are *open* 7, *ones* 8, *oponed, you, (no)on* 10, *long, on* 11, *counfort* 12, *non* (Latin) 15, *come* 17, *other* 20, *on* 23. We should notice that in all these instances *o* is followed by a letter beginning with a minim. In 9 out of 12 cases the next letter is *u* or *n.* For this reason *faunde,* l. 8, and *withaute,* l. 18, are no safe readings. Con- sidering the comparative material adduced above, I prefer to read *founde, withoute,* although *per se* the disputed letter in both instances is more like an *a* than an *o.*

Paston Letters, No. 415, a. 1461, Brit. Mus. Add. MS 34888 f. 193. See **facsimile** on page 129. The letter is written by James Gloys in a clear and legible handwriting: *with- aught it be sone sesid.* — Here also we find orthographic con- fusion between *o* and *a,* although not quite so conspicuous as in the previous letter. Clear instances of a deteriorated *o* are ·

Facsimile of Paston Letter, No. 485, Add. MSS., Br. Mus. 34889 f. 6.

seen in the spellings *you* 1, *countre* 2, *Glowcetir* 11, *you, from*
13, *on* 15, *sone* 16. *Withought,* l. 16, has every appearance of
being spelt with an *a,* but when not only *countre, from* etc.,
but also *sone* in the same line exhibits a similar *a,* we can
hardly hesitate to give preference to the reading *withought.* It
also follows that *hame* 2, is a somewhat doubtful reading for
home, especially as a clear case of *home* occurs in l. 4.

Paston Letters, No. 485, a. 1464, Brit. Mus., Add. MS.
34889 f. 6. See **facsimile** on page 131. This letter, which
is written by a servant of the Pastons, John Pampynge, is in a
rapid and not very clear handwriting: *abaught his nekke.* —
The correct reading of *abought* or *abaught,* l. 20, is very difficult to determine. At first blush, the letter after *b* certainly
looks like an *a.* It was not until I had scanned every *o* and
every *a* in the letter that I arrived at a different conclusion.
Pampynge has two distinct types of *a.* The most usual one
has the minims carried high up above the line, sometimes with
omission of the semicircular body of the letter. This *a* is entirely different from *o.* Only the ordinary *a,* which is much
less usual, can be confused with *o.* The letter *o* consists of a
ring, which is sometimes open. The less usual *a* is altogether
of the modern type, the minim very seldom overlaps the semicircle (cf. *bad* 15, *retarnabill* 15, *fardell* 17, *saving* 24). So far as
I can judge, the letter after *b* in *abought* is a badly shaped *o,*
in which the one semicircle slightly overlaps the other. There
is no other *o* or *a* of exactly the same type, but this particular
o resembles somewhat more closely the *o* in *on,* l. 9, *so,* l. 10,
somwhat, l. 24, than the *a's* of the modern type in which the
body of the letter is more elongated (cf. *bad,* 15 etc.).

Paston Letters XII, a. 1448, Add. MSS. 34888 f. 57, by
James Gloys: *it whas seysyd withawth licens and leve of here.* —
The correct reading is *withouth* (an *o* with slightly overlapping
topstroke).

Cely Letters, No. 20, c. 1480, Record Office AC. 128, by
H. Stawnton: *let your man . . . . . go to the syne of the Ster*

..... *wher* 𝒖𝜽/ (*aur*) *daggers be mayd.* — The first letter is
certainly *a,* the second looks like an *e,* but a *u* of exactly the
same shape occurs in other letters, e. g. in 𝓮𝓼𝔂𝓹𝓬𝓻𝓭𝓵𝓲
(*understonde*) P. Ls., No. 609 (cf. below). Consequently we have
here a safe case of *au* for *ou.*

Cely Letters, No. 104, a. 1484, Rec. Office, AC. 53, 144,
by William Cely: *we have tydynges* 𝓰𝓸𝔃𝓸 (*hew*) *that the
Frensch men hath goten the cyte.* — The spelling *hew* for *how*
is safe.'

Paston Letters, No. 670, a. 1471, Add. MSS. 27445 f. 45
by John Paston the younger: *I have hey i new of myn owne.* —
In *i new* (= 'enow') *e* can very well be an open *o.* The same
kind of letter occurs in *you* and *your* in several instances.

Paston Letters, No. 708, a. 1472, Add. MSS. 27445 f. 64
by John Paston the younger: *she* ('the hawk') *hathe ben so
brooseid with cariage of fewle.* — The reading *brooseid* ('bruised')
is correct, but we should read *fowle,* rather than *fewle* (cf. *all
syche folk* in the next line with a similar open and carelessly
shaped *o*).

From this survey we can draw the important conclusion
that isolated spellings with *a* for *o* in the printed editions of
15th century MSS. can only be relied upon after a close in-
spection of the manuscripts from which these spellings are
derived. Much of what has been written about the transition
of *o* to *a, ow* to *aw* and occasional forms, such as *halde, hame*
etc. for *holde, home,* will have to be revised in connection with
a minute investigation of the manuscripts in which these forms
occur. The result of the close investigation to which the MSS.
have been subjected, is that there remain only two perfectly
safe cases of *eu* and *au* for *ou* (*heu* and *aur*), which, in all
probability, indicate that ME. *ū* in *house* could be pronounced
as (əu) or (au) by some speakers in the 15th century.'

' Neither can occasional spellings with *au* for *ou* in printed editions
from the 16th century (cf. Zachrisson, 79) be implicitly relied upon without

Professor Wyld (pp. 230 f.) comments upon the extreme rarity of spellings with *au* for *ou,* 'which do not inspire the same confidence as do some others of the kind'. He also remarks that 'the spelling *ou,* if taken literally to mean *o + u,* was by no means a bad representation of the pronunciation of the diphthong as it probably was during the greater part of the 16th century' (cf. *ou* in the Welsh Hymn to the Virgin c. 1560, Salesbury 1547, Hart 1569 etc.). The first unambiguous *orthoepistic* evidence for (əu) or (au) in *house* is Wallis' and Cooper's identification of the first element in the diphthong with *o vel u obscurum* and *u gutturalis.* The rendering of *ou* with *au, aou* by French grammarians is ambiguous, and may indicate either (ou) or (əu), (au).[1]

If the old *ū* in *house* has had a parallel development to that of *ī* in *like,* which is in itself very probable[2], it can hardly be doubted that the stage of (əu) or (au) was reached as early as the latter half of the 15th century, especially as the diphthongisation of *ū* must have begun at the time when *ō* in *do* became (u:). We have already seen that this sound-change dates at least as far back as the second half of the 14th century.[3] The rendering of the English word *rout* with *rhawt* by Salesbury (cf. Williams, p. 208) can hardly indicate any other sound than the present one (au)[4], whereas *ou* for ME. *ū* in Salesbury and the Hymn to the Virgin (1560) *can* be interpreted as (əu), the actual Welsh pronunciation of *ou,* or be due to the substitution of Welsh (əu) for the English diphthong (ou)[5].

an individual examination of the manuscripts, which in some instances have been lost.

[1] That *ou* in *house* was pronounced as (au) by Northerners in the 17th cent. is proved by the evidence of Gill, and a few spellings in 17th century plays. Cf. Zachrisson, 79, Engl. Stud. 52, p. 310.

[2] On (əi), (ai) for *ī* in the 15th century, cf. above pp. 54 ff.

[3] Cf. above p. 59, n. 2.

[4] According to Williams, *rhawt* is also found in the writings of Dafydd ap Gwilym.

[5] Salesbury's *awr* for 'hour' may represent an unusual development of Lat. *ō* to Welsh *aw,* as in *nawn* from *nōna* (cf. Pedersen, I, p. 206), especially as, according to Professor J. Glyn Davies, there existed in Middle Welsh a diminutive of *awr,* i. e. *owran.*

III. Spellings with *a* for ME. *ō* < *ā*, as in home.

Stonor Letters, No. 220, c. 1478, Record Office, AC. 46, 186, written by Richard Page: *My lord Chamberleyn rides to morue hame to Leycestre.* — The correct reading is *home, a* and *o* being often confused before minim letters.

Paston Letters, No. LXXVII, a. 145—   , Add. MSS., 33597 f. 4, by John Paston the youngest: *John Pampyng hathe had hame* ('home') *to Carter as good as X^{ml} tylle.* — The letters *o* and *a* being often much alike (cf. *o* in *reparacyon* and *recovering*), the correct reading is no doubt *home* (cf. also *hye you hom hastyly*) in the same letter.

Paston Letters, No. 415, a. 1461, Add. MSS., 34888 f. 193, by James Gloys: *and she seth he was not hame.* — We seem to be justified in reading *hame* as *home,* as in the previous letter (cf. the analysis of the letter on p. 130).

Paston Letters, No. 36, a. 1443, Add. MSS., 34888 f. 8 by Margaret Paston: *tyl I wott that ze ben very hal.* — There is no doubt whatever that the correct reading is *hol.*

The scepticism I have already expressed as to the reliability of isolated spellings with *a* for *o* is amply justified by the examination to which one special group of such spellings has been subjected. One or two instances (*stanys,* Paston Letters 585, *anely ib.* 416) I have not yet been able to examine, because these letters are in the possession of Mr. Pretyman of Orwell Park, Suffolk, but it is not likely that they will prove to be genuine cases of *a* for *o.*

The material does not bear out Dr. Kihlbom's assumption (p. 161) that isolated Northern forms with *a* for *o* were current in the early Standard language. Neither is *scale* necessarily a Northern form, for as is pointed out in NED., we may also have to count with OF. *escale.*

One remaining instance, (*hayme?*) in a letter by Sir John Weston (Cely Letters, No. 64, Rec. Off.,

AC. 53, 83) is no safe instance either. Firstly, the letter seems
to contain several other forms, which may be Northern (*gud* for
good, wallde for *would*, and *sal* for *shall*), secondly, if the letter
is a specimen of Essex dialect (Sir John spent much of his
time in Essex), *hayme* may possibly represent the Scandinavian
word *heim*, thirdly, it is not impossible that *hayme* should be
read as *thayme* (cf. the loose way in which *th* is written in
they sawe, the sonner, the staple, they sal se), fourthly, *home*
occurs in its usual orthographical garb at the beginning of the
letter (*and wallde a sente me home again*).

My own interpretation of the place-name forms *Stane* for
Stone is also made doubtful, owing to the absence of parallel
forms with *a* in the literary language. Perhaps we should look
upon *Stane* as an archaic spelling in which *a* has been preserved
merely on account of the orthography. Concerning such forms
as *leke* for *like*, Dr. Kihlbom (pp. 37 f.) suggests that ME. $\bar{\imath}$,
perhaps owing to reduced stress, was occasionally levelled under
ME. $\bar{e}$, especially in the East and West (Devon). As far as I
can judge, weak stress can only lead to the shortening of $\bar{\imath}$ to
$\breve{\imath}$, hardly to $\bar{\imath}$ being kept as a simple vowel. Some of the
illustrative instances Dr. Kihlbom adduces are not conclusive.
On *e* in French words (5 *desere* etc. NED.), cf. Zachrisson,
pp. 75, 206. Forms with (i:) in modern dialects do not necessarily go back to ME. $\bar{\imath}$. Many of the words quoted by Ellis
(I, p. 291) contain ME. $\bar{e}$ (*mice, mind, friar* etc.), or *i, $\bar{e}$* followed
by a palatal consonant (*eye, high, right*), in which case modern
dialectal (i:) may be the result of various combinative sound-
changes[1]. This also applies to the dialectal material adduced
by Förster (Anglia XXIV, pp. 115 ff.) from Devonshire (1701)
(*ees = eyes, neen = nine, kees = kine*). At least in Devon, (i:)
may sometimes be due to a comparatively recent lengthening
of *i* short to (i:). In the adjacent dialect of West Somerset,
which has many features in common with that of Devon, short
i is often lengthened, as in *itch, kin* etc., and many words

---

[1] Note that Machyn, the Londoner, has almost invariably *hee, de(e)*
for *high* and *die*.

containing ME. *ī* have both (ai), (i:), and (i), the (i:) being often
due to the influence of shortened forms with (i) or to the
lengthening of (i) to (i:). Cf. Kruisinga, pp. 61, 70, 123 f.

IV. Spellings with *ol* for *al,* as in half, and *au* for *o,* as in offer.

Paston Letters, No. 629, a. 1469, Add. MSS., 34889 f. 96,
by Margaret Paston: *I trowe Wretyll hathe told of the pawnte-*
ments. — The MS. has *powtements* for *powntements* (the *n*-
stroke having been omitted), a variant of *appointements* with
apharetic loss of *a* and monophthongisation of ME. *ui* to *ū*.
Cf. Zachrisson, Luick Celebration Vol. p. 147.

Paston Letters, No. 75, *ante* 1450, Add. MSS., 34888 f. 35,
by William Talboys: *and other cause he had non to him as fer*
as I kan knowe, bot awnly for the malissiousness that he hath
unto me. — The MS. has *alonly* not *awnly.* For the early use
of this word see NED. (5—6 *alonly*).

Cely Papers, No. 149, c. 1470: *Thomas Dolton* (twice) is
an error for *Colton,* not a phonetic spelling for *Dalton.*

Stonor Letters, No. 312, a. 1482?, Rec. Off., AC. 46, 208,
by Simon Stallworth. Stallworth's three letters (Nos. 312, 330,
331) are written from Dorchester in Oxfordshire and from
London. Later in life, Stallworth became sub-dean of Lincoln
and prebendary in St. Stephen, Westminster. He cannot have
been a native of the west of England, where *al* became *ol,* as
he uses such forms as *mykyll, hand, land, awne, haith, tayne*

which point to East Anglia or Lincolnshire: *to the 𝓫𝓸𝓱𝓸𝓵𝓸𝓭*

(*beholve*) *of Rychard Idley. —* This is a safe case of *ol* as a
phonetic spelling for *al.*

Cely Letters, No. 50, a. 1475, Rec. Off., AC. 53, 67, by
Richard Cely the younger: *the kynge hath wry(ten) an auffer to*
the lorde master — there come inbassyturs howt of Skotelond
(there had been an incursion of Scots into England), *and the*

kynge whoudde not let them cowm no nar byt sent ther auffer (i. e. offer of peace, there is no talk of an answer) *to New-castell.* — An examination of the MS. shows that *auffer* (= 'offer') is the correct reading, and not *ansser,* as was suggested by Professor Ekwall (Engl. Stud. 49, 279 ff.). The second *f* is provided with the tag which distinguishes it from the long *s.* Compare the double *s* in 〔inbassyturs〕 (*inbassyturs*) with the double *f* in 〔auffer〕 (*auffer*). As for the interpretation of these spellings, cf. above, p. 67.

V. Spellings with *ow* for ME. *ēu* as in new.

Paston Letters, No. 745, a. 1474, Add. MSS., 27445 f. 45,

by Sir John Paston: *or ellys on* 〔figure〕 (*Touesday?*). The

reading is not quite safe, for although the letter looks like an *o,* the tail of *y* in the line above is drawn through it, and it is therefore impossible to decide if an *e,* or an *o* was originally written after *T.* Note also that in *content,* a few lines below, *te* can hardly be distinguished from *to.*

In the previous discussion (p. 63) I have assumed that as early as the 15th century (iu:) could be reduced to (u:) after certain consonants, as in *bruise, jupe, chew.* Dr. Kihlbom (p. 91) adduces 4 *loodly?* NED. (not among the examples quoted from Wyclif), which, however, is not quite safe considering the ME. variant *loʒede* likewise quoted in NED. Dr. Kihlbom thinks this reduction could take place in other positions also, and adduces the spellings *Touesday, boutte* 5 NED., *dewe,* Paston Letters, No. 78, and *doureng,* Stonor Letters, No. 233, in proof of this. We have already seen that *Touesday* may be read as *Teuesday.* In *boutte ou* may be a symbol for (o:) in imitation of the

Continental French pronunciation (cf. *powter*, Paston Letters 429 < French *peutre*, *peau(l)tre*, Zachrisson, 82), in *doureng* ME. (u:) may have been substituted for OFr. (y:) (cf. Zachrisson, Luick Celebration Volume, p. 146). *Dewe* (cf. *du*, *gyudenesse*, 'goodness', Paston Letters, Nos XIX, 826) is most likely to indicate the Eastern dialectal levelling of ME. *ēu* in *new* and *ǭ* in *do* under the same sound (ü:). Note also that the letter in which *dewe* occurs exhibits many other Eastern dialectal features, such as *qu* for *wh* (*quer*, *qheche*), *xuld* for *should*, *meche* for *much* etc. In some Suffolk records we also come across such spellings as *tue* (1600—1700) and *teu* for *two* (Binzel 39).

Traces of this Eastern pronunciation also occur in the Verney Memoirs, as in *one or teu* ('two'), *du* ('do') 1642, pp. 116, 244. Perhaps we ought to interpret all these as phonetic spellings for (dü:), (tü:), so long as no spellings of the type *do(o)* for *due*, and *no(o)* for *new* have been recorded from the same or contemporary sources. This Eastern pronunciation may have occurred in America also (cf. *teu* for *two* in the Southwold Records, 1655 I, 29, Krapp 160).

When *ew* or *u* is written for *o*, as in *teu, du, schule* in specimens of modern vulgar London English,[1] it is difficult to tell whether we have to do with Eastern vernacular forms or with a hyperliterary pronunciation of (u:) as (ju:). Such hyperliterary forms were usual in the rustic speech of New England (Krapp, 160). Cf. Additions.

VI. Spellings with *e* for ME. *ă a*, as in man.

The letter *e* can easily be confused with *o*, when the upper loop of *e* is missing or carelessly written. An open *e* can also be confused with *a, o,* and *u*.

Paston Letters, No. 305, a. 1457, Add. MSS., 3488 f. 133, by Botoner, a servant of Fastolf's: *seth my maister ꝓgꝛ̄ (begen) to kepe house.* — This is a clear case of *begen* for *began*.

---

[1] Cf. Zachrisson, Engelska Stilarter, p. 101.

Paston Letters, No. 534, a. 1465, Add. MSS., 34889 f. 36—7, by Margaret Paston: *The Duck ys men* ~~pomsackyd~~ *(rensackyd) the church.* — Another safe case of *e* for *a*.

Paston Letters, No. 78, a. 1450, Add. MSS., 27, 443 f. 105, by Margaret Paston: *in as meche as I fend them ontrew in other thyngs.* — This is a certain case of *fend* for *fand*, *e* and *o* being quite distinct in this letter. The context shows that *fend* is the past tense.

Paston Letters, No. 609, a. 1409, Add. MSS., 34889 f. 78—9, by R. Calle: *I undrestende, lady, ye have hadde as-moche sorwe for me as any gentelwoman hath hadde in the worlde.* — It is possible to read both *undrestende* and *undrestonde*. As Calle has an equal number of *a*- and *o*- spellings for 'understand' (Kihlbom), it is impossible to make a decision between the two readings. Preference ought perhaps to be given to the normal form *undrestonde*.

Paston Letters, No. 619, a. 1469, Add. MSS., 34889 ff. 86—7, by Sir John Paston (written by an amanuensis, Kihlbom XII): *Neverthelesse I understend by your wryting.* — It is also possible to read *understond*, the letter being either an open *e* or an *o*. No decision can be made, for in the same letter we find both *understand* (p. 369, 2×) and *understond* (p. 371).

Paston Letters, No. 656, a. 1470, Add. MSS., 34889 ff. 105—06, by Sir John Paston: *and as worshypfull as few be lengyng to Norff.* — The correct reading is *be longing* (*lang* for *long* does not occur in the Paston Letters proper, cf. Kihlbom, p. 124). The letter resembles *e*, simply because the upper part of the semicircle somewhat overlaps the top-stroke, which merely serves to join *o* on to the next letter, *n*.

Paston Letters, No. 66, a. 1449, Add. MSS., 27, 443 f. 102, by Margaret Paston: *The frere that cleymyth Oxned was in this town zastyrday.* — The correct reading is probably *zustyrday*, with *u* for *i* owing to the labial influence of (ʒ) (cf. *yister evyn* in the same letter, and Zachrisson, Change of *ts* to *ch*, p. 130).

Paston Letters, No. 144, a. 1451, Add. MSS., 27444 f. 1,

Memoranda for Prosecution: *Item to indyte the baly of Swaffham* etc. *of felonye as excercarys; he* (Sir. T. Todenham) *were worthy to be indyted as* *(excercary)*. — The readings are perfectly safe. As I have already pointed out (Engl. Stud., 52, p. 317, n. 2) *exercary* is a phonetic spelling for *accessory* with the stress on the first syllable, and the *e* in the second syllable pronounced with the vocal murmur (ə). The writer found it difficult to spell this learned word, for in the MS., it is first written *exorcar - - - s,* which has been crossed out and replaced with *exócarys.*

Cely Letters, No. 118, a. 1483, Rec. Off., Anc. Corr., 53, 163, by William Cely: *soudears* ('soldiers') of *Mexymelyans.* — Read: *Maxymelyans.* The *a* has the shape of an inverted *v* exactly as in *name* (p. 142, l. 18).

Although some spellings with *e* for *a* have had to be eliminated, the remaining ones (*begen, rensack, fend, exercary*) in conjunction with those which have been adduced in Engl. Stud., 52, *l. c.,* prove that *a* in *man* had been raised to (æ) or (e) in the pronunciation of some speakers in the second half of the 15th century.

Lists of Verified or Corrected Forms in Early Letters and Documents.

The Paston Letters, ed. J. Gairdner.   London 1875.

No. 36, I 48 *hal*   read *hol.*
  »   66, I 81 *zastyrday*   »   *zustyrday* ('yesterday').
  »   75, I 96 *awnly*   »   *alonly.*
  »   78, I 112 *dewe* ('do'), *fende (= fand).*
  » 144, I 190 *exercary, exercarys* ('acessory, accessories').
  » 283, I 388 *faunde*   read *founde.*
  » 283, I 389 *withaute* »   *withoute.*
  » 305, I 415 *begen* ('began').

No. 415, II 50 *withaught* read *withought.*
»   415, II 50 *hame*   »   *home?.*
»   485, II 150 *abaught*   »   *abought.*
»   534, II 251 *rensackyd* ('ransacked').
»   609, II 351 *undrestende* read *undrestonde?.*
»   609, II 351 *son*   »   *sin* ('since').
»   619, II 368 *understend*   »   *understond?.*
»   620, II 372 *gunnepowder* »   *gonnepowder.*
»   620, II 372 *gannes* (twice) » *gonnes* (twice).
»   629, II 386 *pawntements* »   *pow(n)tements* ('appointments').
»   656, II 415 *belengyng*   »   *belongyng.*
»   670, III   7 *inew*   »   *inow?* ('enough').
»   708, III 68 *brooseid* ('bruised').
»   708, III 68 *fewle*   read *fowle.*
»   745, III 115 *Touesday*   »   *Teuesday?.*
»   XII (ed. 1901, Introd.) *withawth* read *withowth.*
»   LXXVII (ed. 1901, Introd.) *hame*   »   *home.*

The Cely Papers, ed. H. E. Malden. London 1900.

No. 12, p. 12 *Tamas* read *Tomas* (Kihlbom, 138, n. 2).
»   20, » 20 *aur* ('our').
»   23, » 23 *haver syth* read *hover syth* (Kihlbom, 138, n. 2).
»   50, » 55 *auffer* ('offer') (twice).
»   53, » 59 *brahut* read *brohut* ('brought') (Kihlbom, 170, n. 2).
»   64, » 69 *vayage* for *viage* ('voyage').
»   64, » 69 *sende hayme* read *sende thayme?.*
»   73, » 82 *Sent Tamos*   »   *Sent Tomor* ('St. Omer') (Kihl-
                                       bom, 141, n. 1).
» 104, » 120 *hew* ('how').
» 118, » 143 *Mexymelyans* read *Maxymelyans.*
» 120, » 145 *camyth*   »   *comyth?.*
» 123, » 152 *naw wull*   »   *new wull* (Kihlbom, 170, n. 2).
» 149, » 203 f. *Thomas Dolton* read *Thomas Colton* (twice)
                                       (Kihlbom, 78, n. 2).

The Stonor Letters and Papers, ed. Ch. Lethbridge Kingsford. London 1919.

No. 165, II 6 *no* ('know').
» 220, II 59 *hame* read *home*.
» 312, II 144 *beholve* ('behalf').

Diary of Machyn, ed. J. G. Nichols. London 1848.

p. 38 *Chamley* ('Cholmley').
» 182 *Samersett* ('Somerset').

Edmund de la Pole, Orig. Letters, ed. H. Ellis, Orig. Letters, Third Series, Vol. I. London 1861.

p. 133 *tame* read *teme* ('time').
» 138 *barges* » *borges* ('burghers').

Approximate Phonetic Value of Bullokar's Symbols.

a in man: (æ) rather than (a).
á » nám: (ɛ:) » » (æ:).
á » bárn: (æ:)?.
ay » day: (ɛ:i), possibly with a half long (ɛ:).
æ » mæl: (e:).
e » men: (e).
e' » be': (i:).
ý » wrýt: (ei) rather than (ij).
i » sit: (i).
u̟ » lu̟k: (o) rather than (u).
o̟w » ho̟ws: (ou) rather than (uw).
oo » do: (u:).
au̟ » au̟tor: (au)?.
o » not: (ɔ) with slight rounding.
ó » gót: (o:).

o   in thórɴ:. (ɔ:)?.

ow   » blow: (o:u).

e'w, u » ne'w, due: ('iu) or (i'u:).

ew   ·» few: (e:u).

oi   » ịoy: (ɔi).

ooi   » booil: (ui) rather than (u:i).

uy   » ịuic', ịuyst: (əi)?.

ù   » natùr: (o), (ə).

ɭ   in aɭ, tụmbɭ: (ul), ([ə]l).

ᴍ   » caɭᴍ, charᴍ: ([u]m), ([ə]m).

ɴ   » daɴc', báɾɴ: (un), ([ə]n).

ʀ   » fiʀ*i*ng, natʀal: (ər).

ż   » owerż: (z).

ʒ,ʒ̃ » proofʒ, pe'c'eʒ, hedʒʒ̃: (s), (z).

c' in c'æs: (s).

c   » can: (k).

g   » go: (g).

g' » g'entɭ: (dʒ).

h   » he': (h).

h   » liht, browht: (ç), (χ).

ị   » ịoy: (dʒ).

q   » qe'n: (kw).

s   » se': (s).

ṣ   » diu'erṣ: (z).

t   » too: (t).

ṭ   » naṭion: (s).

th » this: (đ).

tḥ » think: (þ).

u' » hau': (v).

v' » v'ery: (v).

w   » will: (w).

wh » what: (ʍ).

y   » yes: (j).

ʒ   » iʒ: (z).

Specimen Page

(see **facsimile** opposite p. XIV, and Fables, p. 53).

81. Of Jupiter and the Aap.

Jupiter græt/y-deȝýr*i*ng ţoo know whoo of mortaɭ [creátừrż] browht-fọrtħ the trim*e*st ħọng-ónż, commaɴdęţħ whatsoeu'er liu'*i*ng tħing iȝ any-whær ţoo be' caɭ*e*d-toogether. They rụn-toogether too Jupiter from-eu'ery-whær, the kýnd of fọwlż and bæst⁊ ɯær pre$ent ọr cọm*m*:] among whooɱ when the aap cám-thither, toó, bær*i*ng hir il-fau'ọr*e*d kitling⁊ on hir arм, no-man coụld temper*a*t ọr mæȝur [him-self] from laụh*i*ng, bụt Jupiter him-self laụhęd v'ery-exc'e'd*i*ng/y toó. The aap her-self sayęţħ thær by-and-by, ħe mary, Jupiter toó oụr įụdg' knowęţħ that my kitling⁊ græt/y exc'el aɭ họw many soeu'er be' he'r.

The moral.

Ónż-owɴ iȝ faier too eu'ery-ón: aȝ the prou'erb iȝ. And elc'-whær in Ţheocritụs. Thóȝ tħing⁊ that be' læst fair ọr fọwl*e*st] se'm fair too ón lọu'*i*ng them.

82. Of the ók and the re'd.

'The ók be'*i*ng v'ery-fụl of disdain and prýd goęţħ too the re'd, say*i*ng, if thụ hau' a cọrag'*i*ọs brest ọr stọmak,] cọm-on ţoo the fiht

In phonetic transcription:

ɔv dȝiu:pitər ænd đe e:p. dȝiu:pitər gre:tli dezeiriŋ tu: kno:u *мu: ɔv mɔrtaul kree:tərz *brouχt forþ đe trimest joŋ o:nz, kɔmaundeþ *мætso:evər liviŋ þiŋ iz æniмe:r tu: bi: kauled

---

[1] The unstressed vowels have been rendered more in accordance with Bullokar's spelling than with the actual pronunciation. I have used (ə) only before *r*. The starred forms indicate words the pronunciation of which cannot be shown in Bullokar's amended orthography. Naturally the colloquial pronunciation came much closer to Present English speech than this specimen of Bullokar's quaint and old-fashioned English.

tu:geðər. ðɛ:i ron tu:geðər tu: dʒiu:pitər frɔm evəriʌe:r, ðe
keind ɔv foulz ænd be:sts we:r prezent ɔr kom, æmɔŋ *ʌu:m
ʌen ðe e:p ke:m ðiðər tu: be:riŋ hər ilfævə(re)d kitliŋz ɔn hər
ær(ə)m, no: mæn ku:ld tempəræt ɔr me:ziur himself frɔm *lauχiŋ,
bot dʒiu:pitər himself *lauχed veri eksi:diŋli tu:, ðe e:p hərself
sɛ:ieþ ðe:r, bei ænd bei, ji: mæri, dʒiu:pitər tu: our dʒodʒ
kno:ueþ ðæt mei kitliŋz gre:tli eksel aul hou mæni so:evər bi:
hi:r. ðe mɔræl. o:nz o:un iz fɛ:iər tu: evəri o:n, æz ðe prɔvərb
iz. ænd elsʌe:r in þeɔkritos. ðo:z þiŋz ðæt bi: le:st fɛ:ir ɔr
foulest si:m fɛ:ir tu: o:n loviŋ ðem. — ɔv ðe o:k ænd ðe ri:d. ðe
o:k bi:iŋ veri fol ɔv disdɛ:in ænd preid go:eþ tu: ðe ri:d, sɛ:iiŋ,
if ðo hæv æ kore:dʒios brest ɔr stomæk kom ɔn tu: ðe fiçt.

Additions of Corrections.

p. 12, n. 1. — read ME. *i* for ME. *oi.*

p. 22, l. 19. — read: Cootes 1596.

p. 34, l. 11. — read: Spenser.

p. 51 ff. — The following additional instances showing the
change of *er* to *ar* and the orthographic interchange between
ir, er, and *ur* have been kindly communicated by Dr. Wallen-
berg for Kent and by Mr. H. Orton for the northern counties.

1. *er* for *er.*

13th century. — *Marchesden, Marchdene* 1246 Ass. R.
= Marsden, Lancs. (OE. *mercels,* Ekwall p. 86); *Casterne*
1256 Ass. R. = Caistron, Northb. (ME. *kers,* Mawer, p. 37);
Charring 1243 Cl. R., *Charring* 1298 Pat. R. = Charing
(Cross), Mds. (OE. *c(i)erring*); *Hartlep,* 1219 Book of Fees
= Hartlip, Kent (OE. *heor(o)t*); *Merdenn, Mardenn'* 1275 HR.
= Marden, Kent (OE. *mere* or *mēre*); *Margate* 1293 RBE.
= Margate, Kent (OE. *mere* or *mēre*); *Bakeshore* 1275 HR.
= Barksore, Kent (OE. *Beor(n)ric?*).

14th century. — *Barton* 1388 Cl. R. = Barton (lost) in Boughton, Kent (OE. *beretun*); *Charleton* 1326 PF., 1354 Pat. R., 1387 Cl. R. = Charlton (115 A 6), Kent; *Charleton* 1327 IPM., *Charletone* 1320, *ibid.* = Charlton (lost) near Dover, Kent; *Sarre* 1313 Pat. R., 1339 Cl. R. = Sarre, Kent (OE. *Serræ, Seorre* 761 CS. 189); *Margate* 1316 Pat. R., 1345 Cl. R. = Margate, Kent.

2. Confusion between *ir, er, ur*.

13th century. — *Scoland* 1242—3 Book of Fees = Shulland (lost) in Newnham, Kent (*Shirelond', Schirlande* 1278, 1293 QW.).

14th century. — *Sholond* 1337 Cl. R. = Shulland, Kent.

16th century. — *serples* 1552 Church Inventory of Relington, 16; *tirkes* ('Turks') 1586 Durh. Wills (Surtees Soc., 38, p. 156); *perse* ('purse') 1587, *ibid.*

The early change of *ir* to *ur* in Shulland, Kent, is probably due to special causes. Note also spellings in early American English such as *pursin* ('person') 1686, *survice* ('service') 1658, *sturling* ('sterling') 1664, *surtifi* ('certify'), 1670, *porson* ('person') 1670 (Krapp, pp. 170—172).

p. 55, l. 9. — read: Wallis 1653, Gill 1621.

p. 59, n. 1. — Thurot I, pp. 244 ff., adduces numerous early French forms with *ou* for *o*, not only when unstressed, but also in a stressed position, e. g. *voutre, noutres* (Meigret), *chouse* ('chose') (H. Estienne), *giroufle* (Lanoue), *estouffe* (Tabourot). Similar instances from 'the popular language' are noted by Rosset, p. 81 (*roube, tresour, grous, drougue* etc.). This vacillation may also account for Bullokar's o in *stomach, comfort* (cf. p. 74) and for his ó in *astóned* (cf. p. 78).

p. 66, n. 2. — I do not consider it improbable that *ew* in Standard English *drew, slew* (cf. *slew3, slewen*, Wyclif, and the material adduced by Price, p. 154) is merely an inverted spelling for (uː), on the analogy of *brew, blew* etc. where *iu* had been reduced to (uː).

p. 74. — The vacillation between ǫ and o in *word* etc. may also be due to the fact that Bullokar's pronunciation of ŭ from ME. *wŭr* differed from his pronunciation of ME. ŭ from other sources, as in *come* etc. In the former case he may have used (u) or (ə), in the latter (o)?

p. 91. — During a recent visit to Teignmouth I took a great deal of pains to analyse the dialectal sound used for *o* in *do* and for *ew* in *new*. In this part of Devonshire the old vernacular forms are dying out rapidly. In point of fact, I made the same observation here as in Dorsetshire a few years ago: dialect is looked down upon as an inferior kind of language. People born in Teignmouth or in the neighbouring towns and villages seem to have a fair knowledge of the dialect, but they carefully avoid making any use of it, at least when they talk to people belonging to the educated classes. Vernacular features crop up occasionally, especially in the pronunciation of local names. I often heard (nü:tn) for Newton Abbot, (lü:tn) for Luton, (nü:mən) for Newman — the present owner of Mamhead House — (pəudrəm) for Powderham etc. ME. *o* in *do, two*[1] etc. is pronounced with exactly the same sound as ME. *eu* in *new*. This sound, which I heard from at least a dozen different Devonians and once from a young girl born in Taunton in Somerset, is identical with (ü:) in the Swedish word 'hus', possibly somewhat lower.

In some cases, as in *do, two,* it is preceded by a faint vocal murmur. It deserves being pointed out that Mr. W. Weeks, who has written several books in Devonshire dialect, remarks in his preface to Devonshire Yarns (Exeter, 1926): 'The French '*u*' is perhaps a nearer approximation to the Devonshire 'u' or 'oo' than any other English sound, but, of course, it is not quite the same.'

It will be seen from this survey that the southern vernaculars agree with the eastern dialects in rendering ME. *o* in *do* and ME. *eu* in *new* with (ü:). On one occasion I heard (a) for (ɔ) in *top,* and I was informed that (o) for ME. *u* in *come* also

---

[1] 'Do you know him?', becomes in the vernacular (dü:i′nɔ:im).

occurs in Devonshire, e. g. in *purse*. Consequently it looks as if the western and the eastern dialects have a good many phonetic features in common.[1]

In his EDG. § 162, Professor Wright notes *iu*, i. e. (ü:), for *ō* in Bedfordshire and Hertfordshire, and, according to Professor Wyld, this sound, or a near approch to it, is occasionally heard in Oxfordshire also. This may account for the sporadic spellings with *eu* and *u* for ME. *ō* which I have quoted from the Verney Memoirs (the family owned land in Oxfordshire) (cf. above, p. 139).

Lastly it should be noted that Wright's dialectal [jiu, jiü] for *you* and [jiu] for *yew-tree* (EDG., pp. 694, 695), in all probability, are due to a wrong analysis of (jü:) (cf. above, p. 99).

p. 103. — My explanation of (ai) for (ɔi) in *employ* and *rejoice* gains in probability by the occurence of similar forms in modern English dialects, e. g. (tʃais) for 'choice' and (naiz, nəiz, nʌiz) for 'noise' (Wright, EDG., pp. 375, 543 f.).

p. 121. — After closer consideration I am inclined to derive *rather*, vb., from the adverb *rather*, dial., in the sense of 'earlier'; hence *rathered* = 'quickened', 'early'. Note also that *r* in *gester*, possibly is a printer's error for *n*, these two minim letters being much alike in contemporary writings.

p. 134, l. 7. — For the date of the MSS. in which the Hymn to the Virgin is contained, see Förster, Archiv, 1926.

p. 139. — Additional instances of e. NE. *ou* for ME. *eu, u* are *oumer* ('humour') in a letter by Lady Southampton (1599) (Hist. MSS. Comm. III), and *dowkes* 1463, *Touesday* 1722, *ousse, stowarde, vallow* (no date) in Suffolk records (Binzel 47). As the dialectal form *trʋu* (+ *trü:*) noted by Wright (EDGr. p. 657) for Suffolk, and quoted by the present writer in the Luick Celebration Vol. (p. 146), may be an inaccurate notation for (əü:) or due to ME. *trow < trēow* (cf. e. NE. [au] in *toward* and Wright EDGr. § 193)[2] it is most probable that all the South-

---

[1] As for *a* for *o* and (o) for *u* in Eastern dialects, cf. above, pp. 58, 70.

[2] The form *chow*, vb. (see NED.) = 'chew' I have heard in colloquial use in London.

ern spellings with *ou* for *ęu, u,* and with *ew, yu* for *ǭ* indicate
that ME. *ō* in *do,* and *ęu* in *new, duke* had been levelled under
a common sound, although it is extremely difficult to settle, on
account of the scanty material, if this common sound was
Standard English (u:) or the dialectal (ü:).   As the spellings in
question are not entirely confined to Eastern letters and documents (cf. *sowertes* 93, *Ƶowll* 123, *contenow* 134, Cely Papers,
oumer, Lady Southampton, *acoused,* Paston Letters 252, written
by Worcester, who was born at Bristol)[1], and as *ou* is no likely
graphic representative for (ü:), we may, after all, have to reckon
with an early levelling of *ęu* and *ǭ* under the same sound not
only in the East but also in other dialectal areas.

The ME. instances of *ou* for French (y:) in Northern texts
(cf. Behrens, p. 118, Luick HEG. § 412, Jordan p. 206), on the
other hand, are best explained as due to the substitution of the
undiphthongized Northern (u:), as in *house,* for the French sound.
I look upon *dour,* which is first evidenced in Northern texts
(see NED.) and often applied to people of Scotch origin, 'a dour
Scotchman', as a Northern form, which has been introduced into
Standard English.

---

[1] Cf. also the instances given by Diehl, p. 176, and Grünzinger, p. 84.

WORD-LISTS

Word=Lists.

The word-lists have been collected from all Bullokar's texts (FA., BL., BG., PG). They do not comprise all words used by Bullokar; I trust, however, that no forms of importance for our knowledge of the contemporary pronunciation have escaped my notice. To words always written in the same way only one or two references have been given; of words spelt in more ways than one a greater number of forms have been noted. BG. has been excerpted with particular care, this being Bullokar's last and consequently most reliable text. Bullokar's symbols have been rendered according to the principles adopted by Plessow in his reprints. The figures after the words refer to the page in Plessow's reprints; the figures at the top of the words refer to critical notes placed after the lists. These notes should always be consulted by those who intend to use the lists.[1]

Before using the word-lists the reader should carefully go through the remarks on pp. 14—21.

Note especially that Bullokar's *oṷ* may stand both for ME. *ū* and *ọ̄*, more seldom *ŭ*, and that his *e'* in certain words may stand for *ĭ* short.

All forms of irregular verbs are given under the infinitive.

Adverbs are as a rule given together with the adjectives from which they are derived.

I must ask the reader's indulgence for several inaccuracies in the alphabetical order of the words.

---

[1] To collect and arrange the words has been a very laborious and time-absorbing task. I have taken great pains to make the lists as correct as possible. A few variant symbols for *f, r, s, sh* as well as certain inflection marks under the first letter of strong verbs etc. have been omitted, as they are useless for settling the pronunciation.

A.

a: a, an 3.
abbreviation: abbreu'iaţion 339.
abhor: aḃŏr 379.
abide: abód 69, abýdd³⁾ 98, abýddn³⁾ 5.
ability: ability 5.
ablative: ablatiu'*ly* 392.
able: ábĺ 5, 348.
abominable: abŏminábĺ 373.
about: aboųt 340, 371.
above: aḅọu' 348.
abroad: a-bród 4, 366, 371.
absolutely: absolut*ly* 341, 364.
abundant: aboųndant³⁾ 142.
abuse (*sb.*): ab-vc' 374.
abuse (*v.*): ab-vȝ 374.
accept: acc'ept*e*d 11.
acceptance: acc'eptanc' 338.
according: accord*i*ng 3, 342, 381.
accordingly: accord*i*ng*ly* 6.
account (*sb.*): accoųnt 382.
account (*v.*): accoųnt*e*d 17, 118, 168, accǫmpt*e*d¹⁾ 112.
accusative: Accuşatiu' 340.
accuse: accuȝ 221, 383, accu-şed 9.
accustom: accųstǫm*e*d 385.

ache: ák*e*d 108.
acknowledge: acknow*l*edg'*i*ng 74³⁾.
acquaint: acqeint*e*d 6.
action: acţion 5.
active: actiu' 353.
Adam (*n. pr.*): Adam 319.
add: ad*e*d 3.
adder: adder 33.
addition: ad*i*ţion 340.
adjective: Adjectiu' 340.
administrator: administrátorȝ (cf. p. 7).
advance: au'aɴc'*i*ng 70.
advantage: adu'antag' 145.
adverb: adu'erb 290, 348.
adverbial: adu'erb*i*al 348.
adverbially: adu'erb*i*al*ly* 348.
adversative: adu'ersatiu'ʔ 357, 369.
advice: adu'ýc' 3, 347, adu'yc'²⁾ 106.
advise: adu'yȝ²⁾ 29, adu'iȝest²⁾ 70, adu'yȝetḥ²⁾ 71.
advisedly: adu'iȝed*ly*²⁾ 7.
Æsop (*n. pr.*): Æşopʔ 5, 8.
affair: affairȝ 8.
affirm: affirᴍ 39, affirᴍ*i*ng 348, 366.

afford: affórd 377, 379.
aforesaid: afór-said 315.
after: after 3, 8, 370.
afterward: afterward 6, 9.
again: agein 10, 11, 338.
against: ageinst 5, 14, 371, against 15.
Agathopus (n. pr.): Agathopus 9.
age: ág' 4, 8.
ago: ago[2)] 366.
agreeable: agre'abl 3.
ague: agu 139.
ah: ah hah ha (laughter) 373, aá-horṣnż (interjection) 373.
aid: aided 374.
air: air 56, ayr 78, aiʀ 97.
alarm: al-arm 52.
alas: alas 373.
ale: ál-hows 191.
alive: a-lýu' 128.
all: al 4, 360.
alledge: alleg' 23.
allow: alow 379, aloweth 379, alowed 6, alow or low 382.
allure: allured 19.
ally: alýż 76.
Almaine = Germany (n. pr.): Almain 188.
almond: almond̦ 137.
alms: almż 102.
aloft: a-loft 31.
alone: alón 62, 337.
along: along 371.
aloud: alowd 26.
already: alredy 362.
also: also 3, 8, 378.

altar: altarż 21.
alter: altered 4, 5, 6, altering 337.
although: al-thowh 357, 369.
altogether: altoogether 367.
always: alway 340, alwaiż 320.
amaze: amáżed 81, 316.
ambush: ambush 160.
amend: amended 4.
amendment: amendment 3.
amiss: amis 343.
Ammarius (n. pr.): Ammarrius 8.
among: among 316, among 5, 367, 378.
amply: ampli 350.
ancestor: aɴc'etorż 145.
ancient: aɴc'ient 69, 78.
and: and 3.
andiron: aɴdýʀn 292.
anger: anger 264.
angry: angri 10, 11, 354.
anguish: anguish 274[1)].
annex: annexed 369.
answer: answer[1)] 339, answereth[1)] 365, answered 5[1)],
answeratively: answeratiu'ly[1)] 357.
antecedent: antec'edent 345, antec'edenț 13.
any: any 4, 381, 220.
any more: any-mór 9.
any one: any-ón 349, 382.
apart: a-part 366.
ape: Aap 34, 53.
aphæresis: Apheresis 382.
apish: ápish 46.

Apollo (*n. pr.*): Apollo 128, Apolloż ib.

apparel: apparel 31, appareled 72.

appear: appe'r 83, 386, appe'- ręth 4, appe'rż 299.

appease: appæʒ 182, a-pæc'ęd²⁾ 123.

appellatively: appellatiu'ly 340.

appertainant: apperteinant 381.

appertainingly: apperteiningly 381.

appliable: appliabl⁽²⁾ 380.

apply: applyed²⁾ 9, 345.

appoint: appooint 44, appoointed 20, appoointtḥ 334.

apposition: appoṣition 370.

appositively: appoṣitiu'ly 372.

approach: aproch 326, aproching 49.

aptness: aptnesɟ 380.

archbishop: arch-bishopɟ 188.

archer: archorż 110.

argue: argu 381.

argument: argument 6.

Argus (*n. pr.*): Argus 107.

Arion (*n. pr.*): Ario 80.

arise: aróʒ 78.

armour: arмǫor 104.

army: army 87.

array: aray or ray 382, araied 57.

arrow: arrowż 370.

arsehole: ars-hól 108.

art: art 3, 337, árt Tab. II.

artichoke: artichokɟ 262.

article: articl 339, articlż 5, 339.

as: aʒ 3, 373.

ashamed: a-shámed 12.

ask: asking 10, 11, 349, 365.

aspiration: aspýrac'ion³⁾ 322.

ass: as 16.

assailing: assailing 90.

assault: assaltɟ 14.

assay: assaying 27.

assign: assignż¹⁾ (cf. p. 7).

Assyrian: Assirians 287.

assuage: aswag' 89.

astoned: astóned 15, astǫned 79.

asunder: asŭnder 62, 366.

at: at 86.

at last: at last 366.

at least: at-lǣst 370.

at the least: at the-lǣst 370.

attain: attain 333.

attending: attendíng 370.

attorney: attŭrnyż 5.

audible: aŭdibl 8.

August: Aŭgŭst 3.

author: autǒr¹⁾ 6, aŭtor 219, aŭtǒrż 6, 7, 8, 382, Autǒrż¹⁾ 7.

antumn: autŭm 324.

avoid: au'oyd 347.

awake: awák 326, awákęth 9.

away: away 9, 366.

awe: aw 218.

axe: ax 27.

B.

Baal (*n. pr.*): baal 287.

babble (*sb.*): babl 268.

babbler: bablorż 93.

babe: báb 343.

bachelorship: bachiler-ship 92.

back (*sb.*): bak 343.

bacon: bácɴ 269.

bad: bad 334.

bailie: baily 10, 11.

balance: ballanc' 287.

bald: bald¹⁾ 195, bałd 59, 139, 195, 287.

bale: bál 287.

ball: bałź 97.

balm (*ointment*): bałᴍ 287.

balm (*plant*): baulᴍ 287.

band: band 66, 317.

bank: bank 380.

banquet: banket 11.

barbarous: barbarǫs 323.

bare: bär (or læn) 288.

bar (*legal term*): bar 218, 343.

bark: bark 24, 326.

barley: barly 13.

barn: bárɴ 269, 288, 315, barnź, barɴ 344.

baron: Baron 380.

barren: barren 269, barenꭍt 334.

base: bás 337, 382, básest 21.

battle: battełź 23, battailź 104.

bay (*colour*): bay 287.

bay-tree: bay-tre' 287.

be: be' 3, 4, am, art, iȝ, ar, 358, ar 4, 6, 8, ár 260, 264, 312, be'ɪng 3, be'n 5, 6, waȝ 5, 6, wær 3, 4.

beak: bæk 78.

beam: bæm 22.

bean (*sb.*): bæn 274.

bear (*v.*): bær 20, 28, 336, 349, 378, bár (= bore pt.) 99, bór 106, 60, borɴ 9, 23, 107, 189, 293.

born (*natus*): bórɴ 11, 24, 292, borɴ 88, 334.

bear (*sb.*): bár 97, 122, 132, 288, bárź 101.

beard: berdꭍ 84.

beast: bæst 10, 338.

beat (*v.*): bæt 14, bætɴ 9.

beautify: bewtify 325.

beauty: bewty 127.

beautiful: beụty-fʉl 28.

beaver: beu'er 134, 163.

because: bicaụȝ 4, 5, 315, by-caụȝ 346.

beck: bekɪng 190.

become: be'cǫmęth 21.

bed: bed 324.

bed-gear: bed-ge'r 83.

bee: be'e'ź 195, be'e' 122, 171.

beef: be'u'ꭍ (pl.) 344.

before: be'fór 3, 4, 5, 8, 347.

beg: begęth 69.

begin: be'gin 8, be'ginɪng 4, be'gan 3, 38, be'gʉn 21.

behalf: be'hałf 6.

behave: be'hau'ed 73.

behaviour: be'hau'ǫor 187.

behind: be'hýnd 371.

behold: be'hóldɪng 10, 100, 101, be'hóld 96, 333, be'hołd 325, beholdn 36, be'held 32.

behove: be'hoou'ęth 71, 363.

believe: be'le'u' 39, be'left 46.
Bellinshurst (*n. pr.*): *h* can be
   distinctly pronounced 277.
belly: bely 11.
belong: be'long*i*ng 380.
beloved: be'-lǫu'*e*d 348.
bend: bend*e*d 92, bend*i*ng 17,
   bent 98.
beneath: be'næth 13.
benefit: benefit 9.
bereave: be'reft 60, be'ræu'*e*d
   333.
beseech: be'se'chẹd 14.
besiege: be'se'g'*d* 338.
best: best 7.
bestow: be'stow*e*d 381.
betoken: be'tókNẹth 347, 373.
betray: be'tray 35.
better (*a.*): better 6.
better (*v.*): bettʀ*i*ng 334.
between: be'twe'n 3, 8, 313,
   370.
betwixt: twixt for be'twixt 382.
bewray: be'wrayẹth 232.
beyond: be'ɦond 371.
bid: bidẹth 12, 353, bidḍ 11.
bill: bil 349.
bind: boụnd 58.
bird: bird 349, bird7 7, 18.
bird-lime: bird-lým 77.
birth: birth 8, 29.
bite: být 43, 126, býtţ³⁾ (pp.) 155,
   býtţN³⁾ 16, být*t*N³⁾ 155, 294.
black: blak 8.
blame: blám 95, blám*i*ng 18.
blast: blast 62, blast7 157.

bleat: blæt 120.
blight: bliht 325, bliht7 78.
block: blok 10.
blood: blụd 55.
blow: ble'w 19, blowℜ 10.
boar: bór 16, 67.
board (*sb.*): boord 17, 161.
board (*v.*): boord*e*d 82.
boast: bóst*e*d 17.
body: body 9, 325, 335, bodýȝ
   319.
Boethius (*n. pr.*): Boeţiụs 21.
boil: booil*i*ng 90.
bold: bóld 21, 66, 347, bóld*l*y
   44.
Bonacius (*n. pr.*): Bonac'iụs 185.
bond (*a.*): bond 43.
bondage: bond-ag' 8.
bondman: bond-man 8.
book: Book 5, 370.
booth: boụth 291.
borderer: borderorż 79.
Bosham: *h* can be distinctly
   pronounced 277.
bosom: bǫȝom 72, boȝǫm 258.
both: bóth 3, 7, 319, 335, 337,
   340, 350, 360, 370, both¹⁾
   351, bóth 315, 325, 326.
botts: bot7 290.
bottle: botĺ 10.
bough: bǫwh 49, bǫwż 18,
   bowh¹⁾ 291.
bourn: boụrN¹⁾ 293.
bow (*sb.*): bow 48, 92, 341.
bow (*v.*): bǫwẹth 62.
bowels: bǫwelż 288, bǫwel 291.

bowl: bowl 291.
bowl (= *ball*): boṵl 291.
box: box 343.
boy: boy 46, boyż 10.
boistious (*see NED.*): bo̢stio̢s 25, boystio̢s 258.
brace: brac', brac'ęd, brac'ṭ 363.
brag: bragíng 24.
brake: brâk (for a hors) 288.
brake: bräk or ferɴ-tṵf 288.
brake: braak (for hemp) 288.
brake: brák (or cros-bow) 288.
brack: brak (ruptura) 288.
bramble: brambĺ 145.
branch· (*sb.*): braɴcheʒ 78.
branch (*v.*): braɴched 32.
brand-iron: brondýrɴ 292.
brass: bras 60.
brave: O-bráu' 373.
brazen: braʒɴ 60.
bread: bred 24, 43.
breadth: bredtḥ 348, 381.
break: bræk 131, brák 341 (pt.), brókɴ 18, 27.
breast: brest 54, 98, 125.
breath: bretḥ 59, 264, bretḥ 132, brætḥ 74, 155, bræthtḥ[3] 129.
breathe: bræthíng 8.
breed: bre'd 326, bre'dḍ 69[3].
breeder: bre'dor 49.
bridge: bridg' 343.
brief: bre'f 5, 8, bre'fĺy 4, 8.
bright: briht 13.
brim: brimż 84.
brine: brýn 172.

bring: bring 334, 370, bringętḥ 9, browht, browht 16, 380.
Britain (*n. pr.*): Britain 326.
broad: bród 78, 348, 365, bródwiʒ 367, bróder 94.
broach: brocheʒ 166.
brood: brood 24.
brook: brook 26.
broom: broomż 82.
broth: brotḥ 67, 172.
brown: bro̢wn 43.
brow: browż 17.
bruise (*v.*): bruʒętḥ 69, brou̢ʒd 103.
brute: brut 158.
brutish: brutísh 324.
bucket: bu̢cket 65.
buckler: bu̢cler 293.
bud: budʒ 325.
build: bild[2] 59, býld 77, 82, býldíng 82, 88.
building: bildíngʒ[2] 59.
buoy: booy 285.
bulk: bu̢lk 215.
bull: bu̢l 19.
bullock: bu̢llokʒ 340.
Bullokar: Bu̢llokar 3.
bulrush: bu̢l-rish 14.
burden: bu̢rdɴ 18, 34.
burn: bu̢rɴíng 11, 91, bu̢rɴd 324.
bury: buryíng[1] 107, 212.
bush: bu̢sh 59.
but: bu̢t 4, 5, 8, 276, 334, 348.
butcher: bu̢tchor 135.
butt (*sb.*): bo̢t 349.

butt (*v.*): bǫǫt (aȝ a she'p) 291, 349, bųtẹd 114.
buttock: bųttok͆ 34.
button: bųtɴ 260.
business: bųȝiɴes[1] 22, 44, 156, bųȝiɴes͆[1] 52.
buy: biy 10, 11, 38, 90, byiɴg[2] 101, 132, 312, bowht 291.
buyer: biyor 191.
by: by[2] 3, 8.
by and bye: by[2]-and-by[2] 366.

C.

cabin: caben 146.
calamity: calamity 50.
calf: caĺf 87.
call: caĺ 338, caĺed 5, 372.
callet (*sb.*): callet 288.
calm: caĺm 268, caĺmɛr 85.
camel: camel 58.
can: can 4, 353, canst 11, coųld[1] 3, 6, 8, 11, 353.
cankered: cancerd 325 (2×).
cane: cán 156.
capable: cápabĺ 7, cápábĺ 375.
capital: capitaĺ 3.
capon: cápɴ͆ 87.
captive: captiv' 20.
care: cár 7, cár͆ 18.
carefulness: cárfųlɴes 17.
cark (*sb.*): cark 334.
carl: cárĺ 268.
carman: car-man 31.
carrion: carain 155, carren- 52.
cart: cart 66, cart͆ 90.

Carthage (*n. pr.*): Cartḩag' 223.
carver: caru'or͆ 28.
cask: cask 10.
cast: cast 323, castẹtḩ 9, cast�860t 22.
catch: catchiɴg 159, caųht 16.
caterpillar: caterpillar 325.
Cato (*n. pr.*): Cato 5, 213, 215, 216, 217.
cattle: cattel, 10, 345.
caul: caųl 288, cawl 16.
cauldron: cawdern͆ 166, caų-dorɴ 292.
cause (*v.*): caųȝ 45, 338, caų-sẹtḩ[1] 323.
cause (*sb.*): caųȝ 368.
causey: cawsy 288.
cave: cáu'͆ 29.
cavil: cau'il 288.
cease: c'æs 182.
celebrate: c'elebrat 53.
Ceres: C'eres 84.
certain: c'ertein 3, 9, 371, c'erten 15.
chafe: cháfiɴg 30.
chaff: chaf 82.
challenge: chaleng' 15.
chamber: chaмber 273, bed-chamber 130.
chance: chaɴc' 15, 366.
Chancellor: Chaɴc'elor 380.
chancery: chaɴc'ery 3.
change: chaɴg' 19, 343, 345, 362.
chap = *chop*: chap 14.
charge (*sb.*): chárg' 189, charg' 312, chárg'e͆ 4, 5, 155, charg'e͆ 318, 342.

charge (*v.*): chárg' 107, charg'-
   *e*d 8.

chariot: chariot 90.

charitable: charitabl 81.

charm: charм 306.

chasten: chastn 306.

chastise: chástic'*e*d 138.

chastity: chást*i*ty[3] 102.

check: chekẹtḫ 70.

cheese: che'ʒ 19.

cherish: cherish*e*d 334.

cherry: che'rýż 262.

chest: chest 84.

chicken: chikñ 190.

chide: chýd*i*ng 66.

chief: che'f 350.

chief ruler: che'frul*o*r 9.

child: chýld 157, 334, chýld-
   dẻrɴ 10[3].

chimney: chimny 182.

chine: chýn 108.

chink: chink 190.

chitter: chitter 78.

chisel: che'ʒĺ 306.

choicative: choic'*a*tiu' 353, 362.

choice: choic' 8, 383.

choke: chóked 324.

choose: chuʒ[1] 106, 179, choo-
   ʒẹth 156, che'wʒ*i*ng[1] 366,
   370, chuʒ*i*ng[1] 106, chooʒ*i*ng
   121, chóʒ 23, chóʒɴ 48, 50,
   choʒ*ɴ* 106.

chop: chop*t* 262.

church: chụrch 178, 370.

churl: churĺ 16, 234, 262, 306,
   chórĺ 221.

Cicilian (*n. pr.*): C'ic'il*i*anż 32.

citizen: c'iti*s*en[3] 192, c'iti*s*enż[3]
   14.

city: c'ity 3, 339.

civil: ciu'il 321.

clad: clad 325.

claim: claim 13.

clap (*v.*): claptḫ 59.

Clapham (*n. pr.*): h can be distinctly pronounced 277.

clause: claụʒ 356, 368 etc.,
   claụse7[1] 350.

clay: clay 174.

clean: clæn 42.

clear (*v.*): cle'r 45.

cleave (= *stick*): clæu'ḍ 55.

clemency: clemenc'y 21.

cliff: clif 12, 65.

climb: clým 254, clim*i*ng[2] 95,
   143, climb*i*ng[1][2] 132, clim-
   ẹtḫ[2]66, clim*e*d[2] 59, climḍ[2]155.

close: clóʒ*e*d 72.

clothe: clóth*e*d 81, 104.

clothes: clóth7 82, 349, clótḫ7 337.

clothing: clóth*i*ng 104, clóth-
   *i*ng7 113.

cloud: clọwḍ7 61.

clown: clọwn 168, cloụnż 254.

club: clụb 20.

cluster: clụsterż 178.

coarse: coorc' 82.

coat: cót 66.

cocker: coker*i*ng 69.

cockle: cockĺ 18.

cod: cod 192.

coif: coif 297, coif7 297.

coin (*v.*): cooynęd 222.
cold: cóld 16, cóĺd ˙254.
collar: coller 288.
collect: collected 8.
collective: Collectiu'ʃ 340.
collier: cóĺꞇ̨or³⁾ 41, 127.
colour (*sb.*): cǫler 293.
colour (*v.*): cǫlǫred 71.
comb (*v.*): comb¹⁾ 296.
comb (*sb.*): comb¹⁾ 380.
come: cǫm 3, 5, 8, 335, cǫm-
    *i*ng 339, cám 10, 353, 372,
    cǫm 57, 363, cǫmm 25.
comeliness: cǫmlines 325.
comely: cǫmly ˙381.
comfort (*sb.*): comfort 334.
comfort (*v.*): cǫmfortęth 4.
comfortable: comfortabĺ 335.
command: commaᴜnd 337, com-
    maɴdęth 11, 353.
commandment: commaᴜndment
    361, commaɴdment 374.
commit: committed 4, commit-
    tęd 4, 9.
commodity: commodity 4, como-
    dity 381.
common: comᴜnest 6, commᴜ-
    nest 369.
commonly: commᴜnly 4, co-
    mᴜnly 339.
communication: communicac'ion
    67.
companion: cǫmpanionż 15.
company: cǫmpany 347.
comparative: compáratiu'³⁾ 347,
    367, -ĺy³⁾ 347.

compare: compárɪng 367, com-
    páred 335, 365.
comparison: compáriƺon³⁾ 71,
    100, 157, compárɪʃon³⁾ 347,
    367.
compass (*sb.*): cǫmpas 84, 372.
compass (*v.*): cǫmpased 25.
compel: compelęth 324.
complain: cǫmplainɪng 51, cǫm-
    playned 51, 189, cǫmplaynęd
    88.
composer: compóʃǫr 5, 385.
composition: compoƺic'iō 290,
    compoʃiꞇ̨ion 362, cómpoʃi-
    ꞇ̨ionż 368.
compositive: compoʃitiu' 348,
    compoƺitiu'ʃ 315.
compound: compoᴜndɪng 347,
    ˙compoᴜnded 362, compoᴜndd
    383.
conceit: conc'eit 5, 8, 337, 382.
conceive: conc'eiu' 335, conc'-
    eiu'ed 3, 375.
concern: conc'erɴɪng 4, conc'ern-
    ɪng 371.
concord: concordʃ 384.
condemn: condemɴ 383, con-
    demnęth 17, condemɴed 123.
conditional: condiꞇ̨ionaĺż 357.
coney: cǫnyż 115, coniż 288.
confer: confer 7.
conferrable: conferabĺ 337.
conference: conferenc' 346, 383.
confess: confes 6.
conjugation: coniugaꞇ̨ion 355.
conquer: coɴqer¹⁾ 371.

conqueror: conqeror[1] 37.

consanguinative: consanguina-tiu'7[1] 6, consanguinatiu'7 348.

conscience: consc'ienc' 336.

consider: consider 4.

consideration: consideraţion 5.

consist: consist 319.

consonant: consonant7 3.

Constance (*n. pr.*): Constanc' 185.

constrain: constrained 101.

construction: consrRuɔion[3] 372.

consume: cons'umed 325.

contain: conteining 5.

contempt: contempt 17.

content: content 383.

continue: continu 319.

continually: continually 5.

continuance: continuanc' 4, (*obsol.*): contʀ-adjectiu' 383.

contrarily: contrarily[3] 14, 20.

contrary: contrary 341.

cool (*v.*): cool 75.

coop: coop 87.

coot (*bird*): coot 292.

copulative: copulatiu' 350, 380, copulatiu'7 368.

cord: córd 40.

Corinth (*n. pr.*): Corinţh 80.

Corinthian: Corinţhianż 80.

corn: corɴ 13, córɴ 29, 45, 55, 64, 119, 159, 258, 364.

corpse: córs 162.

correct: corrected 4.

correction: correcţion 5.

corrupt: corrupt 8, corrupting 320.

costly: cosʒly 87.

couch: cooch 140.

council: coụnc'ĺ 9, 380.

counsellor: coụnsɫorż 5.

count: coụnt 382.

countenance: coụntenanc' 19, 373.

counter: coụnterż 370.

counterfeit: coụnterfeteţh 26.

country: coɳtrýż 319, -iż ib, coɳtry 381, coɳtryż 338.

couple: cop̣ĺ 350, cop̣lĭng 377, 378.

courage: cọrag' 8, 335.

courageous: cọrag'iọs[3] 54.

course: coụrs[1] 4, 7, 336, coụrc'[1] 324.

course (*v.*): coụrsĭng[1] 90.

court: coụrt 5[1].

courteous: coụrtiọs[1] 98.

courtesy: coụrtiọsi[1] 12.

cousin: cọʒɴż 50.

covenant: cọu'nant 57.

covetousness: cọu'etọosɴes 15.

crab: crab 254, crab7 56.

cradle: crádĺ 268.

crafty: crafti

crane: crán 15.

crave: crau' 32, cráu' 34, 51, 65, 333, 337, 379, 384, cráu'-ĭng 118, 182, 381, crau'ĭng 259, cráu'eţh 9, 79, 384, cráu'ţh 378, 379, 383, crau'ed 32, cráu'ęd 118, 192, cráu'ed 381.

creak: cræ̆kĭng 117.

create: creátẹd 115.

creature: creatừr 43, creátừrʒ 53, creatừrż 61, cræturż 319.

credit (*sb.*): credit 24, 338.

creek: cre'k 254.

creep: cræp 37, cre'píng 56, cræpíng 56, cre'pẹtħ 17, 29, cræpẹtħ 21, cræpţt³⁾ 36, 74, crept 321.

crime: crým 383.

Crinitus (*n. pr.*): Crinitụs 78.

crocodile: crocodil 145.

crook-backed: crook-bakt 8.

crooked: crookẹd 92, 325.

crook-legged: crook-legẹd 8.

crop: crop 22, cropţ 344.

crouch: crǫwchẹd 8, croocht 110.

crow: crow 18, crowíng 169, crawẹth 164.

crown: crǫṇż 190.

cruel: cruel 19.

cry: crying²⁾ 10, 373.

cub: cụb 44.

cuckoo: cụccoo 86.

cudgel: cụg'g'elẹd 74.

culver: cǫlu'er 41, cǫlu'erż 23.

Cumæ (*n. pr.*): Cuma (3×) 73.

cunning: cụníng 62.

cunningly: cụníngly 374.

curb: cụrb 254.

cure: cuʀ 58.

curse: cụrsíng 373, cụrsẹd 140 (pp.).

cut: cutt 63.

D.

daintiness: deintiɳes 17.

dale: dálż 105.

dam(e): dám 325, dam 326.

dance: daɴc' 72, daɴc'íng 72.

dancer: daɴc'ǫrż 72.

danger: daɴg'er 14, 17, daɴg'-erż 18, 22.

dare: dárẹtħ 141, dụrst 78.

dart: dart 36.

date: dátʔ 137.

dative: datiu' 383.

daughter: dauhter 89, 103, 162.

daub: dawbẹd 54.

day: day 3, 6.

dead: ded 16.

deaf: dæf 23.

deal (*sb.*): dæl 80.

dealing (*sb.*): dælíng 15.

dear: de'r 43, de'rer 190.

dearly: de'rly 154.

death: detħ 12, 338.

debt: det 26, 349.

deceased: dec'esẹd 102.

deceit: dec'eitʔ 24.

deck (*v.*): dekt 10.

declare: declár 365.

declinative (*gr. term.*): declýnatiu' 315.

decline: declýnẹd 339.

decree (*sb.*): decre' 187.

decrease: decræc' 382.

deed: de'd 17.

deer: de'r 345.

deface: defác'ẹd 375.

defalk: defalk 344.
defend: defend 381.
defer: defered 124.
deformed: deformedst 8.
degree: degre' 337.
delicately: delicatly 77.
delight (*v.*): deliht 336, 382, delihted 8.
delightable: delihtabl 375.
deliver: deliu'ered 8.
deliverance: deliu'ranc' 335.
Delphi (*n. pr.*): Delphi 12.
Delphian: Delphianż 12.
demonstratively: demonstratiu'ly 340.
den: denż 32.
Denbigh: Denbih 380.
deny: denyıng²⁾ 366, denyętḫ²⁾ 26, denýd 221, denýḍ 224.
depend: dependıng 365.
deride: derýd 228.
derivative: derýu'atiu'³⁾ 315, deriu'atiu' 348, derýu'atiu'ʒ³⁾ 348.
derivation: derýu'ation³⁾
description: descripțion 8.
desert (*sb.*): deʒertʒ 41.
deserve: deʒeru'ıng 4, deʒeru'-ed 9.
desire (*v.*): deʒýr 5, deʒýr 333, deʒýręd 9.
desirous: deʒýrǫos 43, 348.
desolate: deʒolat 326.
despair (*sb.*): dispair 312.
despise: despýʒ 63, 68, despýʒęd 31.

destitute: destitut 33.
destroy: destrooy 44, 47.
destruction: destrucțion 50.
detract: detract 5.
device (*sb.*): deu'ýc' 10, 216, 382.
devise (*v.*): deu'yʒ²⁾ 3, 48, deu'ýʒ 216, deu'ýʒed 75.
devil: diu'l 105.
devour: deu'oųr 9, 53, 79, deu'ǫred 48, deu'oųręd 113.
dice: dy²⁾ 259, dyż²⁾ 218.
dictionary: dicționary 6.
Diana (*n. pr.*): Diana 9, Dianaż²⁾ ib.
die: dy²⁾ 29, dięd²⁾ 12.
difference: differenc' 4.
dig: dig 9.
dignity: dignity 381.
digress: digres 324.
dike: dýk 158.
diligence: dilig'enc' 354.
diligently: dilig'ently 7.
diminish: diminished 347.
diminutively: diminitiu'ly 369.
dirt: dirt 101.
dis-: dis- 348, 374.
disallow: dis-alǫw 374.
discharge: dis-charg' 149, dischárg' 169.
discipline: disc'iplin 8, disc'iplin 78.
discomfort (*sb.*): dis-cǫmfort 312.
discrete: discre't 323.
discretive: discretiu'ʒ 369.
disdain (*sb.*): disdain 325, 373.

disease: dis-æȝeȝ 84.
dishonest: dis-ónest 374.
disjoin: dis-ĵooiniṇg 378.
disjunctive: dis-ĵṇunctiu' 350.
disobedient: disobei*d*ient[3] 255.
disorder: dis-order 6.
distinction: distincc'ionż 318.
distinguished: distinguiṣhed 364.
distinguish: distinguiṣhiṇg 345, 364.
dive: de'u' 175, de'u'*e*d 26, 175.
divers: diu'erȝ 321, diu'erṣ 336.
diversely: diu'erṣ*l*y 334.
divide: diu'ýd 15, 167, diu'ýd*e*d 339, 372.
division: deu'iȝionż 318.
divine: diu'ýn 8.
divinity: diu'ýn*i*ty[3] 6.
division: diu'iṣion 3, diu'iȝionż 312.

do: doo 4, 6, 10, 355, 362, did 16, 355, 362, didst 355, dooṣt 362, dootḥ 112, 362, dooth 376, dooṇn[3] 8, 362, doo*n*n[3] 9, 374.
doer: dooorż 12.
dog: dog 10, dogȝ 43
dolphin: dolphin 81.
dolt: dolt 16.
doltish: dolt*i*sh 16.
door: door 26, 192, dór 85, 108, 287, 297, dórż 85, doorż 120, 135.
dor (*insect*): dór 74, 97, 141, 198.
dormouse: dor-ṁýc' 96, 198.

dote: dótẹd 121.
double (*a.*): dọbĺ 345.
double (*v.*): dụbliṇg 57, 364, dụbĺed 65.
doubtful: doụt-fụl 8, 345.
dove: doou' 41.
down: dọwn, dọwn*e*r, dọwn*e*r-móst, dọwn-móst 371.
dozen: dọȝN 340.
draw: dre'w 17, 69, drawẹtḥ 69.
dress: dres, drest 12.
drink: drinkẹtḥ 9, drank 170, drụnk 169.
drive: driu'[2] 126, driu'iṇg[2] 32, drýu'ẹtḥ 41, 37, driu'ẹtḥ[2] 57, dryuℜ[1] 37, driu'*n* 133, 338, driu'en 320, drýu'*n*[3] 375.
drown: drọwn*e*d 156.
dry: dry[2] 82.
dubitative: dubitatiu'ȝ 369.
Dudley (*n. pr.*): Dụdley 380.
due: du 375.
duty: du*i*ż 319.
dumb: dụm 164.
dunghill: dụng-hil 13.
during: duriṇg 6.
dust: dụst 90.

E.

each: æch 317, 376.
each other: æch-ọther 40.
eagle: ægĺ 18, 31.
ear (*sb.*) (*auris*): ær 375, ærż 57, ærżȝ 344.
ear (*v.*): áriṇg 157.

ear (*sb.*) (*spica*): eerż 84, 197.
earl: Erl 380.
early: ærly 64, érly 77.
earnest (*subst.*): ernest 382.
earnest (*a.*): ernest 365.
earnestly: ernes*t*ly 11.
earnestness: ernest*n*es 374.
earth: erth̭ 59, 79, 380.
earthen: erth̭n 60.
earthly: erth̭ly 324.
easy: æʒi 3, 7, æʒier 339, æʒilier 7.
Easter term: Ester-term 5.
east wind: est wýnd 32.
eat (*v.*): æt 9, ætṱ[3] 149, 157, ætʀ 9.
Edmund (*n. pr.*): Edmṷnd 213.
eel: e'ĺ 90, 199.
effect: effect 4, 350.
effectual: effectu*a*l 72.
egg: eg7 68.
Egypt: Eg'ypt 72.
eight: eiht 339, 389.
eighteenth: eihte'nth̭ 275.
eighth: eiht*t*h̭
either (*pr.*): either 93.
either (*conj.*): ether 21, 369.
either or: either-or 320, either-or 340, ether-or 364, 378.
eke: æk 325, æk and -æk 368.
elder: elder 70, 215.
elective: electiu'7 369.
element: element7 318.
Eliot's Court (*n. pr.*): Eliot7 Coṷrt[1] 213.

elm: eĺm 199, 287, elm 287, 289.
elmen: elm*e*n 380.
else: elc' 338, 353.
embracing: embrac'*i*ng7 69.
emmet: emot 28, 325.
emperor: emperoṷr 326.
empire: empýʀ 94.
employ: imploy*e*d 381.
empty (*a.*): empty 383, empt*i* 41.
end (*v.*): end 62, end*i*ng 342, end*e*d 366.
endeavour: endeu'o̭r 8, 17.
endue: ende'w*e*d 71, ende'w*d* 383.
enemy: enimy 14, enemy 23, 338.
enforce: enforc' 163, 323, enfórc'*i*ng 31.
England: e'ngland 348.
English: E'nglish 3, 7, 8, 337.
English (*v.*): e'nglish*e*d 381.
Ennius (*n. pr.*): Enniṷs 77.
enough: ino̭wh 12, yno̭wh 14, 367.
ensample: ensampĺż 324.
ensign: ensýn 335.
entangle: entangĺed 46.
enterprise: enterpryc' 29.
entertainment: interteinm*e*nt 9, enterteinm*e*nt 9.
entice: entyc'ed[2] 48.
enticement: entic'ment[2] 75.
entrappings: en-trap*i*ng7 22.
entreat: entræt 21, intræt*e*d 4.
entreaty: entréti̭ż 122.

entry: entʀ*i* 167.

envy: enu'y 12.

Ephesus (*n. pr.*): Epheṣus 10.

Epimetheus (*n. pr.*): Epime-
theu̯s 22.

epistle: epistl*ż* 28.

equal: eqal 15, 167, 186, æqal
155, y̯n-eqal*ż* 103.

equivocal: eqiu'ocal 349.

equivoke: eqiu'oc 349, eqiu'oc⁊ 6.

err: er 145, erḍ 338, erḍd 381.

error: erọorż 162.

erst: erst 228, 235, ærst 221.

eschew: eshe'węth 152.

espy (*obs.*): espýd 324.

estate: estát 381.

esteem: este'm 13, 324.

estimation: estimaṭion 84.

-eth (*ending*): And, ȝ, for, ęth,
may chaɴg'*e*d be' ṭoo ṇe'ld
sọm v'érs hiȝ grác' tru*l*y 382.

etymology (*sb.*): etimolog' 316.

Eutrapelus (*n. pr.*): Eu̯trapelu̯s.

even (*adv.*): eu'ɴ 34, 338, 348,
374, eu'ɴ-aȝ 366.

even (adj.) e'u'ɴ 167.

evening: e'u'ning 23, eu'ning
107.

every: eu'ery 3, 348, eu'ry 315,
382.

every one: eu'ery-ónż 8.

evil: e'u'l̦ 17, 31, 357, e'u'l̦ż
347.

ewe: ew-she'p 289.

example (*sb.*): exampl̦ 3, 55,
343, exaᴍpl̦ż 8, 344, 368.

example (*v.*): exaᴍpl̦*e*d 372.

exceed: exc'ed 193, exc'e'd*i*ng
348, exc'e'dęth 347, exc'e'd-
*e*d 116.

exceedingly: exc'e'd*i*ng*l*y 54.

excel: exc'el 8.

except: exc'ept 4, 369.

exceptive: exc'ept*i*u'⁊ 357, ex-
c'eptiu'⁊ 369.

excess (*sb.*): exc'es 347.

exclude (*v.*): exclud*i*ng 367.

exercise (*sb.*): ęxerc'ýȝ 5, 258,
318, exerc'iż²⁾ 312.

exercise (*v.*): exerc'ýȝd 334.

excuse (*sb.*): excus 9.

excuse (*v.*): excuȝ 291.

execute: execut 326.

executor: execùtorż 125.

exhort: exȯrtęth 22.

explain: explán 8 (2 ×), explán-
*i*ng 7, explain*e*d 372.

express: expres*e*d 3.

extol (*v.*): extol*i*ng 90, extolęd
158.

extortion: extorṭion 123.

extract (*v.*): extract*e*d 339.

extremity: extrém*i*ty³⁾ 338.

eye (*s.*): yiż 35, 78.

eyed (*a.*): yi*e*d 107.

F.

Fable: Fábl̦ż 5, 8.

fade: vádęth 232.

fagot: fagot 40.

fail: fail 317.

faintness: faintɴes 335.

fair: faier 10, fair 325.

fall: faĺ 157, falę̣tḥ 9, fel 19, faĺɴ 9.

false: faĺs 19, 353.

familiar: familiar 8.

famine: famin 338.

fancy: fansy 99.

fardel: fardĺż 129.

farrow: farow 24.

farther: farder 5, 11, 315, 366.

fashion: fashon 8, fashion 189, fashionż 152.

fast (*v.*): fasti̇ng 56.

fasten: fastɴed 16.

fat: 52, 348.

father: father 14, 341, 353, 363, fatherż 148.

fatling: fatli̇ng 348.

fault: faĺt꜡ 74, 385.

faultless: faĺtl̸es 41.

fautor: faụtorż 219.

favour: fau'ǫr 29, 350, fau'ǫri̇ng 6, 8, 11, fau'ǫred 11.

fawn (*v.*): fawɴi̇ng 43, fawnę̣tḥ 20.

fear: fær 17, 373, færi̇ng 9.

feast: fæst 11.

feat: fæt꜡ 336.

feather: fetherż 18, 28.

feed: fe'd 26, fe'dd[3] 20, fe'dd̨[3] 46.

feel: fe'ltt[3] 339.

felicity: felic'ity 21.

fell (*v.*): feli̇ng 64.

fellow: felowż 31.

female: femál 345 (3×).

feminine: femenin 345.

fen: fen 14.

feoffee: feoffe[1] 381.

feofment: feofment꜡[1] 381.

fern-tuft: ferɴ-tụf 288.

few: few 4, 345, 374.

field-fare: fe'ld-fár 163.

fierce: fe'rc' 30, 43, 55, 151, fe'rc'er 133.

fierceness: færc'ɴes 19, fe'rc'ɴes 43.

fiery: fiʀi[2] 44.

fifteen: fifte'n 192.

fig: fig꜡ 9.

fight: fowht (pt.) 14, 123, 169.

figure: figur 341, figurż 3, 8.

figured: figùred 344, 381.

file: fýl 33.

fill: fil 17.

filthy: filtḥi 10.

finally: finall̸y 41, 366.

find: fýnd 5, foụnd 13, 370, 380.

finger: fingorż 55.

finish: finished 5.

fire: fier[2] 4, fiʀi̇ng[2] 44.

fir-tree: fir-tre' 63.

first: first 3, 9, firṣt (cf. p. 5).

fish: fishe꜡ 7.

fit (*a.*): fit 376.

fitly: fitl̸y 347.

five: fiu'[2] 322, fýu' 340, 353, 370.

Flaccus (*n. pr.*): Flaccụs 23.

Flanders (*n. pr.*): Flanderž7 380.
flat: flat 8.
flattery: flatteri 19.
flax: flax 21.
flea: flæž 107.
flee: fle'*d*d[3] 26.
fleece: flýc' 46, fle'c' 117, 141.
flesh: flesh 14.
flight: fliht 61.
float: flótęth 224.
flood: flụd 60, 162, 297.
floor: floor 109.
Florentine: Florentin[3] 185.
flourish: flọwR*i*sh*i*ng 78, flọr- ishęd 81.
flow: flow 46, flowN 86.
flower: flọwrž 78.
flush: flụsh 76.
flutter: flụtter 47.
fly: fly[2] 28, flyž[2] 85.
fly up: fly[2]-ựp 18.
foal: fól 268.
foam: fóm*i*ng 30.
foe: fọž[2] 335.
fodder: fodder 109, 289, food- *d*er[3] 190.
fold: fọld 326.
folk: folk[1] 92, 345, fólk7 114.
follow: folow*i*ng 5, 7, 8.
folly: fool*l*y[3] 223.
food: food 29.
foolish: fool*i*sh 13.
foot: foot 22, 349, fe't 9.
for (*prep.*): for 3, 337, fór[3] 350.
forbear: forborN 6.

forbid: forbid*i*ng 366, forbidd̦ 47.
force (*sb.*): fórc' 27, 30, 65, 103, 116, 157, 338, forc' 112, forc'7 218.
force (*v.*): fórc'*i*ng 373, forc'ęth 254, forc'ęd 102.
forehead: fórhed 32.
foreign: foren 335.
forge: fórg' 33, 92.
forgive: forge'u' 27.
fork: fork 40, 190, 307.
forlay: for-lay 5.
form (*v.*): forM 152 (2×), 342, 345, 371, fórM 367, forM*i*ng 363, 372, form*e*d 317, forM*e*d 344, 364, 366, 388.
formative: forMatiu' 343, 349, 382.
former (*adj.*): fórmer[3] 3, 5, 334, fórmer[3] 143, 318, 322, 370, 371, 374, 385, 387.
former (*sb.*): forM*o*r 343, fórM*o*r 349.
foremost: fórmóst 370, 371.
fore-named: fór-námed 6.
fore-oppress: fór-oppres*t* 338.
forsaken: forsákN 20.
forsooth: for-sooth 366.
forth (*adv.*): fọrth 7, 9, 366, foorth 382, (cf. p. 5).
forthwith: fọrthwith 53.
fortune: fortùn 8, 19, 20, for- tùnž 62.
forty: forty 387.
forward: fórward 323.

foul: fǫwl 11.
found (*v.*): fųndᴇd 6.
founder: fųndor 3.
four: fowʀ 31, 350, fower 63, 341, 387.
fourteen: fourte'n 273.
fourth: fowʀ*t*h 15.
fowl: fǫwl 345.
fowler: fouͅlor 41, fǫwlor 41.
fox: fox 18, foxê7 44.
frame: frám 124, frámęd 77.
France: Fʀᴀɴᴄ' 348.
fray (*v.*): fray*i*ng 86, 373.
free (*a.*): fre' 8.
free (*v.*): fre'ed 105.
French: french 348.
fret: fræt 324, frætʲng 325, freted 43.
friend: fre'nd 222, fre'nd7 5, 333.
friendly: fre'ndl*y* [3] 43.
friendship: fre'nds͟hip [3] 15.
fro: too and fro [2] 33, fro [2] 371, 383.
frog: frog 14, frog7 22.
from: from 4.
front: frųnt7 122.
frost: frost 74.
froward: froward [2] 67.
frowningly: frǫwn*i*ngly 142.
fruitful: frut-ful 25.
fry: fry*i*ng [2] 90.
full: fųl 8, 370, 383, fųler 362.
fuller (*sb.*): fųlor 41.
furnish: fųrnish 3.
furniture: fųrnitùr 30.

furrow: fųrowż 60.
further (*adv.*): fųrther 124.
further (*v.*): fardʀ*i*ng 333.
future: futùr 354.
fy or fie: fy [2] 373, fy [2]-fy [2]-for-shám 373.

G.

gain (*v.*): gain 341.
gainative (*gr. term*): gainatiu' 340.
Galen (*n. pr.*): Galen 58.
gall: gaſ 17.
gallant: galant 12.
game: gám 119, 382.
garden: gárdɴ 269.
gardener: gardnor 51, 174.
garrison: gariʒon 336, garis̨onż 380.
garner (*sb.*): garnerd 109.
garter: garter 380.
gate: gát 26.
gather: gather*i*ng 362, 370, gathered 8.
Gaudanus (*n. pr.*): Gaͅudanųs 49.
geld (*v.*): geld*i*ng 255.
gender: g'enderż 345.
general (*adj.*): g'eneraſ 317, ge'neral 345.
general (*sb.*): g'eneral 95.
generally: g'enerall*y* 341.
generation: g'eneraţionż 94.
gentle: g'entſ 9.
Gepp (*n. pr.*): Gep 255.
gep (*interjection*): gep 373.

grave (*sb.*): gráu' 177.

grave (*a.*): gráu' 382.

graveness: gráu'*n*es 259.

graver: gráu'*e*r 303.

gravel: grau'el 65.

graze: gra3 295.

great: græt 4, 6, 8, 337, 339, great[1] 182, græt*e*r 4, græt*e*r 337.

greatly: græt*l*y 374.

Greece: Gre'c' 12.

greedy: gre'dy 19.

Greek: Gre'k 8.

green: gre'n 20.

grey (*animal*): gray 326.

greyhound: gre-ho*y*nd [2] 25 (2×).

grieve: gre'u'*e*d 19.

grievous: gre'u'*o*os 10.

grip (*sb.*): gre'p 335.

grind: grýnd 16.

groan (*v.*): gró*n*ing 56.

ground (*sb.*): gro*y*nd 9, 380.

grove: gró*u*' 152.

grovel: gro*y*'*l*ing 41.

grow; grow*e*t*h* 324.

grudge: gr*y*dg' 23.

guard: gárd 78, gárd*e*d 113, gard*e*d 170.

guest: gest 17.

guide (*sb.*): gýd 4, 9, 384.

guise: gý3 216, 379, gy3 [2] 274.

gulf: g*y*lf 52.

gut (*sb.*): g*y*t 291.

gutter: g*y*tter 40.

H.

habendum (*legal term*): haben-d*y*m3 381.

hacker: hak*o*r 146.

hair: hær 43.

hairy: hær*i* 59.

half: half 3, 10, 313, 343, 382, half[1] 314, 315.

hall: ha*l* 83, 339.

halt (*v.*): halt*e*d 136.

halter: halter3 21.

ham: ham 288.

hame (*of a horse-collar*): hám 288.

hand: hand 3, hand7 5, 364.

handful: hand*f*ul 348.

handle: hand*l*ed 6, 365.

hang (*v.*): hang*i*ng 8, hang*e*t*h* 62.

handsome: hans*o*m 77.

hap (*sb.*): hap 42.

happen: hapɴ*e*d (pp.) 6.

happy: happy 9.

harbour: harb*o*r 84,! harbo*y*r*e*d[1] 324.

hard: hard 49, 338, 340, 347, hard*e*r 320.

hardly: hard*l*y 4, 17, 323.

hardness: hard*n*es 104.

hare: hár3 25.

hark: hark 193.

harlot: harlot7 89.

harm: harᴍ 16, 315.

harp: harp 80.

harsh: harsh 216.

hart: hart 15.
harvest: haru'est 64.
haste (*v*.): hást 64.
hasten (*v*.): hastₙ 61, hástₙ 163.
hastily: hástɪly 11.
hate (*v*.): hát 24.
hatred: hátred 10.
haulm: hám 289.
haunt: haụntẹtḥ 29, haɴtẹtḥ 41.
have: hau' 8, 362, hau'ɪng 3,
    hast 10, 221, hatḥ 5, 381,
    10, 362, hath 363, 381, haʒ
    381, had 3.
haven: hau'ɴ 181.
haw (*in the eye*): haụ 285.
hawk: hawk 336.
hawthorn-tree: haụ-tḥórɴ-tre'
    293.
hay (= *net*): hay 285.
hay (= *dry grass*): hey 285.
hazard: haʒard 42, haʒardʔ 86.
he: he' 63.
head: hed 8, hedʔ̃ʔ̃ (gen. pl.)
    344.
(*hard*)-*headed*: hedₑd 349.
heal (*v*.): hæl 349.
health: hæl*l*tḥ [3] 106.
heap: hæp 31.
hear: hæ'r 17, 364, he'arɪng [1]
    322, hæ'rẹtḥ 21, hæ'r*d*d [3] 15,
    hæ'r*d*d [3] 364, he'ar*d*d [3] 320.
hearer: hæ'rorż 71.
hearken: harkɴ 26, herkɴ [1] 186.
heart: hart 15, 102.
heat (*sb*.): hæt 16.
heavy: heu'ɪer 63.

heed (*sb*.): he'd 4, 24, 383.
hele (*v*.): he'l 349.
heel: he'lż 19.
heifer: hekfer 157.
heir: ĕirż 194.
hell: hel 289.
helm: helᴍ 292.
help: helpɪng 325, hoĺp 324,
    holpₙ 322.
hen: henż 87.
hence: henc' 355.
henceforth: henc'-fǫrtḥ 366.
her (*pers. pr*.): hir 333, her
    333.
her (*poss. pr*.): hir 333, 380,
    hirż 338, 352, her 380.
herb: erb 324, erbʔ 121.
Hercules (*n. pr*.): Hercules 68.
herd (= *shepherd*): hærd 326.
herd (*of cattle*): herdʔ 57.
here: he'r 160, 316, 333, 340,
    366, 379, 381.
hereafter: hær-after 77, 269,
    he'r-after 356, 360, 361, 366,
    372.
herein: he'r-in 5, 8, 318, 367,
    381, hær-in 314.
hereunto: he'r-ɥntoo 375, hær-
    ɥnto 313, 314.
heron: hærɴ 22.
hew (*vb*.): rǫwh-hewₑd 4.
het (*interj*.): het 373.
hide: hýd*d* [3] (pp.) 14.
hie: hy [2] 324, hyẹtḥ [2] 14, 41.
high: hih 11, 337, hihₑst 347.
highly: hi*h*ly 4.

highness: Hih*n*es 380.

hill: hilż 24.

hinder (*comp. of hind, a.*): hýnder 158, hýnder 371.

hindmost: hýndmóst 370, 371, hýnder-móst 371.

hinder: hinder*e*d 4.

hip (*sb.*): hip7 174.

hire: hýrż 44.

hire (*v.*): hýręd 364.

his: hiʒ 3, 351.

hiss: his*i*ng 16.

hither: hither 354, 364, 366.

Ho (*interj.*): Ho²⁾ 31, 162, 367, 373, hów 341, how 373.

hoar: hoar¹⁾ 185.

hoarse: hórc' 23, 47.

hoarseness: hórc'*n*es 47.

hog: hog 121.

hold (*sb.*): hóld 338.

hold (*v.*): hóld 56, 194, hołd 323, hółd*i*ng 15, hołdN 55, hółd*N* 105.

hole: hólż 21.

holiness: holi*n*es 109.

hollow: hólow³⁾ 109.

holm (*tree*): hólM 268, 287, hółM 287, hołM 388.

holmen (*a.*): hołMen 388.

holy: holy 21, 46.

home: hóm 9, 353, 372.

homeward: hóm*w*ard 372.

honest: ŏnest 78.

honesty: onest*i* 305.

honey: hǫny 17, 53.

honour: ŏnor 12, 338.

(*right*) *honourable*: riht-ŏnorábł 380.

hoof: hoou'7 20.

hook: hook 54.

hoop (*vb.*): hoop 293.

hope: hóp 4.

hop (*interj.*): hop 373.

Horace (*n. pr.*): Horac' 20.

horn: horN 19, hornż 159, hórnż 58, 114, hornʒ 32, 125, 143, 171, hornż7 344.

horrible: ŏrribł 126.

horse: hors 341, horse7 17, horsé7 (gen.) 30, hors7 380.

horse-comb: hors-comb¹⁾ 380.

hose: hóʒ, hóʒe7, hóʒń 345.

hospitality: ŏspital*i*ty 9.

host: ŏst 82, óst 160, 352.

hostess: óstis 111.

hound: hǫund 336.

hour: ǫwer 325.

house: hǫws 340, hǫwʒe7 29, 77, 83, hǫwse7¹⁾ 63, 97, 340.

household: hǫws-hóld 334.

how: hǫw 341, 363.

howl: hǫwled 15.

ho(w) sirrah (*interj.*): how-sir-a 373.

howsoever: hǫw-soeu'er 321.

hu (*interj. to frighten*): hǫh 373.

hugeness: hug'nes 44.

humble (*a.*): ǔmbł 56.

humble (*v.*): ǔmbłętħ 45.

hundred: hǫnderd 150.

hungry: hǫngRi 100.

hurl: hǫrł*i*ng 147.

hurt: hṵrtę̣sṭ 14, hṵrt (pt.) 341.
hurtful: hṵrtfṵl 316.
husband: hṵsband 9, 89, hǫus-
band 94, 102, 115.
husbandman: hṵsband-man 113.
hush (*interj.*): hṵsh 373.
hutch: hṵtch 36.
Hypocrates (*n. pr.*): Hypocrates 58.

I.

I: I 3, 351.
ice: yic' 109.
idle: idl²⁾ 68, ýdl̄ 70.
idleness: ýdl̄nes 10, 70.
if: if 5, 8, 370.
ignorance: ignoranc' 318.
ignorant: ignorant 17.
ill: il 4, 65, 347.
illatively (*gram. term*): illatiu'ly
368.
imparlance: imparlanc' 338.
imperative: imparatiu' 353 (2×),
356.
imperatively: imparatiu'ly 363.
imperfectly: yn-perfetly 318.
imperfectness: ynperfetnes 320.
impersonal: Im-persnalẑ 363.
imprint: im-printing7 3, imprinted 3.
impression: im-presionẑ 3.
in: in 3, 334, 371.
include: included 318.
increase: encrǣc'ę̣th 4, incrǣc'-
ed 347, encrǣc'ed 347, 364.

indifferently: indifferently 365.
infect: infected 325.
inferior: inferiorẑ 318.
infinitely: infinitly 373.
infinitive: infinitiu' 349.
infancy: infanc'y 320.
infant: infant7 124.
inflame: en-flámed 14.
injury: injury 45.
inmost: in-móst 371.
inn: inn 74.
inner: inẹr 371.
innermost: inẹr-móst 371.
inquire: enqýr 94.
inspiration: inspýrațion³⁾ 8.
instead: instæd 13, 383.
instruct: instrṵcted 319.
into: intoo 8, 339.
interjection: interjecțion 339, in-
terjecționẑ 366.
interpretation: interpretațion 22.
interrogatively: interrogatiu'ly
357.
invade: inu'ád 86.
invent: inu'ented 4.
invite: inu'ýtę̣th 53.
inward: inward 372.
inwardly: in-wardly 372.
iron (*sb.*): ýrɴ 161.
iron (*v.*): ýrɴed 136.
island: iland²⁾ 10, ýl̄-land 162.
isle: ýl 80, yil 127, yl²⁾ 326.
issue: issu 5.
it: it 3.
Italian: Italian 3.
Italy: Italy 80.

J.

Jacob (*n. pr.*): ḭacob 320, ḭaco-
bus 320.
jag: ḭagʒ 74.
James (*n. pr.*): Jámż 194, Iamʒ
256, Jámʒ 320.
jangle: ḭangḷ 256.
jaw: ḭawż 3, 14.
jay: ḭay 28.
jealousy: ḭelǫʒi 258.
jest (*v.*): g'est 335, ḭesti̭ng 93.
jet (*v.*): ḭeted 125.
John (*n. pr.*): Jŏn 341.
join: ḭooin 3, ḭoin 317, ḭoinęth
368, ḭooinęth 45, ḭooined 3,
340, 360, ḭoined 315.
jolly: ḭoily 103.
Joseph (*n. pr.*): Joʒeph 298.
joist (*sb.*): ḭuyst 274.
joint (*sb.*): ḭoint 297.
journey: ḭǫrny 11, 43.
joy (*sb.*): ḭoy 256.
joy (*v.*): ḭoyd 333.
judgement: ḭṷdg'mentʒ 5, 6, 7.
juggler: ḭṷgḷorż 256.
juice: ḭuic' 274.
June: Jun 5.
Jupiter: Jupiter 22, 23.

K.

Kate (*n. pr.*): kát 333.
keep: ke'p 3, 357, 372, ke'pi̭ng
6, ke'pṭt[3] 7.
keeper: ke'por 4, 24.

kernel: kernelż 137.
kettle: ketḷ 380.
key: key 17.
kid: kid 26, 119.
kill: kiled 12.
kiln: kill 109.
kind: kýnd 11.
kindred: kýnddred[3] 14.
king: kingʒʒ (gen. plur.) 29.
kinsman: kinz-men 50.
Kit (*n. pr.*): kit 333.
kite: kiht 14, 21, 23.
kitling: kitlingʒ 54.
knave: knáu'ʒ 9.
knee: kne'ż 192.
knife: knýf 101, 307.
knight: kniht 380.
knit: knitṭ (pp.) 93.
knitter: knitor 85.
knot: knotʒ 21.
know: know 11, kne'w 10,
knowɴ 336.
knowledge: knowledg'[3] 4, 23.
knuckle: knṷcḷ 297.

L.

labour (*sb.*): labǫr 20, 29.
labour (*v.*): labǫri̭ng 10, 20, 29.
Lacedæmonian: Lacedemonian
48.
lack: lak 5, lakṭ 364.
lade: ládɴ 100.
lamb: lamb[1] 13, lambʒ[1] 46.
lament: lamentęth 20.
lamentably: lamentabḷli 37.

lamentation: lamentac'ion 326.

language: languag' 274, langag' 342, langag'e꠸ 7, 339, 368, 386.

languish: languish[1] 274.

lap: lap 66.

lapidary: lapidary 13.

lapwing: lapwing 99.

large: lárg' 5, 339, 361, 372, 386.

largely: larg'ly 83.

lark: lark 75.

last: last 337.

later: láter 5, 367.

lath: laţħ 299.

lathe (= *grange*): láţħ 299 (error?).

Latin: Latin 7, 383.

latten: laten 380.

laugh: lauħ*i*ng 10, 373.

laughter: lauħter 19.

lawyer: law*i*or 119, law*i*orż 381.

lay: layęţħ 9, ley 317.

lea-bound (*side of a hill*): leibound 297.

lead: lædęţħ 9, lædḍ[3] 9, 335, lædd[3] 39, 42.

league: læg 22, 33.

leak (*v.*): læk 285.

lean (*a.*): læn 348.

leanness: lænnes 348.

leap: læp*i*ng 14, læpęţħ 20.

learn: lærn 354, lærn*i*ng 339, lærɴed 4, lærɴęd 363.

learner: lærɴor 7, lærɴorż 6.

least: læst 85, 347.

leave (*sb.*): læu' 364, 370.

leave (*v.*): læu'*i*ng 378, læft[3] 10, left 12, 51, 365.

leave off: læu'-of 24, left-of 365.

leave out: læu'-out 363, left-out 378.

lechery: lechery 112.

leek: le'k 285.

Leicester (*n. pr.*): Lec'ester 380.

leisure: leiʒurż 5.

length: lengţħ 16, 381.

lentil: lentil 11, lentilż 12.

leopard: libard 71 (3×).

Lesbos (*n. pr.*): Lesbos (2×) 80.

less: les 347.

lesser: leser 347.

lesson: lesɴ 81.

lest: lest 9.

let: let 17.

letter: letterż 3.

lewd: lewd 17.

liar: lyor[2] 18.

liberal: liberal 13, 43.

library: librari 2, 75.

lick: lyk 285.

lie (*sb.*): ly[2] 174.

lie (*v.*): ly[2] 35, 346, 380, ly*i*ng[2] 14, lay 21.

liefer: leu'er 13, 106, 353, 362, le'uer[1] 111.

lieutenant: lieu-tenant 380.

life: lýf 4, 8, 324, 336, 377, lif[2] 326.

light (= *bright*) (*a.*): liht 43.

light (= *not heavy*) (*a.*): liht 17.

like (*a.*): lýk 4, 7, lýker 4.

like (*v.*): le'k 233, 350, le'k*i*ng
    191, likẹtḥ[2] 27, lýkẹtḥ 255,
    le'k*e*d 102.
liken: lýk*N*ed 5.
likeness: lýkn*e*s 366.
likewise: lýk wyʒ 38, 43, 115,
    228, lýk-wýʒ 76, 95, 148,
    317, 348.
link (*of a chain*): lync 297.
link: link or litĺ torch 297.
linnet: linnet 99.
lion: lion[2] 15, lyonż[2] 48.
lip: lipʔ 8.
liquor: licǫr 27.
Liricus (*n. pr.*): Liricụs 33.
little: litĺ 347.
live: liu'*e*d 12.
livelihood: lyu'*ly*h*o*od[2] 101.
lo: ló 19, 78, 366, lo 178.
loaf: lof, lou'ʔ 344.
loath (*a.*): lotḥ 264.
loathe (*v.*): lóth 264, lóth*e*d 73.
lock (*of a weir*): lock 297.
lock (*of a door*): lok 285, 297.
loaden: lód*N* 30.
loin: looynż 120.
loiter: loiter*i*ng 312.
loke: a lók or pin-fóld 297.
London: Lǫndon 3, 372.
long (*a.*): long 3, 8, 364.
look (*v.*): look 18, looktḥ 377,
    lookţ 342.
loose (*a.*): lós 111, lóc' 179.
loose (*v.*): looʒ*i*ng 131, lóʒ*i*ng
    191, looʒẹtḥ 40, looʒ*e*d 9,
    107, lóʒẹd 96.

lobster-fly: lopster-flyż[2], 179.
lord: lord 67, 373, lórd 83,
    158, 164, 357, 377, 380.
lose (*v.*): lóʒ 15, 104, 165, 171,
    234, 371, looʒ 55, loʒ*i*ng
    174, lost 14, 104.
loss: losʔ 22.
lot (*sb.*): lót 324, lot 23.
louse: lǫws 349, lýc' 187,
    lyc'[2] 349.
lousy: lǫwsi[3] 187.
love (*v.*): lǫu' 13, 2×, lǫu'ẹd
    361 (in the paradigm pp.
    355—60, always ǫ); lǫu' 19
    etc. etc., loou'ẹd 361.
love (*sb.*): lou'[1] 323, 326.
low: low 11, 337.
lowest: lowest 63.
lubber: lụbbar 30.
Lucan (*n. pr.*): Lucan 223.
luck: lụk 6, 357.
Luke (*n. pr.*): luk 285.
lukewarm: leuk-war*M*[1] 297.
lute: lut 259.
Lydia (*n. pr.*): Lidia 10.
Lyons (*n. pr.*): Lionż[2] 194.
Lysander (*n. pr.*): Lysander 48.

M.

mace: mác' 254, mac' 295.
mad: mad*e*r 65.
magistrate: mag'istrátʔ 318.
maid: maidʔ 51.
mail (*bag*): mál (3×) 370.

maintain: maintain 381, main-
teined 323.

Majesty: Maiestyż 380.

make: mákíng 3, máktḥ 383,
mád 3, 6.

male (*a.*): mál 345.

man: man 345, manż 4, 8, ṁen
4, 345, menż 5.

manhood: manhǫǫd 348.

manifest: manifest 21, 345.

mankind: man-kýnd 347.

manly: manly 367.

manner: maner 4, 353.

Mantuan (*n. pr.*): Mantuan 48.

many: many 4, 5, 8, 335.

maple: mápl 268, mápl-tre' 293.

marble: marbl 127.

mark (*sb.*): mark 8, 349, 383,
mark7 3.

mark (*v.*): markíng 11.

marl: márl 315.

marriage: mariag' 164.

marry (*interj.*): mary 366.

Mars (*n. pr.*): Mars 223.

Marsh (*n. pr.*): Marsh 194 (2 ×).

mart: mart 138.

martial: marṭial 336.

marvel (*sb.*): meru'el 62.

marvel (*v.*): meru'elíng 105,
maru'elíng 138, meru'elętḥ
28, 62, 74, maru'elęd 10, 54,
meru'elęd 188.

masative (*gr. term*): masatiu'7
345.

masculine: masculin 345.

mask: maskíng 73.

masker: maskor 10.

master (*sb.*): maister 9, 354,
380, maisterż 342.

master (*v.*): maister 371.

mastery: maistʀi 338.

match: match 343.

matron: matron 106.

matronly: matronly 334.

matter: mater 3, 6, matter 364.

mattock: mattok7 148.

mattress: matrese7 83.

maund: maɴd or basket 292.

mavis (*poet.*): mau'is 93.

Maximus Planudes (*n. pr.*):
Maximųs Planudes.

may: may 4, 9, 353, 361, maiṣt
361, miht 3, 342, 353, 361,
mihtṣt 361, moųht 353, 360,
363.

maze: máʒ 295.

meadow: medow 380.

meal (*flour*): mæl 36.

mean (*sb.*): mæn 42.

mean (*a.*): mæn 39, 337, mæner
4, 8.

mean (*v.*): mænṭt[3] 75, mæntt[3]
361, 381.

meaning (*sb.*): mæníng 3, 6, 368.

measure: meʒùr 15, 341, 342,
383, meʒur 15.

meek: me'ker 51.

meet (*v.*): me't 20, me'test 3,
me'tṭ[3] 9, 132.

member: member 34.

memory: memory 375, memo-
ryż 7.

mend (*v*.): mend 338.

mention: menţion 8, menţioned 339.

merchandise: merchaɴdýȝ 258.

merchant: merchant 10.

Mercury (*n. pr*.): Mercury 73, 173 (3×), 177, Mercųry 174.

measurable: meȝurabĺ 9.

mere: me'r 314, 369.

merrily: meriƚy 9.

mesh (*v*.): mæshed 151.

mete (= *measure, v*.): mét 46.

metre: me'ᴛʀ 316, métʀ 382, me'ᴛʀȝ 339.

Michael (*n. pr*.): Michael 380.

middle: midĺ 382.

Milan (*n. pr*.): Millan 192 (2×).

mile: mil[2] 380, mýƚȝ 342.

milk (*v*.): milk 117, milkţ 117.

mind: mýnd 4, 6, 8.

mingle: mingĺed 19.

minister (*v*.): ministʀed 4.

mire: mýr 68.

mirror: mirror 333, mirrorȝ 333.

mirth: mirtħ 382.

mis-: mis- 348, 374.

misbelief: mis-be'le'f 374.

mischance: mis-chaɴc' 374.

mischief: mische'f 373.

miserable: miȝerábĺ 258.

miserably: miṣerabƚi 9.

misery: miṣery 50.

mislike: mis-lýk 20, mis-le'kíng 94, mis-le'ked 103, misle'kt 104.

misplace: mis-plác'íng 381, mis-plac'ed 322.

miss: mis 326, misţ 349.

mistake: mis-ták 374, mis-tákíng 381.

mix: mix 73.

mixture: mixtur 318.

mock (*v*.): mok 31, mokt 18.

mould (*v*.): móld 325.

mole (= *animal*): móld 35, 90, 182.

moment: moment 4, 6.

Monday: mǫnday 372.

money: mǫney 371.

monster: monster 24.

month: mǫntħ 335.

mood: mood 349.

moan (*s*.): món 333.

moral: moral 13.

more: mór 4, 6, 337, 347, mo[2] 16, 337, 347, 387.

moreover: mór-ou'er 366.

morning: morning 64.

morrow: morow 366.

mortal: mortaĺ 4, 8.

most: móst 3, 15, 347.

mostly: móstƚy 348.

Mothall (*n. pr*.): *h* can be distinctly pronounced 277.

mother: mǫtherȝ 11.

Mountham (*n. pr*.): *h* can be distinctly pronounced[1] 277.

mourn: moorɴ 292, mǫurnętħ 68.

mouse: mǫųc' 14, ḿýc' 20.

mouth: mǫųtħ 71, 116, mǫųthes 326.

move: moou' 6.
mow (= *stack of hay*, *sb.*):
   mǫw 35.
much: mŭch 4, 6, 347.
must: mŭst 5, 348, 353.
muster-book: mŭster-book꓿ 336.
mutual: mútuaĺ 40.
my: my²⁾ 3, 351, 355, mýn 5,
   351.
myself: my²⁾-self 6.

N.

nail: nayl 94.
naked: náked 9.
name (*sb.*): námż 22.
name (*v.*): námed 3.
nape: náp 345.
Naso (*n. pr.*): Naşo 223.
nation: naţion 108, 345, 375,
   nac'ion 316.
native: natiu' 323, 362.
natural: natùraĺ 43, 93, natʀal
   216, naturaĺ 326.
nature: natùr 4, 8, 9, 40.
naught (*a.*): naŭht 100.
naught (*pron.*): nawht 380.
naughty (*a.*): nawhti 10.
nay: nay 374.
near: ne'r 9, 46, 143, 153, 81,
   219, 333, 371, 380, 388, nær
   78, 166, 216, 372, nér 163,
   nærer 22, 72, 335, 372,
   ne'rest 182, 194, nærest 325.
neatness: nætnes 82.
necessary: nec'essary 8.

necessity: nec'essity 370.
neck: nek 8.
need (*sb.*): ne'd 5, 15.
need (*v.*): ne'd 21.
needs: ne'd꓿ 326.
neglect (*vb.*): neglect 326.
negligence: neglig'enc' 324.
negro: neger 11.
neigh: neiɀh 30.
neighbour: neihbǫrż 64.
neighbourhood: neihbǫrhood 46.
neither (*conj.*): nether 13, 95,
   350.
neither (*pron.*): nèither 6, 14.
nest (*sb.*): næst 74, 75.
nest (*v.*): næsted 115.
nether: næther 371.
nethermost: næther-móst 371.
neuter: neŭter 345, 377.
nevertheless: neu'ertheles 11,
   369.
new: ne'w 337.
next: next 349, 372.
nice: nic'²⁾ 70, nýc' 82.
Nicholas (*n. pr.*): Nicolas 341.
niggish: niggish 221.
nigh: nih 87, 366, 372, niher
   372.
nightingale: nihtɀngál 47.
nimbleness: nimblɀnes 26.
no: no²⁾ 5, 8, 366.
nod: nodɀng 190.
noise: noiɀ 17, noic' 326.
noisome: noysǫm 29.
no one: no²⁾-ón 339.
none: nón 334, 361.

nor: nor 14, 337.
north: nortḥ 62.
north-east: nortḥ·est 325.
nose: nóʒ 176.
nostril: nostrelż 8.
not: not 4, 8, 367, nót 338.
note (*sb.*): nót7 4, 6.
note (*v.*): noted 318, nóted 340.
notable: nótábl 80, nótábl 84,
    nótabl 100, 102.
notably: nótabli 10.
nothing: notḥing 4, no-tḥing 9,
    35, 380.
notwithstanding: notwithstand-
    ing 369.
noun: noʋn 339, 364.
nourish: noʋrishęd 27, noʋrished
    34, noʋrishęd[1] 98.
nourishment: noʋrishment 34,
    noʋrishment[1] 96.
now: noʋ 6.
number: noʋmberż 340.
numerative: numeratiu' 378.
nurse (*sb.*): noʋrc'[1] 88, 96.
nut: noʋt7 72.

O.

oak: ók 54, 77, 78.
oaken: ókɴ 293.
oar: owerż[1] 233.
oath: ótḥ 218, 292.
obedience: obeidienc'[3] 323.
obedient: obeidient[3] 76.
obey: obey 76.
obtain: opteined 9, obteynęd 152.

occasion: occaşion 14, 33, oc-
    caʒion 319.
occupation: occupac'ion 316.
odd: ods 233.
of: of 3, 6.
offend: offended 319.
offence: offenc' 337.
offer: offering 5.
officer: offic'or 123.
oft: oft 366.
often: oftɴ 348, 364, 372.
oh (*interj.*): oh 373.
oil: oyl 90.
ointment: ointment 287.
old: óld 63, 337, old 312, 321.
Old Bailey (*n. pr.*): óld Baily
    213.
olive: oliu' 133.
on: on 149, ón 326, ón a tým 71.
once: ónc' 27, onc[1] 78.
one: ón 3, 8, 9, 379.
only: ónly 4, 118.
open (*a.*): opɴ 5, 14.
open (*v.*). opɴ 26, opɴed 26.
optative: optatiu' 353.
or: or 3, 8.
orator: oratorż 151.
order (*sb.*): order 3, 366, 380.
ordinary: ordinary 4.
orthography: ortography 3, or-
    tography 314.
other: oþer 3, 8, 339.
otherwise: oþer-wyʒ 6, 42,
    oþerwýʒ 350, -wýʒ 316, oþer-
    wiʒ 371.
ought: owht 11, 17, 353, 360.

our: oụr 3, 6, 351, oụrż 352.
ourself: oụr-selu'ʒ 77.
out: oụt-of 7, 8.
outward: oụtward 372.
oven: ọu'n 182.
Ovid (*n. pr.*): Ou'id 19.
over: ou'er 348, 371.
overbear: ou'er-*b*orn 188.
overcome: ou'ercọm 57, ou'er-
   cọmed 57.
oversight: ou'er-siht 5.
own (*a.*): own 4, 5, 15.
owe: ow 26, owṣt 16.
owl: ọwl 77, ọwlżʒ 78.
owner: ownor 64.
ox: ox 334, oxń 345.
Oxford: Oxford 372.

P.

pacify: pac'ifi*e*d²⁾ 12.
pack-saddle: pak-sadĺ 20.
page: pág' 3.
pains: painż 334.
pair: paierż 3, 350.
pale: paal 58.
pamphlet: Pamphlet 4.
pang: pang 335.
paper: paper 3.
paradise: paradýc' 325.
parasite: paraṣitʒ 19.
parcel: parc'el 379.
pardon: pardn 95, 337, 381.
parent: parentʒ 69, 323, parentʒ 342.

parse: párc' 386, párc'*i*ng 339,
   376.
part (*vb.*): párt 167, Part*i*ng
   366.
part (*sb.*): part 4, 9, 31, 102,
   334, 349, 373, partʒ 339.
partly: par*t*ly 5.
partative: part*a*tiu' 378.
participle: Partic'ipĺ 339.
particular: Particular 349.
parting: Parting 366.
partner: pártnor 31.
partridge: partrig'eʒ 83.
pass: pas 8, 337, pas*e*d 5,
   pas*t* 5.
passion: passion 350, 373.
pasture: pasturż 37.
pasty: pastyż 29.
patch (*vb.*): patch*e*d 322.
path: paṭh 337.
pathway: paṭh-way 4.
patience: paṭienṭi 218.
Paul (*n. pr.*): Paụl 193.
pay: pay*e*d 11.
peacock: pe-cok²⁾ 47, pecokʒ²⁾
   28.
peace: pæc' 15, 338, 373.
peaceable: pæc'*a*bĺ 177.
pear: pærż 100.
pearl: pærlż 56.
pelt: peltʒ 82.
penny: peny 345, penc' 10, 345.
people: pe'pĺ 23.
peradventure: peradu'entùr 21.
perceive: perc'eiu'*i*ng 11, 26,
   perc'eiu'*e*d 350.

perfect (*a.*): perfet 183, 318, perfect 337, 340, 348, 349, perfect*r* 386, perfet*e*st 319.
perfect (*v.*): perfect*i*ng 338.
perfection: perfec*t*ion 4.
perfectly: perfect*l*y 353.
perform: perfórм 319, performᴇd 375, perfᴑrmᴇd 4.
Periander (*n. pr.*): Periander 80.
periwinkle: pirwincĺ 111.
perk (*up*): perk-ур 217.
perpetual: perpetuaĺ 6, perpetual 375.
person: persꞐ 15, PersꞐż 352.
persuade: perswád 65.
pertain: pertein 380, pertein*i*ng 4, pertain*i*ng 341, 367.
peruse: pervᴣ*i*ng 4, 5.
petticoat: peticót 256.
pewter: pewter 273.
peitrel (*obs.*): pewtrelż 31.
Phalaris (*n. pr.*): Phalaris 32.
pheasant: pheṣant꞉ 83.
Philip (*n. pr.*): phillip 263.
phrase: phráṣ 7, 8, 337, 376, 384.
phtrowh (*interj.*): phtrᴑwh 373.
Phrygia: Phrig'ia 8.
physique: phiᴣik 58.
physician: phiᴣic'ion 30, 162.
pickaxe: pek-axe꞉ 148.
pie: py[2] 50.
piece (*sb.*): pe'c'e꞉ 63.
piece (*vb.*): pe'c'ed 315.
pierce: perc' 41.
pierceable: pérc'abĺ 104.

picture: pictur*i*ng 337.
pike: pýk 116.
pill (*v.*): pilᶁ 123.
pillion: pilion 256.
pillory: pillory 289.
pinch (*vb.*): pinch*i*ng 98, 335.
pine-tree: pýn-tre' 33.
pine (*v.*): pýn*i*ng 338.
pipe: pýp*i*ng 149.
piss: pisᶊ 11.
pitch: pitch 18.
pithy: pitḥi 215.
pity: pity 325, pe'ty 326.
pitifully: pity-fụll*y* 21.
place: plác' 4, plác'e꞉ 3.
place: plác'ᶒd 8, plác'*i*ng 372.
plague: plág 12.
plaice: plais 296.
plain: plain 37, 376.
plainly: plain*l*y 9, 381.
plank: plank 380.
plant: plant 48.
plaster: pláster 234.
plat (*sb.*): plat 192.
Plato: Pláto 41.
play: plaiż 296, play 370.
pleasantness: plæᴣant*n*es[3] 39.
please: plæᴣ 376, plæᴣed 11.
pleasure: plæᴣur[3] 13, 336, 338.
plenteous: plentiọs 75, 383.
Pliny (*n. pr.*): Pliny 80.
plough: plọw*i*ng 157, plọwᴇd 60.
pluck: plụkᶒtḥ 14.
plural: plural 340.
poet: poet꞉[2] 62, Poet꞉[2] 229.

Poggius (*n. pr.*): Pog'g'iųs 185.
point: pointʒ 313, pooint 3, 4,
350, poointʒ 9, 368, 372.
poison: pooiʒnż 53.
poke: pookṭ 95.
polish: pųlished 5, pǫlished 84.
poll: powl 132.
pomegranate-tree: pómgranat-
tre' 182.
poop: poųp[1] 81, 156.
poor: pọor 27.
porch: porch 167.
porcupine: porkepin 110.
portion: porṭion 119.
position: poṣiṭion 370.
positive: poṣitiu' 347.
possessive: possesiu' 351, 352,
381.
post (*sb.*): post 25, 192, póst 158.
pot: potʒ 60.
potage: potag' 75.
pouch: poųch 191.
pour: poųʀ 65, pǫwrędֿ 98,
poųrędֿ 121.
poverty: pọu'erty 52, 122, 175,
pou'erty 38.
power: pǫwr 10, pǫwer 326.
practise (*v.*): practiʒ 42.
praise: praiʒed 9, dis-praiʒ 383.
prater: prátorż 219.
prattle: pratlïng 92.
pray: pray 9, 366.
prayer: praierż 9, 68.
precept: prec'eptʒ 12.
precious: prec'iǫs 13, prec'ioųs.
prefer: prefered 323.

prejoiningly: præ-ֈooiníngly 369
(2×).
prepare: prepáred 9.
preparative: preparatiu' 215.
preposition: prepoʒic'ion 290.
presence: preṣenc' 24.
present (*a.*): preṣent 4, 21, 355,
360.
present (*sb.*): preʒent 9.
Preterpluperfect: Preter-plu-per-
fect 354.
pretor: prætor 124.
pretty: prety 28.
prey: prey 18.
price: prýc' 11, pric'[2] 383.
prick: prik 88, prikíng 300.
priest: pre'stʒ 9, pre'st 100
Primer: Primar 4, 6.
primitive: primitiu' 348.
prince: princ' 326.
princely: princ'ly 337.
principle: princ'iplż 318.
printer: printor 3.
prison: priʒn 20.
prisoner: priʒnor 21.
private: priu'at[2] 137.
privity: priu'ityż 94.
privy: priu'y 14, 380.
proceed: proc'e'd 7, 338.
proceeding: proc'e'díngʒ 4, 5.
procure: procur 5, 338.
profane: prophán 6.
profit: profit 4, 381.
profitable: profitábĺ 312.
Prometheus (*n. pr.*): Prometheųs
22.

promise: promis 182, 221, pro-
   miseþ 43, promiȝeþ 26, 56,
   promiȝed 26.
pronoun: Pronoųn[2] 339.
proof: proof7 127.
proper: propʀ 321.
properly: propʀly 13.
prophesier: prophisior[2] 135.
proprietary: propʀietary[2] 340.
prosody: Prosody 382.
prosperity: prosperity 19.
prothesis: Protþesis 382.
Prot(h)eus (*n. pr.*): Protþeųs
   67.
proud: proųd 19.
prove: proou' 12, 28.
provide: prou'ýded 318.
provision: prou'iṣion 3, prou'i-
   ȝion 258.
provoke: prou'ók 99, 114, 161,
   prou'ókeþ 15, prou'óked 39,
   54, 74, 93, 182.
Psalter: Psalter 5, 6.
public: pųblik 3.
publish: pųblish 3.
puddle: pųdl 192.
puff: pųft 79.
pulley: pųli 290.
punishment: pųnishment7 9.
puppet: poppet7 147.
pure: puer 324.
purse: pųrc' 376, pųrs 192.
purge: pųrg' 383, pųrg'ed 5.
purple: pųrpl 72.
purpose (*sb.*): pųrpoȝ 3, 6, 347,
   pųrpóȝ 316.

put: pųt 364, pųteþ 25, pųtt
   336, 364.

Q.

quail: qailż 99.
quarrel: quareleþ 16.
quarry: qarry 50.
quarn: qárn 260, 307.
quartern: qartern 260.
quean: qæn 288.
queen: q'en 18.
quench: qench 93.
querulous: qeruloos 117.
quicken: qikned 8.
quickly: qikly 9.
quill: qilż 163.
quince: qinc'e7 260.

R.

race: rác' 333.
rag: rag 343.
rage: rág'eþ 14.
rail (*v.*): rail (at) 51.
raiment: rayment 81, raiment
   382.
rain: rain 78.
Ralph: Ráph 298.
range: rangeð[1] 336.
rank: rank 336.
rankle: rankleþ 324, ranklۤed
   139.
rare: rár 313, rárer 384.
rash: rash 62.
rather: rather 5, 23, 321, 342,
   362, 366 (4×), 386.

raven: ráu'ɴ 39.
reach: ræch 325, ræchęth 318.
read: ræd 370, ræd*i*ng 7, 8, rædd³⁾ 75, 337.
reader: Rædor 3.
ready: redy 9.
realm: relм 326.
reap: ræp 64, ræpţt³⁾ 76.
reaper: ræporż 84.
rearward: re'r-ward 375.
reason: ræʒɴ 4, 353, 355, reʒɴ 320, 324.
reasonable: ræʒɴabl 3, 6, reʒ-ɴábl 325.
recapitulation: re-capitulaţ*i*on 374.
receive: rec'eiu'*e*d 11.
reckon: rekɴ*i*ng 335.
reconcile: reconc'ýl*e*d 12.
recover: recǫu'erd 324, recǫu'er-*i*ng 5.
red: red 98.
Redditive (*gr. term*): Redditiu'ʔ 369.
reed: re'd 54, 156.
reform: reformd 338.
refresh: refresh*e*d 9.
refuse: refuʒ, refuʒ*i*ng 338.
regard: regard 17, regárd 82, regard 321, 373.
regenerate: reg'enerat 255.
region: reg'ionż 127.
rehearse: reherc' 36, 63, re-hærc'ęth 37, 48, rehærc*i*ng 351, reherc'ęd 12, 75, 102, rehærc'*e*d 345.

rehearsal: rehærc'al 40, re-herc'al 41, rehærc'al 374.
reign: rein 326, reyn*i*ng 50.
rein: reinż 335.
relative: relatiu'ʔ 13.
relatively: relatiu'ly 340.
relief: rele'f 335.
remain: remain 365, remainęd 10.
remember: remember 342.
remembrance: remembʀanc'eʔ 8.
renew: rene'w 255.
renown: renǫwm 101, renǫwm 335.
repeat: repétęd 190, 367.
reply: reply²⁾ 5.
report: report 18.
reproach (*v.*): reproch 51, 58, repróch 117 (2×).
reproach (*sb.*): repróche ʔ 160.
reproof: reproofʔ 105.
reprove: reproou' 42.
require: reqýr 353, reqý'ręth 5, reqireth²⁾ 316, reqýręth 361.
requite: reqýt 9.
reserve: reşeru'ęd 50.
resolve: reşolu' 342, reşolu'ed 365, 368.
resort (*v.*): reʒort 312.
respect: respect 7, 8, 345.
respite: respit 9.
rest (*sb.*): rest 9, 337, 367.
restore: restór 45.
retain: reteinęth 5.
return: reţyrɴ 334, reţyrɴ*i*ng 9.
reverence (*vb.*): reu'erenc'*i*ng 9.

reward: reward 16.
Rhodes (*n. pr.*): Rŏds 127.
rhyme: rým 216, 382.
riches: rich*e*s 18.
ride: rýd 355, rýd*i*ng 342, ród
    372.
ridge: ridg'e⁊ 79.
rid (*vb.*): rid*d* 153.
rife: rýf 377, ryu' 383.
right: riht 6.
rightly: riht*l*y 227.
rind: rýnd 325, rýnd⁊ 137.
riotous: riot*o*os²⁾ 172.
ripe: rýp 22.
rise: rýʒ 52, 326, 383, rýʒn³⁾
    76, riʒn 82.
river: riu'er 14.
roam (*vb.*): rowm 292.
roar: rórẹd
roast: rósted 87.
robbery: roboriż 21.
Robert (*n. pr.*): Roberd 380.
Robin (*n. pr.*): Robin 98.
rock: rok 65.
rod: rod 343, rod⁊ 131.
roll: rowl*i*ng 90, 112.
Roman: Roman 3.
Rome: Room 190, room¹⁾ 292.
roof: roof 169, ro*u*f⁊¹⁾ 139.
room: room¹⁾ 268, room 292,
    320.
root: root⁊ 116.
rope: róp 66.
rose: róʒ 183.
rote (*sb.*): by rót 320.
rough: rọwh-hew*e*d 4.

royal: royal 337.
rub: rụbḍ 12.
ruddock: rụddok 98.
rude: rud 323.
ruff: rụf 343.
rugged: rụgged 70.
rule (*sb.*): rul 372, rulż 12.
rule (*vb.*): rul*e*d 337, 377.
run: rụn 11, rụnẹtḥ 16, ran 20,
    rụn*n* 353.
rush: rụsh 260 (*not worth a*
    rush).
rush: rọwsh 22 (< O. Fr. *russher,*
    re(h)usser).

S.

sacred: sacred 337.
sad: sad 12.
saddle: sadĺ 293.
safeguard: saf-gard 323.
safety: sáfty 16.
sail: sailż 19.
salve: saĺu' 325.
same: sám 3, 369.
Samos (*n. pr.*): Samos 10.
sand: sand 65.
satyr: satyr²⁾ 67, satýr 129.
save: sáu' 34, 369, 377, 384,
    sau' 326, sau'*i*ng 312, sáu'*i*ng
    352, 369, 380, sau'*d* 227.
savour: sau'or 17.
savoury: sau'ery 48.
say: say 4, saiẹtḥ 10, 27, saiʒ
    27, sayż 136, 161, sai*e*d 4,
    say*e*d 5, 346.

scant: skant 320, scant 366.
scantily: scant*ly* 366.
scarce: scárc' 27, 50, 324, 366,
 skárc' 324.
scarcely: scarc'*ly* 25, scárc'*ly*
 30, 44, 366.
scatter: scatter*d* 326.
sceptre: sc'eptʀ 344.
scholar: scool*l*or*ż*[3] 11.
science: sc'ienc'[2] 318.
scoff: scof*ʃ* 25.
scoffer: scoffo*r* 104.
score: scór 335.
scorn: scórɴ 217, scorn*i*ng 335,
 373.
scorpion: scorpion 179.
sea: sæ 40, sæż 20.
seal: sæl 70.
searce: særc'*ed* 254.
search: serch 384, særch*i*ng
 233, serchẹd 8.
seat: sæt 337.
secret: secret 150, secret*ʃ* 12,
 386.
Secretary: Secretary 3, secre-
 taryż 188.
see: se' 9, 349, 362, se'*i*ng 4,
 saw 10, 17, 336, 349, 362,
 se'*n* 339, se'ṇ 362.
seek: se'k 48, 362, se'kẹth 21,
 sowht 2ĭ, 84, 362, 380.
seem: se'mẹth 8, 381.
seld: se'ld 215, 366, 377, 344.
seldom: se'ldọm 15, 343.
sell: sell 10, sold[1] 10, sóld 104,
 sowld 291.

send: sent 9, 381.
sense: senc' 7, 337.
sentence: sentenc' 3, sentenc'es
 5, sentenc'e*ʃ* 12.
separate: seperát*ed* 369.
sergeant: Serg'ant*ʃ* 5.
serpent: serpent 90.
serve: seru' 382, seru'*i*ng 340,
 seru'*ed* 8.
servant: seru'*a*nt 9.
set: set*t* 333, 362.
seven: seu'ɴ 375.
seventieth: seu'ɴ*ti*ṭh 92.
sever: seu'ʀ*i*ng 325.
several: seu'er*a*l 50.
severally: seu'er*a*l*ly* 50.
sewer: sewer 291.
shadow: shadow 14.
shall: sha*l* 5, 333, 353, 365,
 sha*l*t 14, 20, shọuld[1] 8, 353.
shallow: shalow 85.
shambles: shambl*ż* 38.
shameful: shám*f*ụl 265.
shank: shank*ʃ* 159.
shape: sháp 324, sháp*ʃ* 3, 333.
shawm: shawᴍ 149.
she: she' 13, 351.
she-bear: she'-bár 155.
sheep: she'p 15, 33, 349, she'p*ʃ*
 47.
sheet: she't 3.
shell: shel 18.
shepherd: she'pp-herd[2] 32.
shift: shift 95.
shine: shýn*i*nġ 14, shýnẹd 14.
shirt: shert 341.

shoe (*sb.*): shoo 52.
shoe (*v.*): shoo*dd*[3] 95.
shoot: shoot 62, 290, shot 276,
    shoott[3] 349.
shore: shór 233.
short: short 8, 364, 383.
shorten: shortN*i*ng 364.
shortly: short*ly* 342.
shortness: short*n*es 365.
shovel (*sb.*): shọu'l 306.
show (*sb.*): shew 18, 345.
show (*vb.*): shew 3, 8, 25,
    sheweth 334, shew*i*ng 3, 340,
    366, shew*ed* 6, 365.
shoulder: shọulder*ż* 105.
shower: shọwer*ż* 85.
showh (*interj.*): shọwh ('fray-
    ing') 373.
shrill: shril 45.
shritch-owl: shrých-ọwl 306.
shuffle: shụfl̄ 306.
shun: shụn 384, shụn*i*ng 373.
shut: shụt*i*ng 367, shụt*t* (pp.) 87.
sick: sik 21, 35, 147, 348.
Sicily (*n. pr.*): Ci'c'il 80.
side: sýd 3.
sigh: sih 326, sihẹth 68.
sight: siht 4.
sign: sýn 340, 370, sýn*ż* 56.
signify: signify*i*ng[2] 347.
simple: simpl̄ 344.
silence: silenc'[2] 228, 373.
sillable: sillabl̄ 348, sillabl̄*ż* 348.
silly: se'ly 9, 19.
silver: silu'er 173.
since: sinc' 369.

sing: singẹth 69, sọng (pt.) 69,
    sụng (pt.) 81.
singer: sing*o*r 10.
singly: singl̄i 367.
singular: singular 340.
sink (*sb.*): sink 192.
sire: sýr*ż* 145.
sit (*v.*): sit*ʒ* 337.
sith: sith 220, 334, 369.
six: six 348.
sixteen: sixte'n 349.
skill: skil 3, 336.
skill (*v.*): skilẹth 363.
slack (*v.*): slak 5.
slave: sláu'*ʃ* 259.
sleep (*sb.*): sle'p 9.
sleep (*v.*): sle'p 43, 370, sle'p*ʧ*[3]
    157.
slide: slýd 294, slýd*d*[3] (pt.)
    294, slýd*d*N[3] 294.
slight: sliht 215, 382.
sloth: slowth 212.
slothful: slowth-fụl 69.
sloven: slọu'in*ż* 99.
slow: slow 8, 347.
slowly: slow*ly* 6.
sluggishness: slụg*i*shn*e*s 22.
sluice: sluc' 291.
slyly: sly*ly*[2] 230.
small: smal̄ 3, 8, 336.
smarid (*a small fish*): smarid
    144.
smart (*sb.*): smart 325.
smith: smith 161.
smooth: smooth 70.
snaffle: snafl̄ 288.

snail: snail 56.
snake: snák 16.
snare: snárż 21.
snatch: snatchẹth 14.
snow: snow 16.
so: so[2] 3, 4, 9, 338, 339.
sober: sóbʀ 229.
Socrates (*n. pr.*): Socrates 59.
sod (*pp.*): sod 12 (pp.).
soever: soeu'er[2] 348.
soft: soft 348.
soil: soyl 334.
soldier: soldŋọr 42, soldŋor 338, soldŋorż 95, 336.
solicitor: sollic'itọrż 5.
some: sọm 3, 8.
some one: sọm-ón 339, 349.
some time: sọm tým 372.
somewhat: sọm-what 5.
son: sọn 258.
song: song 378.
soon: soon 5, 365.
sooner: soonẹr 346.
sooth (*sb.*): sooth 17, 77.
soothe (*v.*): sooth 300.
soothsayer: sooth-sayọr 170.
sorrow: sorow 373.
sorry: sory 32.
sort: sórt, Tabl. I, sort꞊ 4, 8, 317.
soul: sowl 102.
sound (*vb.*): soụnd 42, soụndth 382, soụndẹd 387.
sound (*a.*): sọwnd 79.
sour: sọwer 178.
south: soụth 62, 372, soụth[1] 300.

southwardly: soụth-*w*ard*ly* 372, thowh we' pronoụnc' sọwthẹr*ly*.
sow (*sb.*): sọw 24.
sow (*vb.*): sow*i*ng 76, sowɴ 76, sow*n* 325.
space: spác' 8.
spade: spád꞊ 148.
spaniel: spantŋel 98.
spare: spár 14.
sparkle: sparkl*i*ng 148.
Sparta (*n. pr.*): Sparta 81.
spawn: spawnẹd 64.
speak: spæk 4, 6, 369, spák 9, 370, spók 220, spókɴ 6, 373, 340.
speaker: spækọr 373.
spear: spær 14.
special: spec'ial 350.
specially: spec'ial*ly* 4.
speech: spe'ch 3, 4, 6, 373.
speedy: spe'd*i* 319.
speedily: spe'd*i*ly 365.
spell: spel*i*ng 4, spel*d* 388.
spider: spyder[2] 82, spider[2] 85, spydor[2] 208.
spill (*vb.*): spil 42.
spiteful: spýt-fụl 14.
spoil: spooil 8, 22, spooilẹd 341, spoil 326.
spoon: spónż 273, spoonż 340.
sport (*sb.*): spórt 46, sport 100.
spread: sprædẹth 324, spred*d* 335.
spring (*sb.*): spring 324.

spring (*vb.*): spro̜ng (pp.) 27,
    spru̜ng 215.
spread: sprædd (pp.)[3] 82,
    spredd 232, 335.
spy (*sb.*): spýż 296.
spy (*vb.*): spy[2] 326, spyĭng[2] 18.
square: sqár 192, sqárż 314.
ssh (*interj.*): ssh 373.
stable: stábl 268, 293.
staff: staf 14, 344, stau'ʔ 344,
    (gen.) stáu'ʔ 381 (gen.).
stag: stag 32.
stall: stal 35.
stand: stand 9, 380, stood 60,
    380.
star: starż 56.
stay (*sb.*): stey 6, 375.
stay (*v.*): staie̜þ 5, stay 221.
stayer: stayor 12.
stead: stæd 378.
steal: stæle̜st 87.
steep: ste'p 46.
steer (*taurus*): ste'ʀ 66.
stern: sterɴ of a ship 292.
stick: stike̜þ 68, stu̜k (pt.) 15.
stir: stire̜st 42.
stock (*sb.*): stok 325.
stomach: stomak 26, sto̜mak 54.
stone: stón 13, 348.
stonen: stónen 178, 380.
stoney: stóni 348.
stop: stopĭng 373.
store: stór 379, 384.
storehouse: stór-ho̜ws 336.
storm: storɴ 32.
stormy: storɴi 20.

stout: sto̜u̜t 29.
stoutly: sto̜u̜tly 19.
straight (*adv.*): straiht 81, 88,
    382.
straight (*a.*): strait 37, 325.
straightaway: straith-away[1] 40.
strait (*sb.*): straihtʔ 185.
strange: strang' 126, straɴg' 377.
stranger: straɴg'orż 43, straɴ-
    g'or 345, 363.
straw: straw 344.
stream: stræmż 29.
stretch: stretch 338, stretche̜þ
    324.
street: stre'tʔ 115.
strength: strengþ 14.
strife: strýf 377.
strike: strýke̜þ 27, strák (pt.)
    9, 57, 66, 139, 142, 146,
    187, strók 177, strýkɴ[3] 15.
strike (*sb.*) (*stroke*): strýk 348.
stripe: strýpʔ 98.
strive: striu'[2] 57, strýu' 14, 62,
    72, striu'ʒ[2] 338, strýu'e̜st 57,
    strýu'e̜þ 66, striu'ĭng[2] 73,
    strýu'e̜d 182, stryu'ed[2] 103,
    strau' (pt.) 130, stráu' 145,
    150, 156, stróu' 182.
stroke (*sb.*): strook 96, strók
    102, 104, strókʔ 96.
stuff: stu̜ft 153.
stuffle (= *stifle*) (?): stu̜flędd 172.
stumble: stu̜mblĭng 8.
sturdily: stu̜rdily 168.
subject: su̜bject 101.
subjunctive: su̜bju̜nctiu' 353.

substantive: sụbstantiu' 339.
subtlety: sụtl*t*y 27.
succour: succǫr 33[1].
succour (*vb.*): sụccǫr 61, 155, 163, sụccǫr*d* 325, succǫr*d*[1] 325.
such: sụch 3, 7, 8.
suck: sụkż 325, sụk*i*ng 119.
sudden: sǫden 350, sụdden 373.
suddenly: sụdden*l*y 350.
suet: suet 291.
suffer: sụffer 346, sụffʀi*n*g 62, sụffer*i*ng 353.
sufficient: sụffic'*i*ent 312.
sufficiently: sụffýc'*i*ent*l*y[3] 254.
sufficiency: sụffic'*i*enț*i* 5.
sugar: sugar 291.
sun: sụn 11.
superfluous: superfluǫs 4.
superlative: superlatiu' 347.
superior: superior 30, superiorż 323.
supine (*sb.*): supinż 384.
supper: sụpper 9.
supply: sụpply[2] 340, 379, sụpp-lied[2] 320.
sure: suʀ 365.
surely: suer*l*y 366.
suit: sut 333.
summer: sǫmer 324.
surgeon: sụrg'eon 137.
sustain: sụstein 44.
swaddle: swadl*i*ng 337.
swallow: swalow 21.
swan: swan 88, swanż 18.
sway: sway 336.

sweal: swæl 291.
sweat (*v.*): swet 57, swetț (pp.) 15.
sweeper: swe'porż 82.
swell: sweld 20, swólɴ 79.
swine: swýn 98, 345.
swear: swór 133, swóʀɴ 46.
swim: swim*i*ng 14.
sword: swerd 175.
syncope: syncope 363.

T.

table: tábl 3, 12, 20.
take: ták 4, 5, 337, ták*i*ng 348, tók 62, 156, 323, took 8, tákɴ 150.
talk: talk 4, 64, 67, talkęd 72.
tall: tal 63.
tallage: tallag' 290.
talon: talanț? 56, 111, talanż 169.
tame: tám 325.
tanner: tanor 51.
tarry: tary 10, tary*e*d 342.
taste: tasțed 84.
taverner: tau'erɴor 191.
teach: tæch 353, 364, tæch*i*ng 9, 364, tauht 353, 364.
tear (*sb.*): te'rż 46.
tear (*v.*): tær 33, tár 97, tór 111, torɴ 20, tórɴ 105.
tease: tæʒęth 25, tæʒ*i*ng 366.
tell: telęth 28, told[1] 91, tóld 341.
temperateness: temper*a*tɴes 78.

ten: ten 342.
Tenarus (*n. pr.*): Tenarǫs 81.
tender: tender 333.
tense: tenc' 341.
term: terᴍ 5, 380.
terror: terrǫr 382.
Thales (*n. pr.*): thales 265.·
than: than 4, 23, 344.
thankful: thankfǫl 11.
that: that 3, 8, thaт 4, »dat»
   E. Sussex and Kent 263.
the: the 3, 380.
thee (*v.*): the' 300.
thee (*pr.*): the' 10, 351.
theft: the'f*t*[3] 9, thef*t* 38,
   the'f*ft*[3] 180, the'f*t*ʒ[3] 181.
their: their 3, 4, 351, 372,
   their꙼ 352.
then: then 3, 347, 381.
thence: thenc' 80, 366.
there: thér 4, 10, 339, 347,
   353, 364, 387.
them: them 3, 8.
therefore: thær-for 8.
therein: thær-in 4.
thereof: thær-of 3, 4.
these: thæʒ 6, 7, 8, 338, 350,
   361.
Thessalia (*n. pr.*): thessalia 265.
they: they 4.
thief: the'f 14, 180, thæ'u'ʒ 150,
   the'u'ʒ 182.
thigh: thih 192.
thing: thingʒ 4.
think: think 4, 6, 363, think*i*ng
   8, thowht 3, 363.

third: third 44, 194, 338.
thirty: thirty 4.
this: this 4, 8, 'dis', in E. Sussex
   and Kent 263.
thither: thither 31, 354.
Thomas: Tŏmas 194.
thong: thong 73.
thorn: thórɴ 175, 264, thorɴ
   30, 'dorne' in E. Sussex and
   Kent 263.
thorny: thorɴ*i* 30.
thoroughly: throwhl*y* 6.
those: thóʒ 3, 6, 9, 342, 'dose'
   in E. Sussex and Kent 263.
thou: thǫ 10, 264, 341, 351.
though: thowh 4, 5, 340, 357,
   369.
thought: thowht 336.
thousand: thǫʒand 150, 152,
   264, 340.
thousandth: thǫʒandth 307.
Thraso (*n. pr.*): Thraṣo 19,
   thraʒo 265.
threaten: thretɴeth 13, thretɴ*i*ng
   373.
three: thre' 350.
thrice: thric'[2] 326.
thrive: thrýu' 300.
throat: thrót 15.
throes: throw꙼ 338.
through: throwh 5, 8, thorow
   39, thorowh 40, 78, thorow
   or throwh 308.
through-ripe: throw-rýp 76.
throw: throwɴ 62.
thrust: thrǫst 40.

thumb: thụmb[1] 187, 263, 'dumbe' in E. Sussex and Kent 263.

thus: thụs 8, 336.

thwart: th̦warting 225.

thy: Thy[2] 14, 351, thýn 24, 351.

thyme: tym[2] 65.

tie: ty[2] 382, tymg⸗[2] 21.

tiger: týgʀ 62.

tile: týlż 51.

tiler: týlor 51.

till (*v.*): tilẹd 113.

tillage: tilag' 336.

time: týme[1] 325, tým 3, 382.

tit (= *teat*): tet⸗ 39.

title: týtl 353, týtlȝ 366.

to: too 3, 8.

toe: to[2] 290.

together: toogether 7.

toil: tooil 290, tooyl 334, tooil-ing 334.

toll (*sb.*): tól 290.

toll (= *entice vb.*): towl 290.

tomb: toomb[1] 66.

tongue: tụng 9, 337, tụng⸗ 382.

tongued: tọnged 75.

too: toó 5, 9, too 4, 348.

tooth: te'th̦ 16, 33, 95, 161, 167.

top (*sb.*): top 218, 349, 370.

torch: torch 123.

touch: tụching 4, 6, toụching[1] 319, tụchẹth̦ 8, 24, tụcht 338.

tough: tọwh 290.

tow (*sb.*): tow 290.

toward: toward 371, Toward íȝ sọm tým diu'ýdẹd by hiȝ cá-sụal word, o be'ing chaɴg'ẹd too oo 372.

towel: tọwel 290.

tower: tọwerż 63.

town: tọwn 8, 353.

trade: trád 104.

traffic: Trafik⸗ 41.

train (*sb.*): train 335.

transitory: transitory 319.

translation: transláțion 6, 7, 194.

translate: translát 7, translátẹd 7, translátẹd 8.

trappings: traping⸗

travel: trau'el 4, 338.

tread: træd 30, 323, trod 163, trodɴ 136.

treasure: træȝùr 60.

treatise: Trætiȝ 312, Trætic' 312, trætic' 374.

treaty: trety 33.

thresher: th̦reshorż 84.

tree: tre' 18.

tremble: tremblẹd 13.

trial: trial[2] 5.

trier: tryor[2] 364, tryer[2] 364.

trifle: triflż[2] 319.

trifler: trýflor 68.

trim: trimd 30.

trimly: trimly 11, 62.

triphthong: triphth̦ong 314.

trish trash: trish trash 265.

triumph: triụmphing[2] 54.

trouble (*sb.*): trọbl 343.

trouble (*v.*): trọblẹd 13.

utter: ӯttered 373.
utterly: ӯtter*ly* 322.

V.

valiant: v'aliant 22, 23.
valiantly: v'aliant*ly* 381.
valley: v'alyż 105.
vanquish: v'anqish*t* 62.
vary: v'ary 319, v'ariẹd 6.
variance: v'arianc' 5, 40.
varlet: v'erlat⁊ 259.
vault: ṭoo v'aụlt on a hors, too
  v'aụt or mák v'aụt⁊ 292.
vehement: v'eëment 138 ²⁾.
vehemently: v'eëment*ly* 74 ²⁾.
venom: v'enim 16.
Venus: V'enụs 39, 130, 152
  (3 ×).
verb: v'erb' 370.
verse: v'érs 81, 344, 370, 376,
  382, v'érse⁊ 77, 219.
versify: v'ers*i*fy*i*ng ³⁾ 382.
virtue: V'ertu 26.
very: v'ery 8.
vessel: v'esĺ 10.
vicious: v'ic'ịọs 258.
vineyard: v'ӯn-ŋard 148.
violate: v'i'olat ²⁾ 141.
violence: v'iolenc' ²⁾ 103.
Virgil (*n. pr.*): V'irg'il 20.
visor: v'iʒer 10, v'iṣọrż 72.
vizard: v'iʒard 147.
vocative: v'oca'tiu' 340.
voice: v'oic' 115.
void: v'oid 259, 383.

volume: v'olùm 5, v'olụm 337,
  v'olùmż 6.
vomit: v'omiteṭḥ 9.
vouchsafe: v'oụchsáf 116.
vowel: v'ọwel 343 (2×), v'ọwelż 3, 314, 382.
voyage: v'yag' ²⁾ 138.

W.

wag: wag*i*ng 147.
wail: wail*i*ng 56.
walk: walk ¹⁾ 217, waĺkẹd 11,
  12, 82.
wall: waĺ 109, 380, waĺż 83,
  342.
wallow: walow 100.
Waltham (*n. pr.*): *h* can be
  distinctly pronounced 277.
wan: wan 58.
wand: wan 9, 40, wand 388,
  wanż 187.
wander: wandered 12.
want (*sb.*): want 5.
wanton: wanton 78, 382.
war: war 12, 338, 349.
ware: wár 350.
warm: warᴍ 9, 347.
warn: wárn 269, 288, warɴ
  326, 383, warɴed 15.
warren: warren 269.
warrantee: warrant*e* ²⁾ 381.
warranty: warrant*i*ż 381.
warrior: war*i*orż 14.
washer: wash*o*r 148.
wasp: wasp⁊ 182.

waste: wástęth 67.

water: wáter 9, 14, water 29, 49, 54, 65, 165.

wave: wau' 325, wáu'ʒ 20.

waver: wau'erɪng 29, wau'ʀɪng 221.

waw (*interj.*): waw 373.

wax (*sb.*): wex 104, 171, wax 340.

wax (*v.*): wex 326, waxɪng 22.

way: way 8, 344, waiż 336.

we: we' 351.

weak: wæk· 8, 34.

weaken: wækɴed 4.

weal: wæl 336.

wealth: welṭh 140, 338, welṭh 318.

weapon: wépnż 42, 52, wepɴż 110, 117, 121.

wear: weerɪng 139, weer-oyt 33 (2×), worɴ 70, 105.

weariness: weryɴes 51, We-rines 56.

weary: we'ry 20, wery 23, 41, 109, 146, 149, wæry 270, 316.

weasel: wæʒſ 36.

weave: wæu'ɪng 82.

web: webʒ 82.

wedge: wedg'eʒ 180.

weed: we'dʒ 324.

weep: we'p, we'pṭt[3] 56.

weigh: weih 17, weihed 85, wayęth 70.

weight: weiht 22, 41.

weightiness: weihtines 5.

well (*sb.*): well 66.

well (*adv.*): wel 4.

wellaway (*interj.*): alas and wel away 373.

well-doer: wel-dooorż

wench: wench 92.

Wenthurst (*n. pr.*): *h* can be distinctly pronounced 277.

wet (*v.*): wett (pp.) 132.

wether: wetherż 46.

wharf: wharf 266.

what: what 4.

wheat: whæt 26.

wheaten: whætɴ 308.

wheel: whe'l 31.

whelm: whelʍed 67.

whelp: whelp 266, whelpʒ 33.

when: when 9.

where: whær 5, 344, 366.

whereas: whær-aʒ 3.

whereby: whær-by[2] 4.

whereof: whær-of 8.

wherry-man: whe'ry-man 266.

whether: whether 81, 362, whether-or 369.

which: which 3, 8.

whilst: whýlst 342.

whip: whip 20, 68.

whirl: wherſ 308.

whirlpool: whirl-pool 308.

whirlwind: whyrlɪng-wýnd 157.

whistle: whistſ 266.

whit: whit 139, (not-)awhit 367.

white: whýt 307, whyter[2] 17.

whither: whither 4, 9, 62, 366.

whittle: mantſż or, whitſż 268.

who: whoo 8.

whom: whooṁ 6, 375.
whoop (*interj*.): whoop 373.
whole: whól 3, 36, 349.
wholesome: whólsǫm 12.
wholesomely: whólsǫml*y* 74.
whoop (*v*.): whoop 293.
whore: whoorż 266.
whose: whooż 5, whooż7 21.
whosoever: whoo-soeu'er 4, who-
  soeu'er 321.
whouh (*interj*.): whoụh 373.
why: why²⁾ 10.
wicked: wicked ̣32.
wide: wýd 54.
wield: we'ld 215.
wife: wýf 297.
wile: wýlż 71.
wild: wýld 325.
wily: wýl*i* 324.
wiliness: wýli*n*es 94.
will: wil 4, 361, wilt 361,
  woụld¹⁾ 9, 353, 361.
willing: wil*i*ng 323.
William: William 3, 341.
willow: wilowż 65.
wimble: wimbĺ 308.
win: wǫn 12.
wind (*sb*.): wýnd7 19.
wind (*v*.): wŷnd 289.
winder: wýndo*r* that wýndęṭḥ
  290, a wiynde*r* or winch too
  wiynd ypon 290.
window: window 51, wyndḍoor
  147, wýndór 290.
windlass: wyind*l*as 290.
windy: wýnd*i* 289.

winner: wino*r* 119.
winter: winter 324.
Wintershal (*n. pr*.): h can be
  distinctly pronounced 277.
wisdom: wýʒdǫm³⁾ 12, 78, 146,
  183, 305, 342, wyʒdǫm 50, 65.
wise (*a*.): wýʒ 4.
wise (*sb*.): in no wyʒ 42, 36,
  177, in no wýʒ 133, in what
  wyʒ 189.
-*wise*: flatw*i*ʒ 367, hartw*i*ʒ 367,
  longw*i*ʒ 367, ǫtherw*i*ʒ 367,
  tábĺw*i*ʒ 367.
wish (*v*.): wish 4, wish*i*ng 366.
wit (*sb*.): wit7 8.
with: with 3, 334, 336, 371,
  witḥ 256, 268, 307.
withal: witḥaĺ 318.
withdraw: with-drawɴ 4, 5.
within: witḥin 317, within 335,
  371.
without: withoụt 4, 8, 340, 370,
  witḥoụt 317.
withy: withy 180.
witty: wit*i*est 8.
wo (*interj*.): wo, wo²⁾ 373.
woad: wód 287.
woe: wo²⁾ 129.
woeful: woful²⁾ 326.
wolf: wǫlf 13, wǫlf7 14, 33.
womb: womb 333¹⁾.
woman: wǫ-man 12, 89, wǫ-ṁen
  87, 115, 335.
womankind: wǫ-ṁan-kýnd 338.
wonder (*sb*.): wǫnder 373.
wonderfully: wǫnder-fụll*y* 9.

wont: wǫnt 14.
wood: wǫǫd 25, 41.
wood-beetle: wǫǫd-betl̄ 380.
wood-dove: wǫǫd-dou'[1] 134,
   wǫǫd-doou' 200.
wooden: wǫǫdN 380.
woodness (*rage*): wǫǫdnes 91.
word: word 6, 8, 339, 349,
   wǫrd 316, word7 16, 337,
   363, 365, 368, 370, wǫrd7
   313, 315.
work: wǫrk 5, wǫrk7 4, 8, 9.
world: worl̄d 11, 373.
worm: wǫrM 344, wǫrMż 86.
worse: wǫrs 347, 365.
worser: wǫrser 347.
worship: wǫrship 12.
worst: wǫrst 8, 347, 365.
wort: wort7[1] 82.
worthily: wǫrth*i*ly 19.
wound (*sb.*): woụnd 27, 55.
wound (*v.*): woụnded 62.
wrangler: wranglor 308.
wrath: wrath̠ 21.
wrestle: wrastl*i*ng 54.
wretch: wretch 9.
wriggle: wrigl*i*ng 36.
wrinkle: wrinkl̄ż 55.
write: wrýt 337, 370, wrýting7
   3, wrýtN[3] 3.
wrong (*sb.*): wrong 8.
wrong (*a.*): wrong 337.
wrong (*v.*): wrongęd 6, wrongd
   382.
wrought: wrowht 3, 161
wry: wry[2] 336.

X.

Xanthus (*n. pr.*): Xanth̠ụs 10.

Y.

yard: ŋard 112.
yarn: ŋárN 257, 308.
ye: ŋe' 5, 351, 365, 381.
yea: ŋe' 71, ŋe[2] 5, 8, 25, 72,
   166, 366, 367, 375, 381,
   ŋe[2]-for-sooth̠ 366, ŋe[2]-mary
   366, ŋe[2]-rather 366.
year: ŋe'r 5, ŋe'rż 333.
yellow: ŋelow 76.
yeoman: ŋe'man 257.
yes: ŋes 366.
yesterday: ŋesterday 257.
yet: ŋet 3, 349, 366.
yield: ŋe'ld 29, 368, 372.
yoke (*sb.*): ŋók 66.
yoke (*v.*): ŋoked 257.
yonder(er): ŋonderer 371.
yondermost: ŋondermóst 371.
yondmost: ŋondmóst 371.
you: ŋoụ[1] 8, 348, 351.
young: ŋǫng 10, 24, ŋụng 257.
your: ŋoụr[1] 269, ŋoụr[3] 338,
   351, ŋoụrż[3] 352.
youth: ŋuth̠ 19, 312, 323, ŋuth̠
   257, 333, ŋuth̠7 25.
youthful: ŋuth̠-ful 333.

Z.

zeal: ʒæl 301.
zealous: ʒælǫos 301.
Zenas (*n. pr.*): Zenas 9, Zenas7.

A Second Word=List.

authority: aųtŏrity 58.

bail: bail 287.

barely: bárly 361.

butt (sb.): a bọt or v'esí for wýn 29.

casual (*adj. from case*): cásual 372.

cleave (=*to split*): clæv' 180, cleft 16.

countervail: coųnter-v'ailęd 193.

duck (*vb.*): dųkṭ 187.

eftsoons: eftsons 181.

fet (=*fetch*): fetĭng 155.

forego: forgo[2] 92.

foresire: fór-sýrž 145.

frenzy: phrenȝy 263.

gester (?): a-gestred 148.

gorbellied: gor-belyed 8.

gotling: gótlĭng 65.

helve (*sb.*): hylu' 33.

hew: heų 286.

kemb: too kemb or comb 296.

lask: lask 136.

lease: læȝeʃ or fe'dingʃ 37.

lock (*sb.*): a loc of wųl 297.

mainprize: mainpriȝ[2] 287.

medicine: medc'inż 163.

noble: nóbí 21.

nobility: nobility 145.

overthwart: ou'er-tḥwart 308.

persuasion: perswaṣion 158.

pill: the pil of an apí 289.

philosopher: philosophor 263.

pin-fold: pin-fóld 297.

possession: possesĭon 351.[1]

preter-tense: preter-tenc' 348.

rattle-mouse: ratí-moųc' 31.

rather (*vb.*): ráthʀed 76.

renting: rentĭngʃ 26.

resist: reṣisting 66, reṣistęst 60.

scarcity: scarc'ĭty 17.

shrape: shra'p 48.

splecked: spleked 71.

springle: springlĭng 66.

stud: stųded 31.

suer: suor 291.

teal: tælž 103.

thrall: tḥraí 224.

thwittle (*vb.*): tḥwití 307.

tile (*vb.*): týl 299.

un-fitty: ɏn-fitty 229.

unworthy: ɏnworthy[1] 226.

warily: wárly 221.

wastfully: wástfųlly 94.

whether (*pron.*): weither 73.

viscount: vicount[1] 288.

wit (*vb.*): wit 342.

wroth: wrotḥ 308.

Notes.

[1] The form is due to (or influenced by) the traditional spelling, cf above pp. 15—19.

[2] The length-mark has (or may have) been omitted, cf. above pp. 17 f.

[3] In determining the quantity or quality of the vowel (consonant) due regard must be taken to the inflection or derivation mark, cf. above pp. 19 f.

———————

Index of Words.

Of Present English words only the modern forms, not the early variants, have been indexed. For ME. *olr,* e. NE. *hankerstolkes* etc., see 'alder-tree', 'anchorstock' etc. Forms which have been corrected in Plessow's reprints of Bullokar's works are marked with an asterisk.

belengyng, error for belongyng, 142.

belief 44.

believe 47.

believed 44, 116.

belong 140.

beneath 46, 111.

bequeathed 44.

bereave 46.

beseech 47.

besiege 49.

between 47.

bever 29.

bishop 99. 2.

bit pt. 20.

bite 118.

blame 116, 118.

bleat 46.

blight 118.

blood 30.

blow 6, 75, 76 f., 144.

blue 80, 89.

board 4, 33.

Boethius 110.

body 105.

boil sb. 57.

boil 100, 102, 144.

boist(er)ous 65, 102.

bolster 66.

bolt 66, 77 f.

bond 74.

bone 72, 74.

book 31. 2.

booth 23, 61, 63, 111.

*born 5.

born 29, 116, 119.

bosom 74.

bostious 23.

*both 6.

both 111.

bough 16, 17, 107.

bought 15, 16, 68.

bourn 61.

bow 75.

bowl 63, 77.

boy 102.

brace 28.

brack (dial.) 23.

brack 29, 122.

brahut, error for brohut, 142.

brak 29.

braken 3, 39.

braid 39.

brand-iron 74.

bravo 72.

brazen 29.

bread 31.

breadth 30.

break 30, 39, 40, 43, 46, 78.

breath 30, 46, 116.

breathe 46.

bred 20, 30, 116.

breed 47.

breeder 47.

brew 99.

Brewster 92.

brief 49.

broad 30.

broke 78.

broken 31.

brooch 28.

brood 30.

cleanly 117.
clear 50.
cleave 46.
climb 17.
clothes 111.
*clothing 4.
coarse 50.
coif 102.
coin 102.
*cold 5.
cold 75, 76 f.
collier 20.
colt 66.
Colton 66, 137.
comb 17.
come 57, 78, 90.
comfort 74, 147.
comfortable 74.
commodious 28.
compared 118.
comparison 110.
comparative 20.
complain 104.
complete 67.
compose 28.
composition 18, 105.
conceit 15.
conceive 15.
concern 19.
condemn 19.
coney 64.
conquer 17.
consanguinative 17, 100.
consider 116.
construction 19.
Coultherd 125.

continue 63. 2.
contrary 117.
cord 29.
corn 33. 2, 34.
corpse 29.
couch 64.
cough 16.
could 16.
country 105.
courage 106.
course 14, 61, 64, 118.
court 16, 61.
courtish 116.
cowl 4, 59.
crave 29.
crazy 39.
creak 46.
created 116.
creature 46.
creek 48.
creep 46, 47, 48, 49.
crept 18, 20, 34.
crime 116.
cripple 44.
crouch 14, 64.
crow 22.
cry 17.
culver 122.
curious 101.
curlew 53.
curtain 53.
cut 57.

daily 38. 2, 40.
daisy 42. 1.
dance 73, 144.

danger 116.
dared 34.
daughter 15. 1, 68.
day 143.
dead 30.
deaf 30, 46.
deal 31, 32, 46.
dear 50.
death 30.
decease 28.
deceiue 15, 43.
decrease 46.
decree 49.
defeature 39.
deed 47, 117.
deep 32.
deeper 30. 2.
deepest 44.
deer 50.
default 67.
degree 49, 117.
delight 107.
deny 17.
deride 117.
desire 136.
desolate 106.
despise 119.
destroy 101, 102.
Deus (Latin) 47.
deve (dial.) 122.
devil 56.
devise 18.
devour 28.
dew 82. 1.
die 17, 117.
different 52.

difficult 52.
digress 116, 118.
dike 48, 49.
*diphthong 5.
dirdum 53.
dirge 53.
dirt 52. 2, 53.
discipline 19.
discreet 49.
disdain 39.
disease 46, 110.
dishonest 107.
disjoin 102.
displeased 43.
dive 22, 47.
divel (dial.) 122.
*divers 4.
divers 144.
divide 28.
divinity 20.
do 60, 118, 138, 139, 143.
dolt 23, 74 f.
doltish 23, 74 f.
Dolton error for Colton 142.
done 20, 31, 34, 91.
door 64.
doth 91, 111.
dour 150.
dove 23. 1, 30.
draw 66.
drawbridge 69.
drawing 69.
drawn 69.
drew 66, 147.
drive 32.
driven 17.

drug 59. 1, 148.
dry 117.
due 89, 144.
ducit (Latin) 93.
dull 23. 2, 57.
dumb 17.
during 138.
Durrington, Suss., 124.
duw (Welsh) 83.

each 46.
ear vb. 23, 37.
ear 49.
earl 19. 1.
early 49.
earnestly 117.
earth 116.
earthen 116.
eat 46.
eaten 46.
ease 28, 39.
easily 44.
Easter 30.
east-wind 30.
eel 47.
eels 32.
eftsoons 106.
Egypt 28.
eke 46. 1, 48.
elm 19.
elmen 19.
embrace 28.
emmet 106.
emperor 105.
employ 102, 103.
end 117.

enemy 105.
enough 133.
enroll 77.
enterprise 110.
entertainment 104.
entice 18.
entreaty 46.
entry 19.
Ephesus 110.
equal 28, 46.
erred 118.
erst 49, 116, 118.
eschew 98.
espied 116.
esteem 49.
Europa (Swedish) 95.
even sb. 32.
even 15, 29, 48, 49.
evening 30, 47.
ever 116.
evil 47.
ewe 98.
ewer 98.
ewe-sheep 47.
exalt 38.
*exceed 4.
exceed 49.
*exceedingly 4.
executor 106.
expectation 28.
explain 37.
extremity 46.
eye 136.
eying 16.

led 20.
leek 47.
leisure 43.
leoppe (pt. of leap) 31. 2.
Lesbos 110.
lest 116, 119.
lewd 82. 1.
lewdly 138.
lice 18.
lie 117.
liefer 30, 49.
*life 5.
life 116, 118.
light 144.
like 31, 33, 49, 55, 62, 81 n.,
   90, 100, 103, 136.
livest 116.
loaf 31.
loath 30.
loin 102.
loiter 102.
loke 121.
long 118.
look 30.
loose 78.
lord 33. 2.
lose 29, 78.
losing 29, 32.
loss 116, 118.
lost 78.
lot 33, 116.
lousy 110.
love 17, 74.
*loved 6.
loved 116.
low 118.

loyal 104. 1.
luck 62, 143.
lust 61.

mace 28.
made 38.
magistrate 106.
maid 38.
mail 37.
make 30, 31.
malt 66.
man 143.
Marden, Kent, 146.
Margate, Kent, 146.
marl 29.
Marnhull, Dors., 100.
marred 34.
Marsden, Lancs., 146.
marvel 52.
mate 39.
material 28.
matron 28.
matter 17, 32.
mattock 17.
maundy 67.
mavis 28.
Maximilian 142.
mayest 118.
me 117.
mead 39.
meal 38, 46, 143.
mean 39, 46, 117.
meaning 46.
measure 106.
meat 39.
meek 47.

meet 44, 47.
men 116, 118, 119, 143.
merchandise 110.
mesh 46.
mete 39, 46.
metre 46, 49.
meus 47.
Mexymelyans, error for Maxymelyans, 142.
mice 136.
might 14.
Millbrook, Bedf., 91.
mind 116, 136.
mine 100.
mirror 53.
mischief 49.
*miserable 5.
Miserden, Glouc., 101.
mislike 47.
misplace 28.
mo 18.
mo 118.
moistness 102. 2.
mole 22.
moment 28.
Moreton, Bucks., 91.
Morholm, Lancs., 78.
morn 19.
mortal 105.
mourn 61, 64.
*mouth 4.
mow 123.
much 45.
murderer 56.
murmur 63. 4.
muse 88.

must 116, 118.
myrmidon 53.

nail 40. 2.
name 40. 2, 143.
nap 70.
nation 28, 105, 144.
native 28.
natural 106, 144.
nature 28, 32, 39, 144.
naughty 69.
nave 108.
naw, error for new, 142.
near 49, 50, 118.
nearer 30. 2, 49, 50.
nearest 49, 50.
neatness 46.
need 44, 47, 118.
needs 47.
neger 28.
neglect 116, 119.
nest 30, 46.
nether 46.
nethermost 46.
neuf (French) 79.
neutre (French) 79.
new 79, 85, 88, 144.
news 88.
Newbury 92.
Newton Abbot, 148.
Nicholas 52.
niggish 116.
night 108.
nine 136.
no 18.
noise 102, 110, 118, 149.

state 39.
stave 30.
staves 29.
stay 38. 2, 40.
stead 46.
steak 40.
steal 31, 46.
steep 47.
Steeple cum Stanesgate, Ess.,
    33. 1.
steer sb., 50.
sterling 147.
Stewart 92.
stifle 65, 120.
stir 53. 2.
Stoddart 125.
stole 32.
stolen 29.
stomach 74, 147.
stone 48.
stood 31.
storm 19. 1, 34.
strave 31.
stream 46.
streams 39.
street 31. 2, 47.
stretch 118.
stroke 22, 64.
stuff 59. 1, 147.
stuffle (dial.) 123.
subject 63. 4.
succour 17.
such 116, 118.
suddenly 57. 2, 130.
sue 82.
suet 81.

sufficient 63.
sugar 98.
suit 101.
suitor 82.
sure 94, 98, 109.
surplice 147.
surely 94, 109.
Suthbrun, 91.
sweal 46.
sweeper 48.
swollen 29.
sword 51.
syrup 53.

table 40. 2.
*tables 4.
tact 29.
tail 119. 1.
take 31, 32, 39.
taken 31, 32.
tale 119. 1
*talk 4.
talk 118.
talker 116.
tall 119. 1.
talon 22.
Tamas, error for Tomas, 142.
tame, error for teme, 143.
tasted 28.
teach 46.
*teacheth 6.
teal 119. 1.
tear, sb., 51.
tear, vb., 49.
tease 46.
teeth 47.

ten 51.
tenuis (Latin) 93.
Thales 110.
Thames 39.
*than 5.
that 111.
*thee 5.
thee, vb., 47.
thee 47, 117.
them 116.
there 49, 118.
therefore 49.
therein 49.
thereof 49.
these 46.
they 16.
thief 47.
thieves 44. 2.
thine 116.
think 144.
third 53.
thirteen 52.
thirty 53.
this 111, 116, 144.
*thither 4.
thorn 33. 2, 34, 111, 143.
those 111.
thou 88, 106, 117, 119.
thousand 22, 30.
thousandth 30.
Thraso 110.
thread 30.
three 47.
throes 47.
thumb 111.
Thursday 52.

thus 118.
thwittle 120, 123.
time 116.
timorous 65.
tin 52.
tit 52.
to 18. 1.
toil 102, 119.
token 31.
tomato 71, 72.
tongue 118.
*too 6.
too 117, 118, 144.
took 30, 31, 78.
tooth 45.
torn 33. 2.
touch 28.
Touesday, error(?) for Teues-
    day 142.
tread 46.
treasure 28, 46.
treatise 46.
treaty 28.
tree 47.
Trinity 52.
trot 59. 1.
troth 77.
true 80, 89, 116, 149.
truly 117.
trust 100.
try out 116, 118.
tuck 59. 1.
Tuesday 63. 2, 138.
tumble 144.
Turk 147.
turn 118.

weed 47.
weep 47.
weigh 38, 40.
well 32.
what 144.
wheat 46.
wheaten 46.
wheel 47.
where 49.
whereas 49.
whereby 49.
whereof 49.
wherry 15, 51.
wherryman 50.
whir 50, 51.
whirl 52.
white 32.
whiter 18.
whittle 111, 123.
whole 135.
whore 64.
wield 47.
will 144.
*wind 5.
*winder 5.
window 106.
wine 32.
wise 31. 2, 116.
wit, vb., 32.
with 111.
withaught, error for without, 142.
withaute, error for withoute, 141.
withawth, error for withowth, 142.

within 111.
without 130, 132.
woke 78.
womb 17.
wont 64.
wood-beetle 106.
wood-dove 17, 74, 106.
word 52, 74, 148.
*words 5.
worm 116.
worst 116, 119.
wort 17, 74.
would 136.
wound sb. 64.
wrangler 111.
wrath 111.
wrestle 37, 111.
write 31, 55, 143.
wrong 67, 111.
wynd 35.

yarn 33.
ye 49.
yea 40, 49.
year 32, 50.
yeoman 48.
yesterday 140.
yestereven 140.
yew 85, 97, 149.
yes 144.
yield 47.
yoked 29.
*you 6.
you 94, 97 ff., 149.
young 97.

your 93, 97 ff.   zastyrday, error for zustyrday,
*youth 5.   141.
youth 94, 97 ff.   zeal 46.
                                   zealous 46.

List of Works Consulted.

Letters and Ducuments.[1]

The Cely Papers 1475—1488, ed. H. E. Malden. London 1909.
References are to letters (London).

Holograph Letters of Edmund de la Pole (c. 1500) in H. Ellis,
Original Letters III. 1, pp. 117—141, and Chronicles and
Memorials 24, 1, pp. 253—257. References are to pages.

The Diary of Henry Machyn, Citizen and Merchant Taylor of
London, 1550—1563, ed. J. G. Nichols. London 1848.

Original Letters illustrative of English History, 1418—1726, 1st,
2nd, and 3rd series, ed. Ellis. London 1825 ff.

The Paston Letters, 1422—1509, ed. J. Gairdner. Westminster
1872—75. References are to letters. Roman figures refer
to additional letters in a later edition by Gairdner, published
in 1901 (Mainly Norfolk).

Letters of John Shillingford, Mayor of Exeter, 1447—1450, ed.
S. A. More. London 1871 (Devonshire).

The Stonor Letters and Papers, 1290—1483, ed. Ch. Lethbridge
Kingsford. London 1919. References to letters (Mainly
London and Oxfordshire).

Memoirs of the Verney Family During the Seventeenth Century,
ed. Frances P. Verney and Margaret M. Verney, Second
Edition, abridged and corrected by Margaret M. Verney.
London 1907 (London, Oxfordshire, and Buckinghamshire).

---

[1] Collections of Letters which have been used only occasionally are
not included in this list.

Orthoepists.[1]

Alphabet Anglois 1625.
Anon. 1568 (Dutch Grammar).
Arnold 1757.
Bachmair 1750 (1788).
Barclay 1521.
Baret 1573.
Bellot 1580.
British Grammar 1763 (1784).
Buchanan 1766.
Bullokar 1580, 1584, 1586.
Butler 1634.
Cooper 1685.
Cootes 1596.
Cotgrave 1611.
Daines 1640.
De La Mothe 1592.
Desainliens 1566, 1580 (1597).
Du Wes 1532?.
Dyche 1729.
Eliot 1593.
Elphinstone 1765, 1787, 1790.
Erondelle 1605, 1906.
Expert Orthographist 1704.
Festeau 1675, 1693.
Florio 1578, 1611.
Gill 1621 (1619).
Gres 1636.
Hart 1569, 1570.
Hillenius 1664.

---

[1] For bibliographical details, see Ellis, Early English Pronunciation 31 ff., 819 ff., Zachrisson, Pronunciation of English Vowels VIII ff., Spira, Englische Lautentwicklung, 10 ff., Krapp, The English Language in America, II, 273 ff. and works from which the evidence is quoted. Figures within brackets refer to later editions.

Hexham-Manley 1672.

Hodges 1644.

Holder 1669.

Holyband = Desainliens.

Hume 1611 (?).

Johnston 1764.

Jones 1701.

Lambeth Fragment 1528.

Lediard 1725.

Lye 1677.

Mason 1622.

Mauger 1652, 1656, 1679, 1693.

Maupas 1607.

Meigret 1545, 1550.

Miege 1685 (1728, 1750, 1756), 1688, 1691.

Mulcaster 1582.

Nares 1784.

Nicolai 1693.

Palsgrave 1530.

Peyton 1756 (1765).

Podensteiner 1685.

Price 1665, 1668 (1670).

Richardson 1677.

Rogissard 1738.

Salesbury 1547, 1567.

Sewel 1705.

Sheridan 1780.

Sherwood 1632.

Siret-Parquet 1796.

Smith 1568.

Sterpin 1660.

Strong 1676.

Sylvius 1531

Tiessen 1705.

Vander-Milii 1612.

Walker 1791.

Wallis 1653.

Wilkins 1668.

Wodroephe 1625.

Writing Scholar's Companion 1695.

Literature.

Archiv für das Studium der neueren Sprachen. Hamburg (Archiv).

C. W. BARDSLEY, A Dictionary of English and Welsh Surnames. London 1901.

——, English Surnames and their Significations. London 1906.

A. J. BARNOUW, Echoes of the Pilgrim Fathers' Speech. Amsterdam 1923 (Mededeelingen der Koninklijke Akadémie van Wetenschappen, Afdeelning Letterkunde, Deel 55, Serie A, No. 6).

D. BEHRENS, Beiträge zur Geschichte der französischen Sprache in England (Französische Studien V, 2).

H. S. BENNETT, The Pastons and their England. Cambridge 1922.

A. BINZEL, Die Mundart von Suffolk in früh-neuenglischer Zeit. Darmstadt 1912 (Diss., Giessen).

E. BJÖRKMAN, Scandinavian Loan-words in Middle English. Halle 1900—1902.

J. BOSWORTH and J. TOLLER, An Anglo-Saxon Dictionary. Oxford 1882—1921.

B. BRILIOTH, A Grammar of the Dialect of Lorton (Cumberland). Uppsala 1913.

B. TEN BRINK, Chaucers Sprache und Verskunst. Leipzig 1899.

R. BROTANEK, Mason's Grammaire Angloise. Halle 1905 (Neudrucke frühneuengl. Grammatiken, 1.).

BULLOKAR, see PLESSOW.

K. D. BÜLBRING, Altenglisches Elementarbuch. Heidelberg 1902.

L. CARDIM, Some Notes on the Portuguese-English and English-Portuguese Grammars to 1830. Porto 1922 (Revista da Facultade de Letras da Universidade do Porto, Nos. 5—6).

O. DEIBEL, Th. Smith, De recta et emendata Linguæ Anglicæ scriptione Dialogus. Halle 1913 (Neudrucke frühneuengl. Gramm. 8).

Dictionary of National Biography.

W. DIBELIUS, John Capgrave und die englische Schriftsprache (Anglia, 23, 24).

L. DIEHL, Englische Schreibung und Aussprache im Zeitalter Shakespeares nach Briefen und Tagebüchern (Anglia, 29).

E. Dölle, Zur Sprache Londons vor Chaucer. Halle 1913.

E. Eckhardt, Die Dialekt- und Ausländertypen des älteren englischen Dramas. Leipzig 1910 (Materialen zur Kunde des älteren englischen Dramas, herausg. von W. Bang, 27).

A. Eichler, Ch. Butler's English Grammar (1634). Halle 1910 (Neudrucke frühneuengl. Gramm. 4, 1).

——, Schriftbild und Lautwert in Ch. Butler's English Grammar (1633, 1634) und Feminin' Monarchi' (1634). Halle 1913 (Neudrucke etc. 4, 2).

E. Ekwall, Jones's Phonography. Halle 1907 (Neudrucke frühneuengl. Gramm., 2).

——, Writing Scholar's Companion. Halle 1911 (Neudrucke etc. 6).

——, Historische neuengl. Laut- und Formenlehre. Berlin und Leipzig 1922.

——, Zur. Geschichte der stimmhaften interdentalen Spirans im Englischen (Lunds Universitets Årsskrift, 1906).

——, Contributions to the History of Old English Dialects. Lund 1917 (Lunds Universitets Årsskrift, NF, Afd. 1, Bd. 12, Nr. 6).

——, Notes on the Early New English Pronunciation (Englische Studien 55).

A. J. Ellis, On Early English Pronunciation 1—5. London 1869—89.

Englische Studien, Organ für Englische Philologie. Leipzig.

English Studies, Amsterdam.

H. Faltenbacher, Die romanischen, speciell französischen und lateinischen (besw. latinisierten) Lehnwörter bei Caxton. München 1907. (Diss.).

H. M. Flasdieck, Forschungen zur Frühzeit der neuenglischen Schriftsprache, 1—2. Halle 1922.

M. Förster, Datierung und Charakter des kymrisch-englischen Marien-Hymnus (Archiv 1926).

A. Gabrielson, Rime as a Criterion of the Pronunciation of Spenser, Pope, Byron, and Swinburne. Uppsala 1909.

——, The Development of Early Modern English i/r (+ cons.). Uppsala 1913 (Axel Erdmann Celebration Volume).

E. Gepp, A Contribution to an Essex Dialect Dictionary. London 1923.

Olga Gevenich, Die englische Patalalisierung vor k>č im Lichte der englischen Ortsnamen. Halle 1918.

J. E. B. Gover, The Place-Names of Middlesex. London 1922.

E. Hauck, Systematische Lautlehre Bullokar's (Vokalismus) Marburg 1906 (Marburger Studien zur englischen Philologie, 12).

E. Hauck, William Bullokar. Marburg 1905 (Oberrealschule zu Marburg a. d. Lahn. Jahresbericht über das Schuljahr 1904—1905).

M. Grünzinger, Die neuenglische Schriftsprache in den Werken des Sir Thomas More (1478—1535). Würzburg 1909 (Diss.).

G. Hackman, Kürzung langer Tonvokale vor einfachen auslautenden Konsonanten. Halle 1908.

J. O. Halliwell, A Dictionary of Archaic and Provincial Words. London 1878.

F. Holthausen, Ein mittelenglischer Hymnus auf Maria und Christus (Palæstra 147).

J. Hoops, Englische Sprachkunde. Stuttgart 1923.

W. Horn, Historische neuenglische Grammatik. Strassburg 1898 (= Horn).

——, Untersuchungen zur neuenglischen Lautgeschichte. Strassburg 1905 (Quellen und Forschungen 98).

——, Beiträge zur Geschichte der englischen Gutturallaute. Berlin 1901.

——, Die Entwicklung des mittelenglischen kurzen *u* im neuenglischen (Englische Studien 60).

O. Jespersen, A Modern English Grammar on Historical Principles. Heidelberg 1909—1914 (Jespersen).

——, John Hart's Pronunciation of English (1569 and 1570). Heidelberg 1907 (Anglistische Forschungen, 22).

——, Lehrbuch der Phonetik. Leipzig und Berlin 1904.

J. Jiriczek, A. Gill, Logonomia Anglica (Quellen und Forschungen, 90).

D. Jones, The Pronunciation of English. Cambridge 1911.

——, An English Pronouncing Dictionary. London 1919.

J. D. Jones, Cooper's Grammatica Linguæ Anglicanæ. Halle 1912 (Neudrucke frühneuengl. Gramm., 5).

R. Jordan, Handbuch der mittelenglischen Grammatik. Heidelberg 1925.

K. Kern, Die englische Lautentwicklung nach Right Spelling (1704) und anderen Grammatiken um 1700. Giessen 1913 (Diss.).

Asta Kihlbom, A Contribution to the study of Fifteenth Century English. Uppsala 1926 (Uppsala Universitets Årsskrift).

F. Kluge, Geschichte der englischen Sprache (Grundriss der germanische Philologie, 2:te Aufl., 1901).

G. Ph. Krapp, The English Language in America, I, II. New York 1925.

E. Kruisinga, A Grammar of the Dialect of West Somerset. Bonn 1905 (Bonner Beiträge zur Anglistik, 18).

J. LEKEBUSCH, Die Londoner Urkundensprache von 1430—1500.
Halle 1906.

H. LINDKVIST, Middle English Place-Names of Scandinavian Origin.
Uppsala 1912.

A. LUHMANN, Die Überlieferung von Lagamon's Brut. Halle 1906.

K. LUICK, Untersuchungen zur englischen Lautgeschichte. Strassburg 1896.

——, Historische Grammatik der englischen Sprache. Leipzig 1914
(Luick).

——, Zu den neuenglischen Lehnwörtern (Palæstra 147 = A. Brandl
Celebration Volume).

——, Weitere Studien zu den neuenglischen Lehnwörtern (E. Sievers
Celebration Volume 1927).

——, Beiträge zur englischen Grammatik (Anglia 14, 45).

H. MARCUS, Die Schreibung *ou* in frühmittelenglischen Handschriften.
Berlin 1917 (Diss.).

A. MAWER and F. M. STENTON, The Place-Names of Buckinghamshire. Cambridge 1925 (English Place-Name Society II).

——, The Place-Names of Bedfordshire and Huntingdonshire. Cambridge 1926 (English Place-Name Society III).

Modern Language Review. Cambridge.

L. MORSBACH, Mittelenglische Grammatik. Halle 1896.

——, Über den Ursprung der neuenglischen Schriftsprache. Heil·
bronn 1888.

——, Die angebliche Originalität des frühmittelenglischen 'King
Horn' (Wendelin Förster Celebration Volume 1902).

E. MÄTZNER, Altenglische Sprachproben. Bd. 2. Wörterbuch. Berlin
1878—1900.

CH. MÜLLER, Die englische Lautentwicklung nach Lediard (1725)
und anderen Grammatikern. Darmstadt 1915 (Giessen Diss.).

E. MÜLLER, Englische Lautlehre nach James Elphinstone. Heidelberg
1914 (Anglistische Forschungen, 43).

G. NEUMANN, Die Orthographie der Paston Letters von 1422—1461.
Marburg 1904 (Marburger Studien zur englischen Philologie, 7).

A New English Dictionary. Oxford 1888 ff. (NED.).

A. C. PAUES, Shakespearian Pronunciation (The Times Literary Supplement, Sept. 11th, 1919).

H. PEDERSEN, Vergleichende Grammatik der keltischen Sprachen.
Göttingen 1909, 1913.

M. PLESSOW, Geschichte der Fabeldichtung in England bis zu John
Gay (1726). Berlin 1906 (Palæstra 52). Contains reprints
of Bullokar's works: Æsop's Fables 1584 (F. A.), Booke at

Large 1580 (B. L.), Bref Grammar for English 1586 (B. G.),
   Pamphlet for Grammar 1586 (P. G.).
H. T. PRICE, A History of Ablaut in the Strong Verbs from Caxton
   to the end of the Elizabethan Period. Bonn 1910 (Bonner
   Studien zur englischen Philologie, 3).
A. COMPTON RICKETT, A History of English Literature. London 1918.
TH. ROSSET, Les origines de la prononciation moderne. Paris 1911.
M. RÖSLER und R. BROTANEK, Simon Daines' Orthoepia Anglica.
   Halle 1908 (Neudrucke frühneuengl. Gramm., 3).
W. SEGELHORST, Die Sprache des 'English Register of Godstow
   Nunnery' (ca. 1450) in ihrem Verhältnis zu Oxford und
   London. Marburg 1908 (Diss.).
W. SCHLEMILCH, Beiträge zur Sprache und Orthographie spätalt-
   englischer Sprachdenkmäler (1000—1150). Halle 1904.
MARY S. SERGEANTSON, Distribution of Dialect Characters in Middle
   English. Amsterdam 1924.
E. SIEVERS, Angelsächsische Grammatik. Halle 1898.
E. SLETTENGREN, Contributions to the Study of Aphæretic Words in
   English. Lund 1912.
——, On ME., early NE. oi, ui in French Loan-words containing
   pop. Latin stressed ǫ, o. Lund 1915 (Från Filologiska För-
   eningen i Lund. Språkliga Uppsatser IV).
W. SOPP, Orthographie und Aussprache der ersten neuenglischen
   Bibelübersetzung von William Tyndale (Anglia, 12).
TH. SPIRA, Die englische Lautentwicklung nach französischen Gram-
   matiker-Zeugnisse. Strassburg 1912 (Quellen und Forschungen,
   115).
E. STENGEL, Chronologisches Verzeichnis französischer Grammatiken
   vom Ende des 14. bis zum Ausgange des 18. Jahrhunderts.
   Oppeln 1890.
H. STICHEL, Die englische Aussprache nach den Grammatiken Pey-
   tons (1756, 1765). Darmstadt 1915 (Diss., Giessen).
A. STIMMING, Der anglonormannische Boeve de Haumtone. Halle
   1899.
F. H. STRATMANN and H. BRADLEY, A Middle-English Dictionary.
   Oxford 1891.
K. SÜSSBIER, Sprache der Cely Papers, einer Sammlung von englischen
   Kaufmannsbriefen aus den Jahren 1475—1488. Berlin 1905
   (Diss.).
CH. THUROT, De la prononciation française depuis le commencement
   du XVIe siècle d'après les témoignages des grammairiens, I, II.
   Paris 1881, 1883.

VAN DER GAAF, Notes on English Orthography (*ie* and *ea*). (Neophilologus, 5, 1920).

W. VIETOR, A Shakespeare Phonology. Marburg 1906.

B. WALKER, Derbyshire Place-Names (Derbyshire Archæol. and Nat. Hist. Society's Journal, XXXVI, 1914—1915).

J. WELLS, A Manual of the Writings in Middle-English 1050—1400. New Haven and London 1916. First Supplement 1919. Second Supplement 1923.

F. WILD, Die sprachlichen Eigentümlichkeiten der wichtigeren Chaucer-Handschriften und die Sprache Chaucers. Wien und Leipzig 1915 (Wiener Beiträge zur englischen Philologie 44).

T. H. PARRY-WILLIAMS, The English Element in Welsh. London 1923 (Cymmrodorian Records Series, 10).

J. WRIGHT, The English Dialect Dictionary. London 1889—1905 (EDD.).

——, The English Dialect Grammar. Oxford 1905 (EDGr.).

J. WRIGHT and E. M. WRIGHT, An Elementary Middle English Grammar. Oxford 1923.

——, An Elementary Historical New English Grammar. Oxford 1924.

L. WURTH, Das Wortspiel bei Shakespeare. Wien und Leipzig 1895 (Wiener Beiträge zur englischen Philologie, 1).

H. C. WYLD, A Short History of English. London 1914.

——, A History of Modern Colloquial English. London 1920 (Wyld).

——, Studies in English Rhymes from Surrey to Pope. London 1923.

——, The Spoken English of the Early Eighteenth Century (Modern Language Teaching, 1915).

——, The Surrey Dialect in the XIIIth Century (English Studies III).

R. E. ZACHRISSON, A Contribution to the Study of Anglo-Norman Influence on English Place-Names. Lund 1909 (Lunds Universitets Årsskrift, N.F., Afd. 1, Bd. 4, Nr. 3).

——, Pronunciation of English Vowels 1400—1700. Göteborg 1913 (Göteborgs Kungl. Vetenskaps- och Vitterhetssamhälles Handlingar, F. 4, H. 14—15) (Zachrisson).

——, Engelska stilarter med textprov. Stockholm 1919.

——, Notes on Some Early English and French Grammars (Anglia: Beiblatt, 1914).

——, Shakespeare's Uttal. Uppsala 1914 (Studier i modern språkvetenskap utgivna av Nyfilologiska Sällskapet i Stockholm, 5).

——, Northern English as the Standard Pronunciation? (Anglia, 38).

R. E. Zachrisson, A Contribution to the History of the Early New English Pronunciation, especially in the 15th Century (Englische Studien, 52).

——, Change of *ts* to *ch*, *ds* to *dg* and Other Instances of Inner Sound-Substitution. Uppsala 1921 (Studier i modern språkvetenskap, utgivna av Nyfilologiska Sällskapet i Stockholm, 8).

——, Notes on the English Pronunciation of Greek ʋ and French *oi* in Loan-words (K. Luick Celebration Volume, Die neueren Sprachen, Beih. 61, 1925).

——, Notes on the Essex Dialect and the Origin of Vulgar London Speech (Englische Studien, 59).

——, English Place-Names and River-Names Containing the Primitive Germanic Roots *vis, *vask*. Uppsala 1926 (Uppsala Universitets Årsskrift).

——, Det engelska riksspråkets uppkomst och utveckling (Nordisk Tidskrift 1925).

W. Zopf, Zum Sprachgebrauch in den Kirchen-Urkunden von St.-Mary-at-Hill-London (1420—1559). Berlin 1910 (Diss.).

Table of Contents.